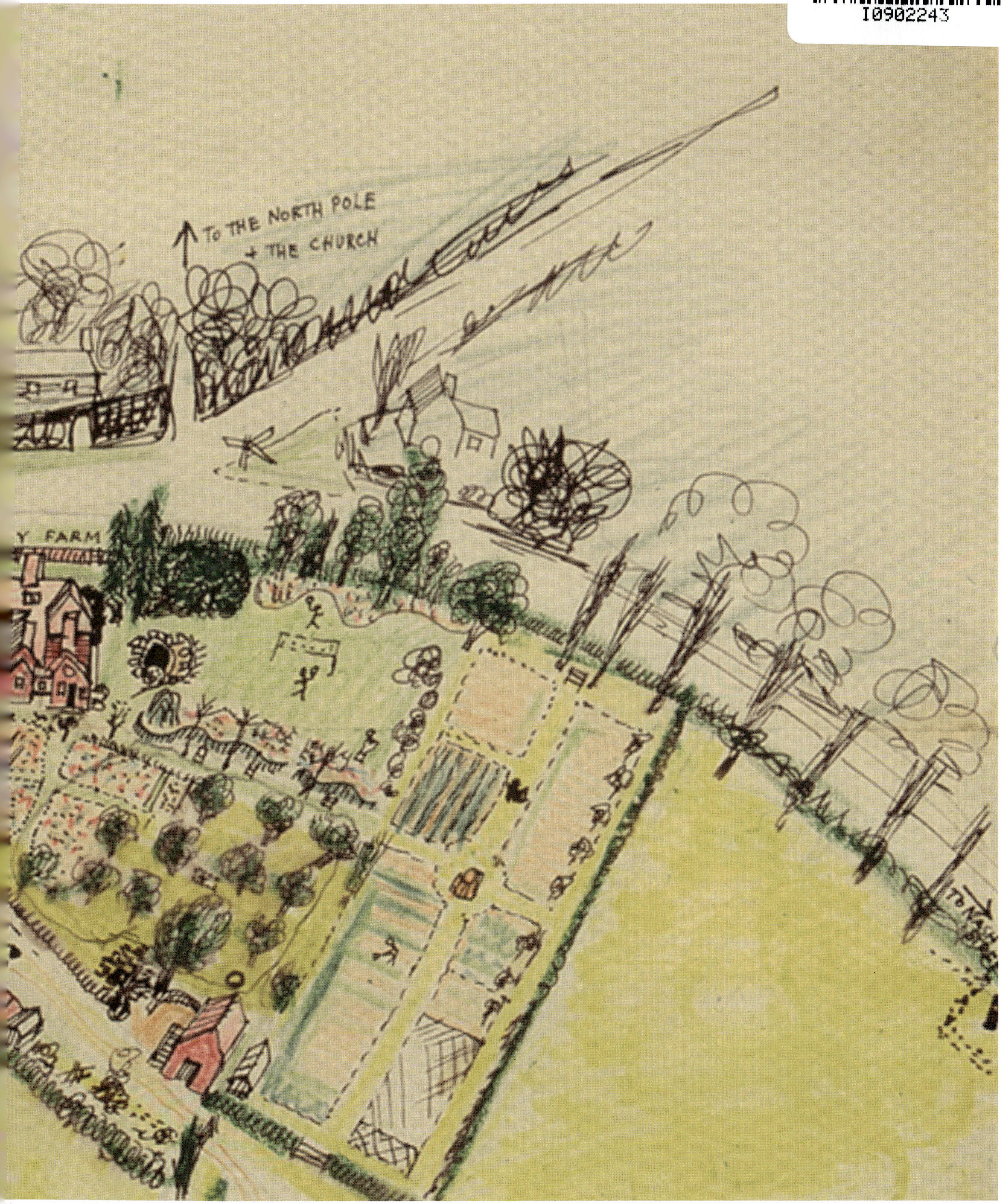
TO THE NORTH POLE
+ THE CHURCH
Y FARM

FRONT COVER IMAGE **Dorothea Tanning and Max Ernst**, Farleys garden, East Sussex, England 1950

INSIDE COVER IMAGE **Map of Farley Farm**, Ink and wash on paper, Muddles Green, East Sussex, England 1956 by Roland Penrose

BACK COVER IMAGE **Detail of Fireplace**, Farleys House, Muddles Green, East Sussex, England 1950

SURREALIST WEEKENDS

FARLEYS IN THE FIFTIES

By Antony Penrose

Supported by the Culture Recovery Fund awarded by:

Supported using public funding by
ARTS COUNCIL ENGLAND

HERE FOR CULTURE

FIRST EDITION: Lee Miller Archives Publishing 2022.

Farleys House and Gallery Ltd are the managing agents of the Lee Miller Archives,
Farleys House, Muddles Green, East Sussex, BN8 6HW England
www.leemiller.co.uk

A catalogue record of this book is available from the British Library.

ISBN 9781 914298 01 1

Designed by FOURLY and Lee Miller Archives Publishing.

Printed in the UK by FOURLY.

DEDICATED TO:

FRED AND JOAN BAKER

Important figures of my youth
and a key part of life at Farleys

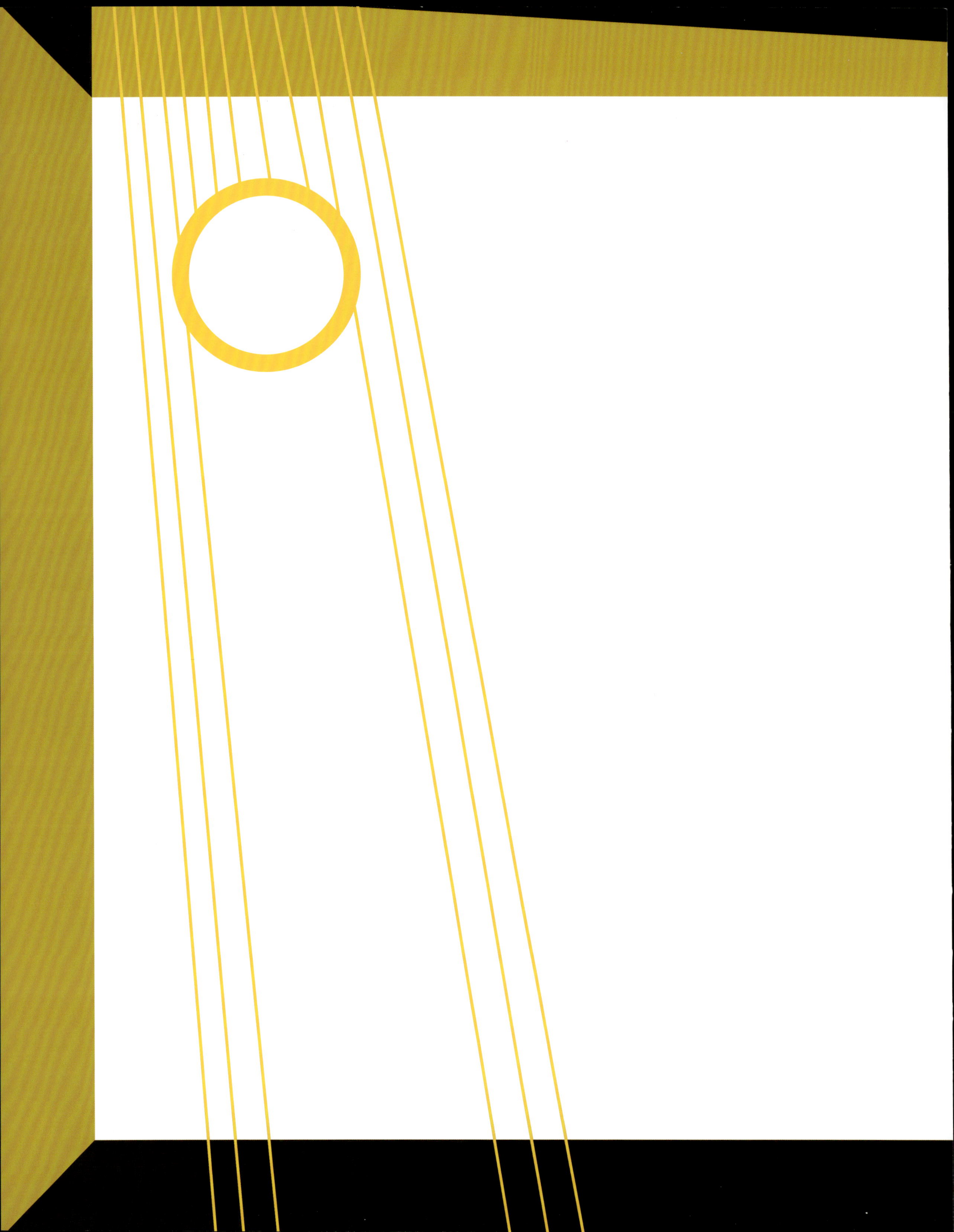

INTRODUCTION

THE EARLY DAYS

LEE MILLER AND ROLAND PENROSE AT FARLEYS

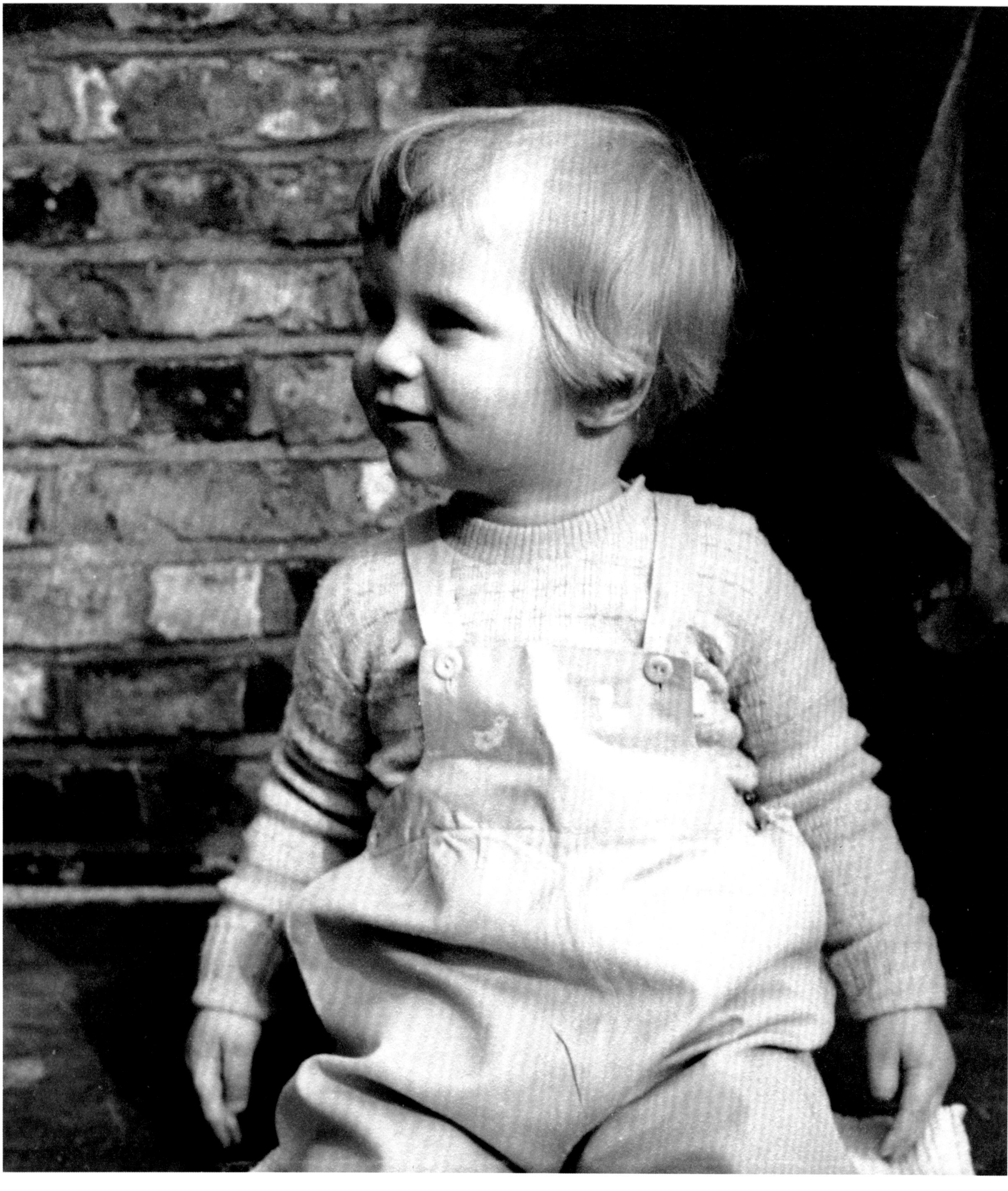

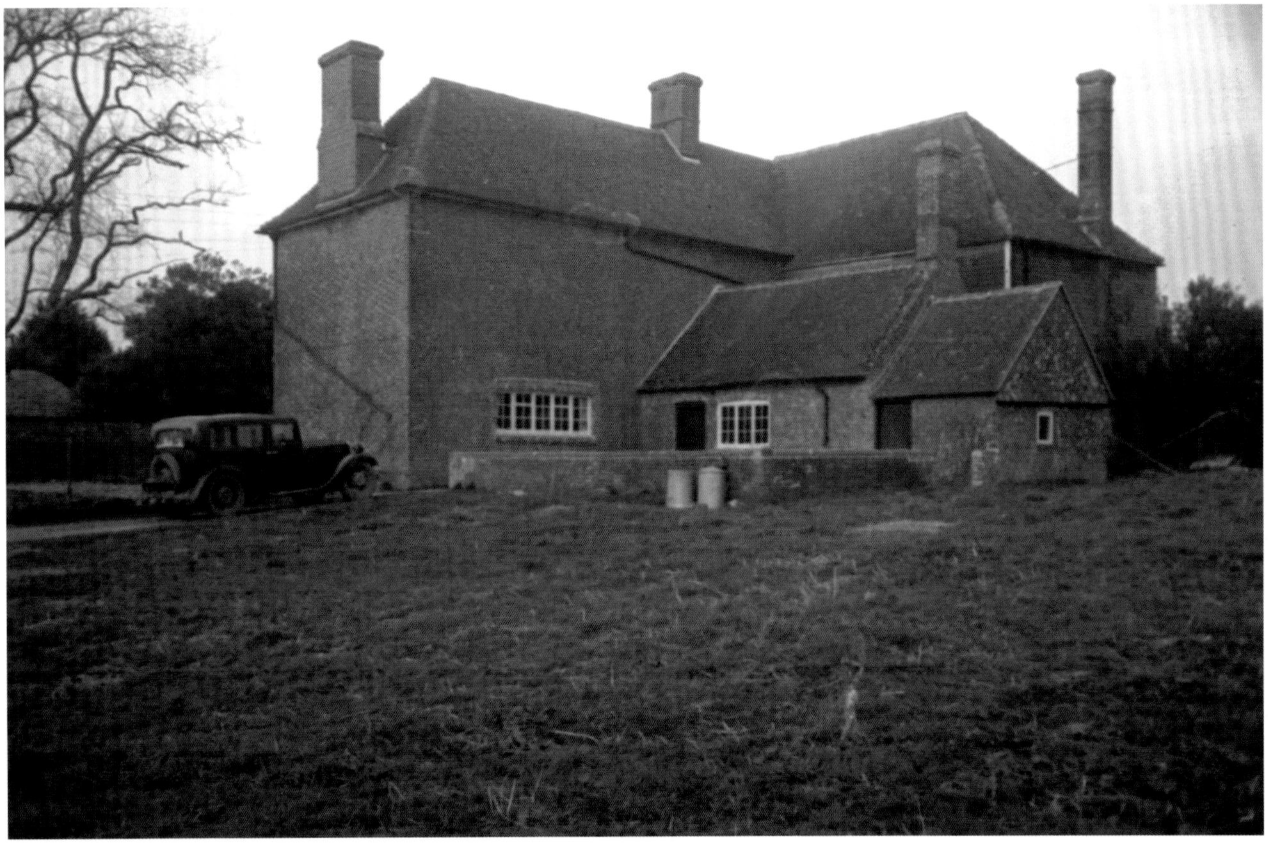

Farley Farm 1949

My second birthday fell on 9th September and we celebrated it at our home in Hampstead, 36 Downshire Hill. That is where my parents, Lee Miller and Roland Penrose had all their close friends, but in truth they may have wanted to avoid taking me to Farleys. It had not been a big success for me when we took possession in February 1949. The old house had no heating and icy draughts swirled in the dark, slamming the doors in damp corridors and comfortless rooms.

The previous owners had kept the place as well as they could, given the constraints of wartime, and although the basic structure dating from about 1730 was sound enough, repairs were needed everywhere. For warmth the woodlands on the farm provided plenty of logs. The open fires smoked incessantly but no one noticed as the air was always thick with cigarette smoke. In later years we were never certain if the nicotine colour tint of the ceilings was from cigarettes or the wood fires.

Antony Penrose,
Farleys garden
February 1949

The warmest place in the house was the kitchen where a Rayburn stove was constantly alight for the cooking and the limited supply of hot water. An unreliable pump drew water from the well, sending it up three floors to a tank in the roof space. When it came out of the taps it had a dark orange colour from the immense concentration of iron oxide in the water. We learned that a few miles away at Gun Hill there had been a foundry making cannons from the local iron ore. When Dorothea Tanning came in June 1950, she wanted to wash her hair but fearing transformation into a red-head she opted to use rain water from the garden tank. She casually fished out the dead leaves, beetles and other debris and heated it in a large pan on the stove. She was entirely satisfied with this arrangement and in Lee's photo of her she resembles one of Max Ernst's collages with her head stuck on back to front.

My mother's first priority was to make sure the garden was planted with the usual range of vegetables augmented

Farleys kitchen 1951

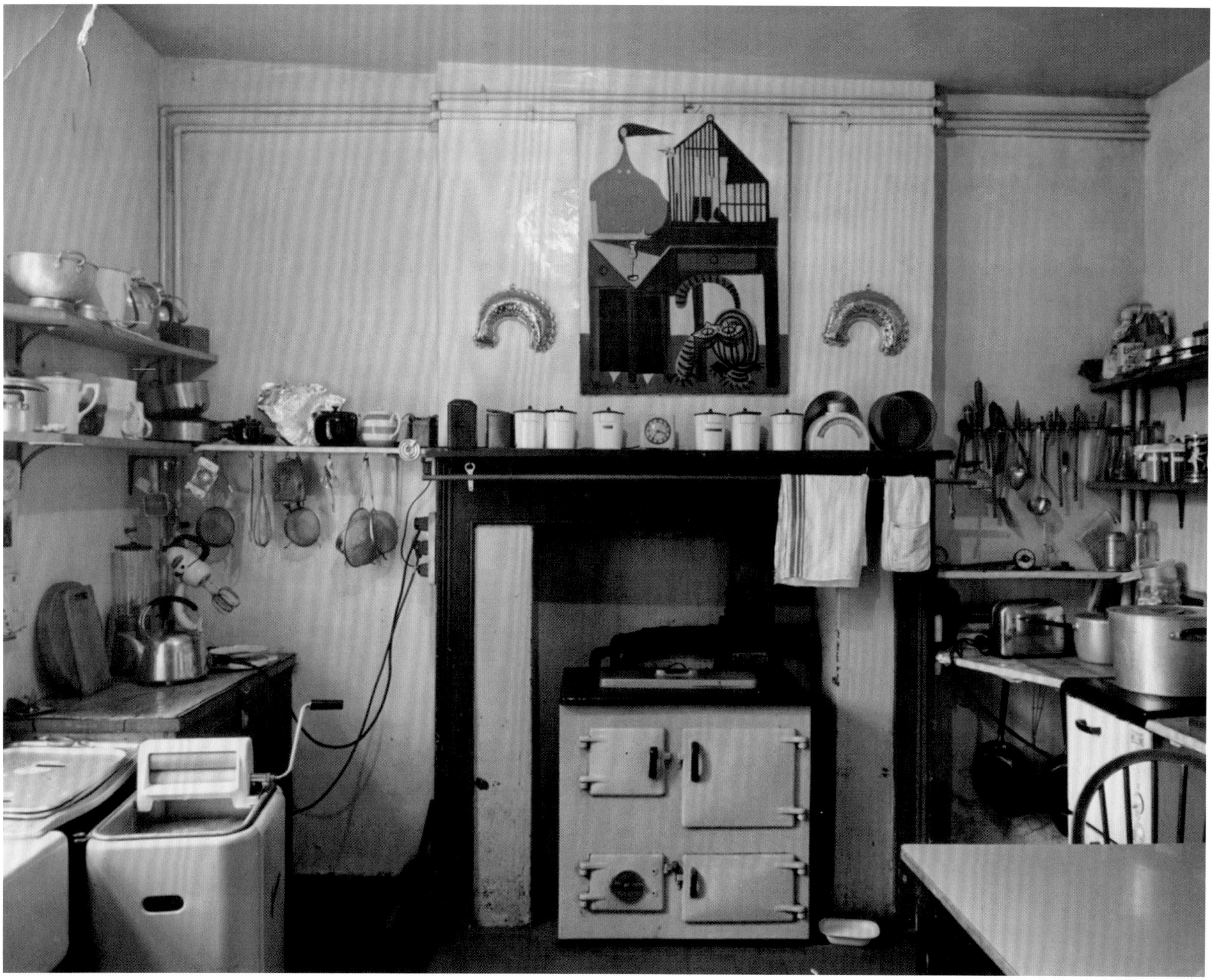

by sweetcorn grown from seed sent from America by her parents, asparagus and artichokes begged from French friends and a massive range of herbs. For Lee herbs were more than a frivolous luxury. She found them invaluable in hard times, and throughout the war her stash of herbs allowed her to be creative with the most dismal rations.

The first guests bravely arriving in April of our first year were Timmie and Terry O'Brien. Timmie was an editor at *Vogue* and particularly supportive to Lee who was battling post-traumatic stress disorder following her war experiences, coupled with post-natal depression following my birth. Timmie, a wonderfully intelligent South African, had a way of almost mothering Lee that ensured she handed in her articles on time. She was immensely kind to me and we had the most marvellous adventures together. Terry, a solidly practical Australian, was a big help to my father in coaxing the plumbing to work and connecting Lee's 110-volt American kitchen gadgets to crude transformers.

Terry O'Brien, Roland Penrose, Antony Penrose and Timmie O'Brien, Farleys garden 1951

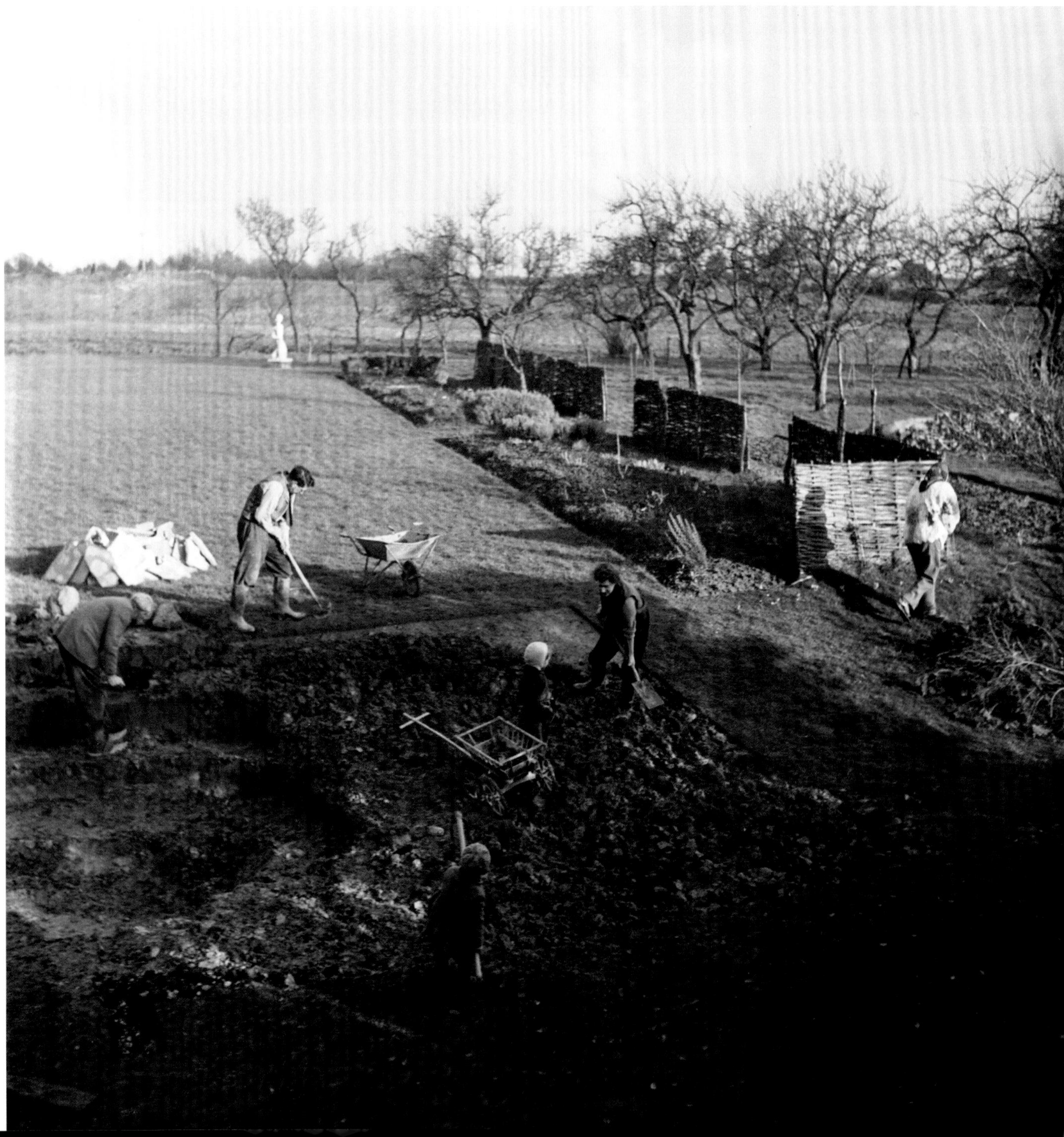

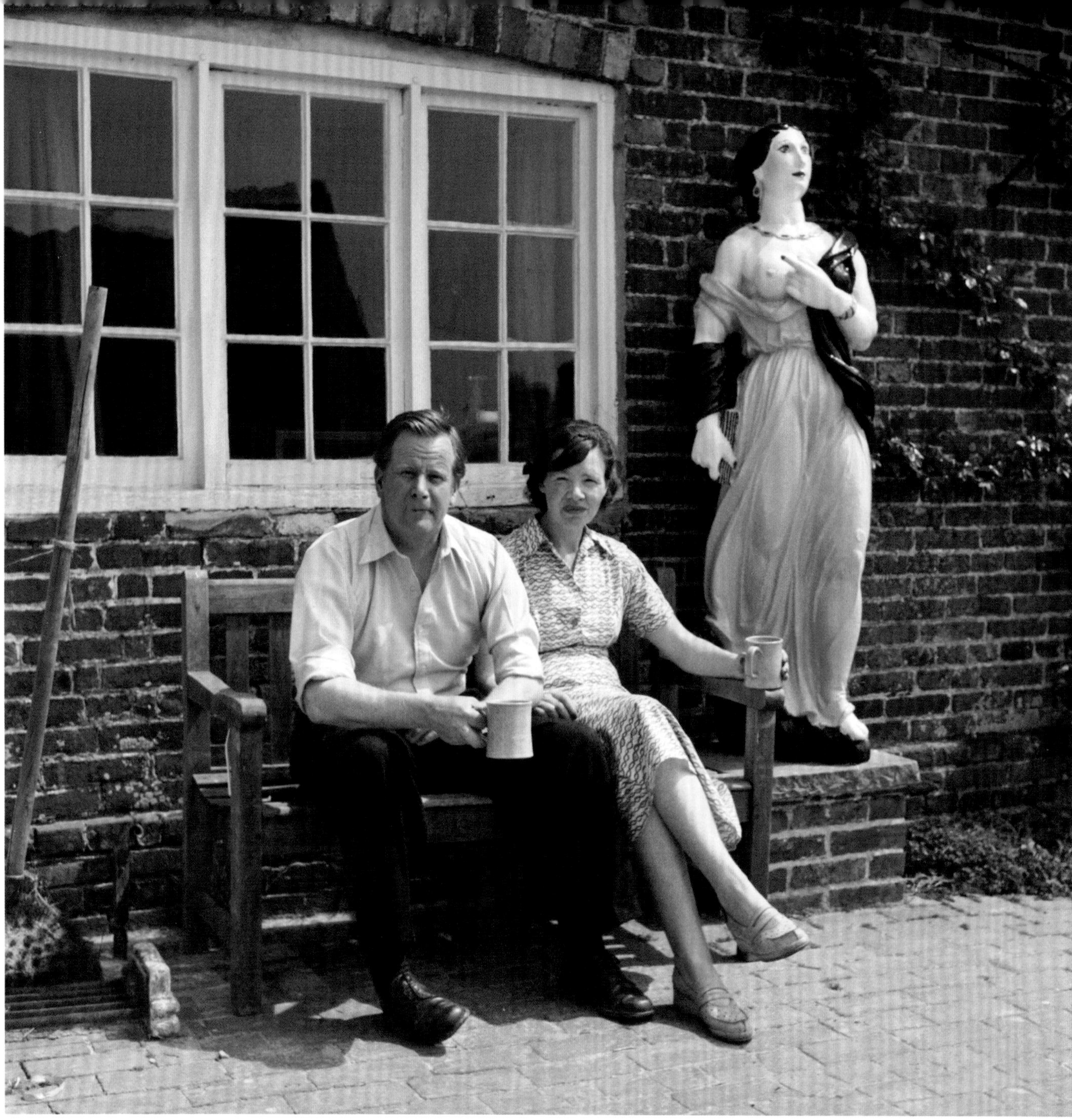

Jim (Editor) & Kit (Artist) Richards, Farleys House

Roland had found an old photo album that had probably belonged to one of his aunts. She had filled the first few pages with formal photographs of the places she had visited but the remainder was untouched. Heavily bound with pages of thick paper it was ideal for use as our visitor's book, and so it became, keeping safe the record of our guests until 1981, three years before my father died.

Other friends from that September and October included the Albanian/American photographer Gjon Mili, who Lee had photographed in New York City in 1946 and John and Cynthia Thompson, two outstanding journalists. Jim (James Maude) Richards, editor of *The Architectural Review* and the new love of his life the artist Kit Lewis. The diplomat Bernard Burrows, Lee's old friend from her Egypt days, came with his Hungarian wife Ines, later with their baby daughter Antonia and the up and coming QC Jeremy Hutchinson with his then wife, the actress, Peggy Ashcroft.

The mix of vibrant and eminent friends bonded by a passion for the arts established the pattern of entertaining at Farleys that was to last for the next 45 years.

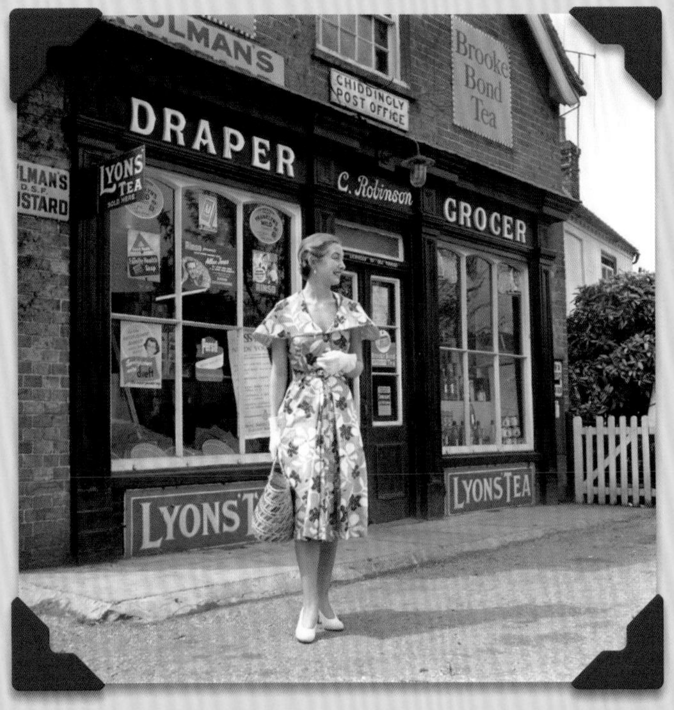

Fashion Shoot, Chiddingly Post Office Store 1950

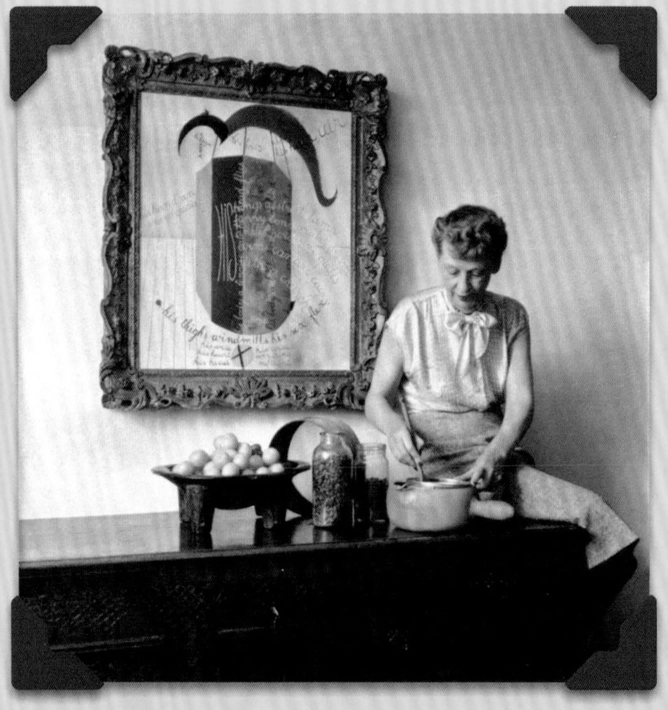

Madge Garland (Professor Lady Ashton),
Farleys House 1950

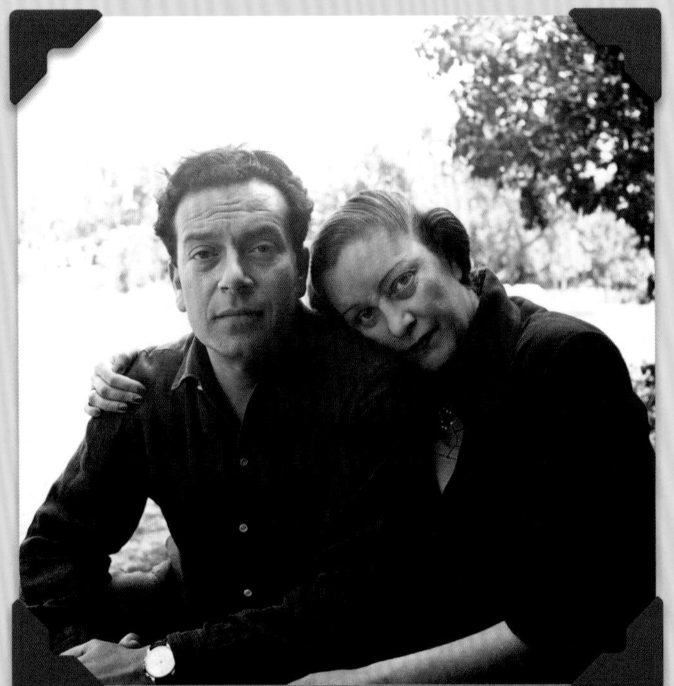

Renato Guttuso (Painter) and Mimise Guttuso,
Farleys garden 1950

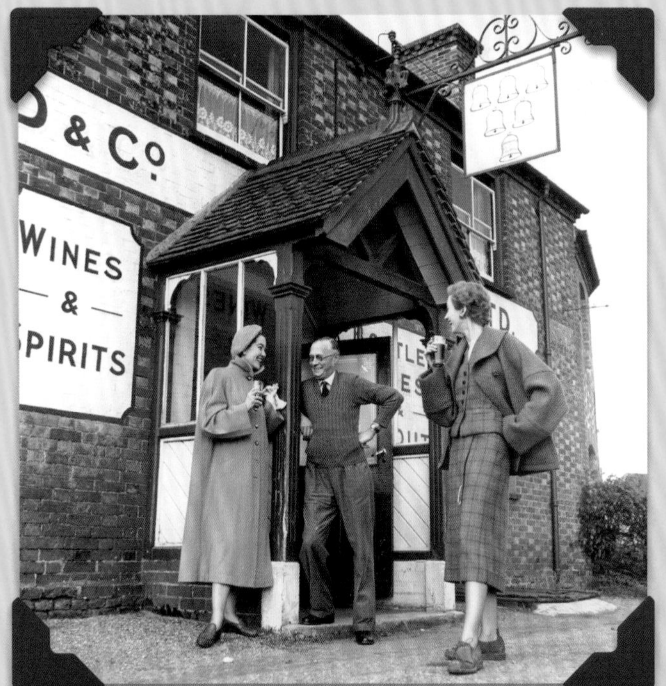

Fashion Assignment, models talk to Charlie Kirby
at the Six Bells pub, Chiddingly 1950

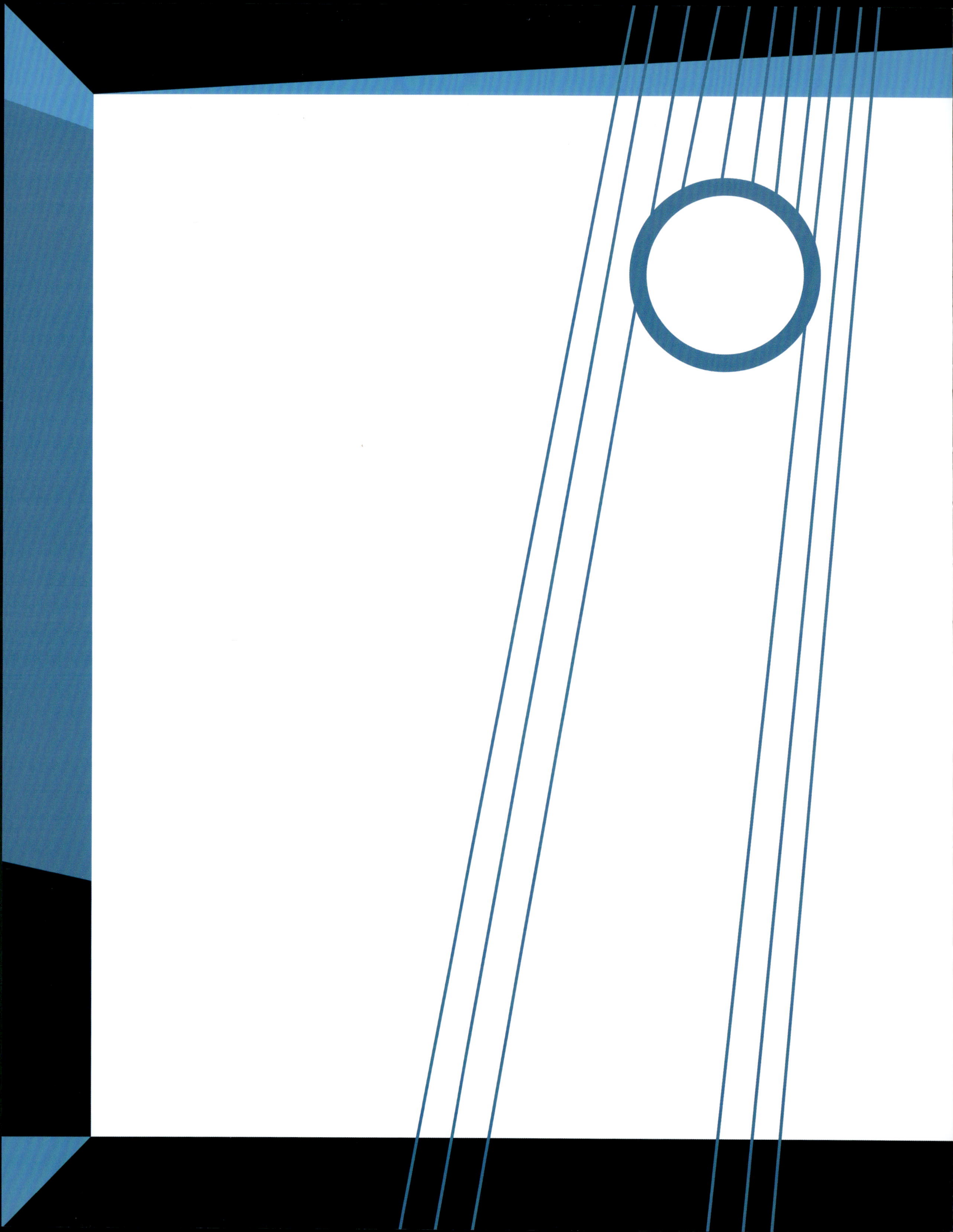

CHAPTER 01

BITING PICASSO

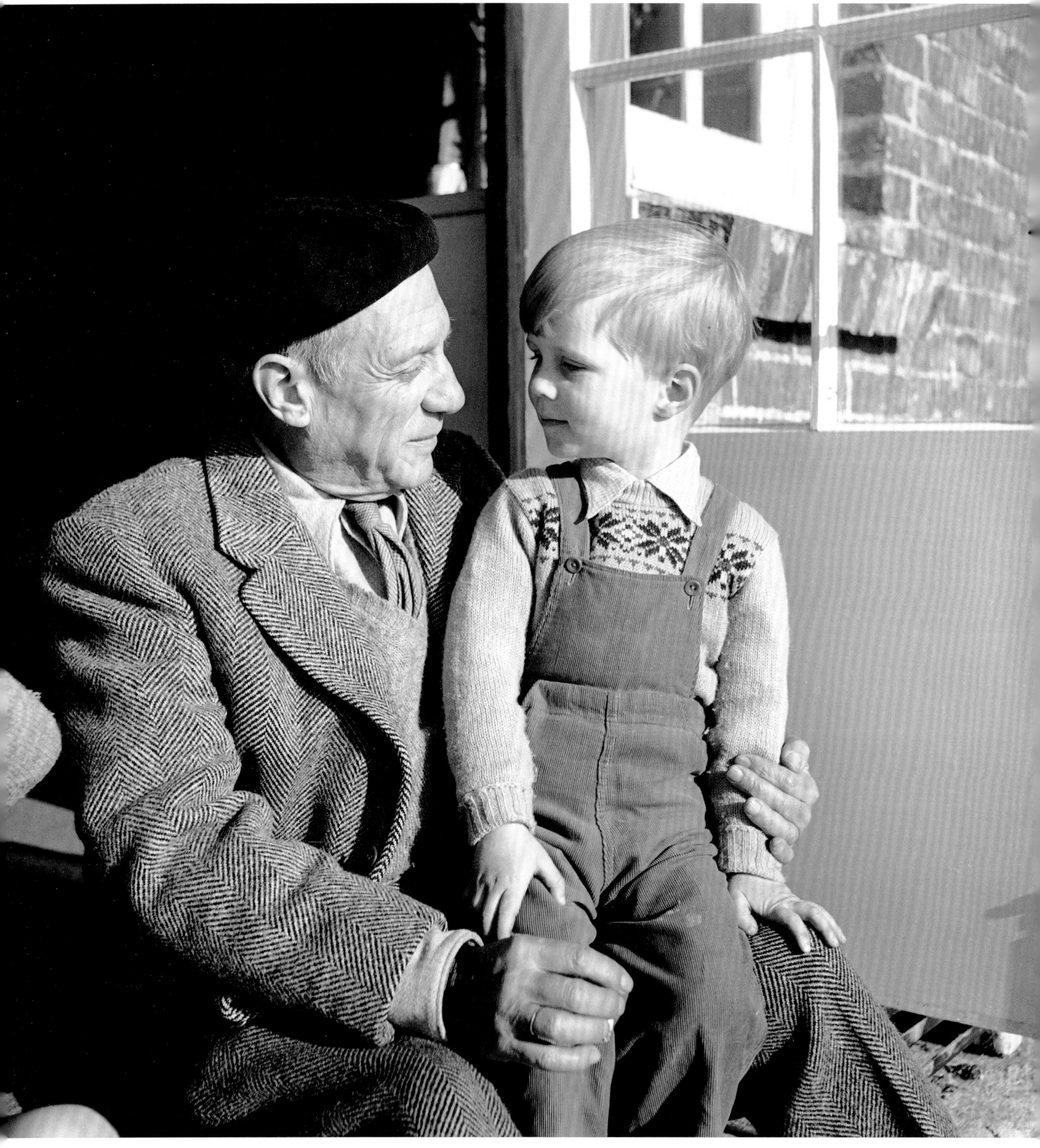

Picasso and Antony Penrose, Farleys House 1950

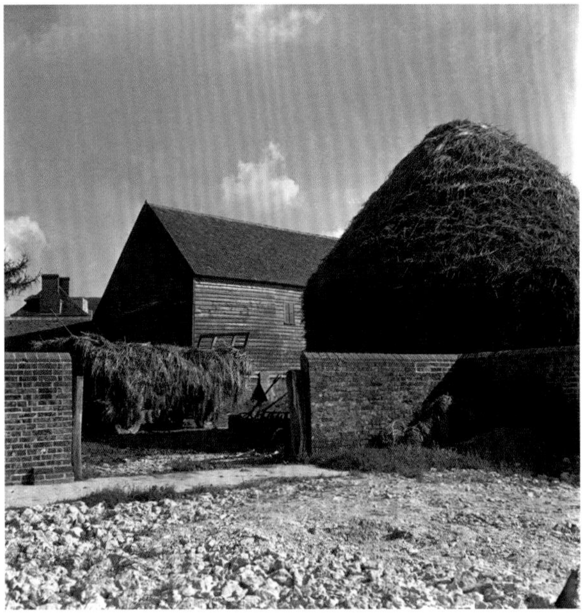

Stack, Farley Farm 1953

I am eternally thankful that Lee wrote about Picasso's visit to Farleys in 1950 for British *Vogue*'s November edition in the following year. Her piece marked my father Roland's Picasso exhibition at the Institute of Contemporary Arts in London, marking the artist's 70th birthday.

I was three years old and Picasso's visit has stayed in my memory as a series of hazy sensual recollections. Picasso smelled good. It might have been Eau de Cologne or some wonderfully perfumed soap from the south of France. It was a distinctive scent blended with the smell of his French cigarettes, probably fixing itself in my memory because it was not associated with any other adults in my life. My other memory is tactile. Picasso's Mediterranean warmth guaranteed he was wonderfully generous with hugs and cuddles and I have a vestigial memory of being held tightly against the coarse scratchy fibre of his tweed coat while immersed in the odour of his scent.

As for me biting Picasso, in our family that did not even rate as a story of minor interest, and would have been forgotten had Lee not written so amusingly about it for *Vogue*. This monumental piece of bad behaviour was prompted by events around our bull called William.

Roland had owned our family farm only eighteen months and wanted to share his love of it with his friend, Picasso. We walked across the field to where our herd of Ayrshire cows were kept, twenty-four of them tied up by the neck in a row of stalls. I am sure Picasso enjoyed their serenity and their quiet munching of their cud in the warm cow shed, but Lee did not document this moment with her camera. My guess is the light level was too low and it would have been hard to get a shot that was more than a row of cow's bums. Instead, she waited until we stepped outside. On the south wall of the barn there was a small hatch where tempting food could be dropped into the manger of William the bull. When he was eating, hauling on a chain closed on a yoke around his neck, making it safe to enter his pen. That day there was no need for this restraint. William was in a good mood and poked his head out through the hatch. He snuffled and extended a long pink tongue, perhaps hoping for a treat to eat. I watched while Picasso gently stroked William's nose. Lee caught the moment with her Rolleiflex camera. In her photograph, the bull, well known for being bad tempered to the point of occasional acts of aggression, seems to enjoy this contact with his new found friend. He has a dreamy look, and Picasso has clearly made a rapport with him. I was later to find that Picasso had an enviable way of charming birds, animals and small children.

Later back in the house Picasso and I invented a game. It was based on a bull fight and in my own defence I have to state it was a decade before I understood how vile the cruelty of bullfighting is in reality. On this occasion it was a wild romp. I was the bull. With my fingers held as pretend horns I charged at Picasso who fluttered his jacket like a matador's cape. Picasso, aged 69, was far more nimble on his feet than I was, and finding myself unable to gore

Antony Penrose and Picasso with William the Bull, Farley Farm 1950

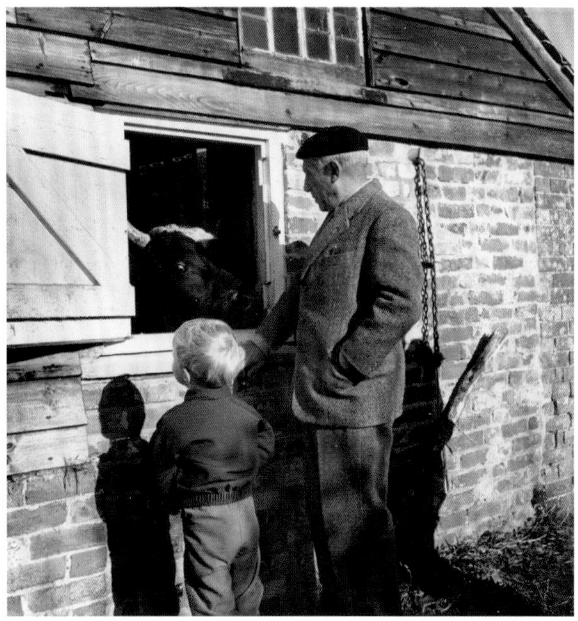

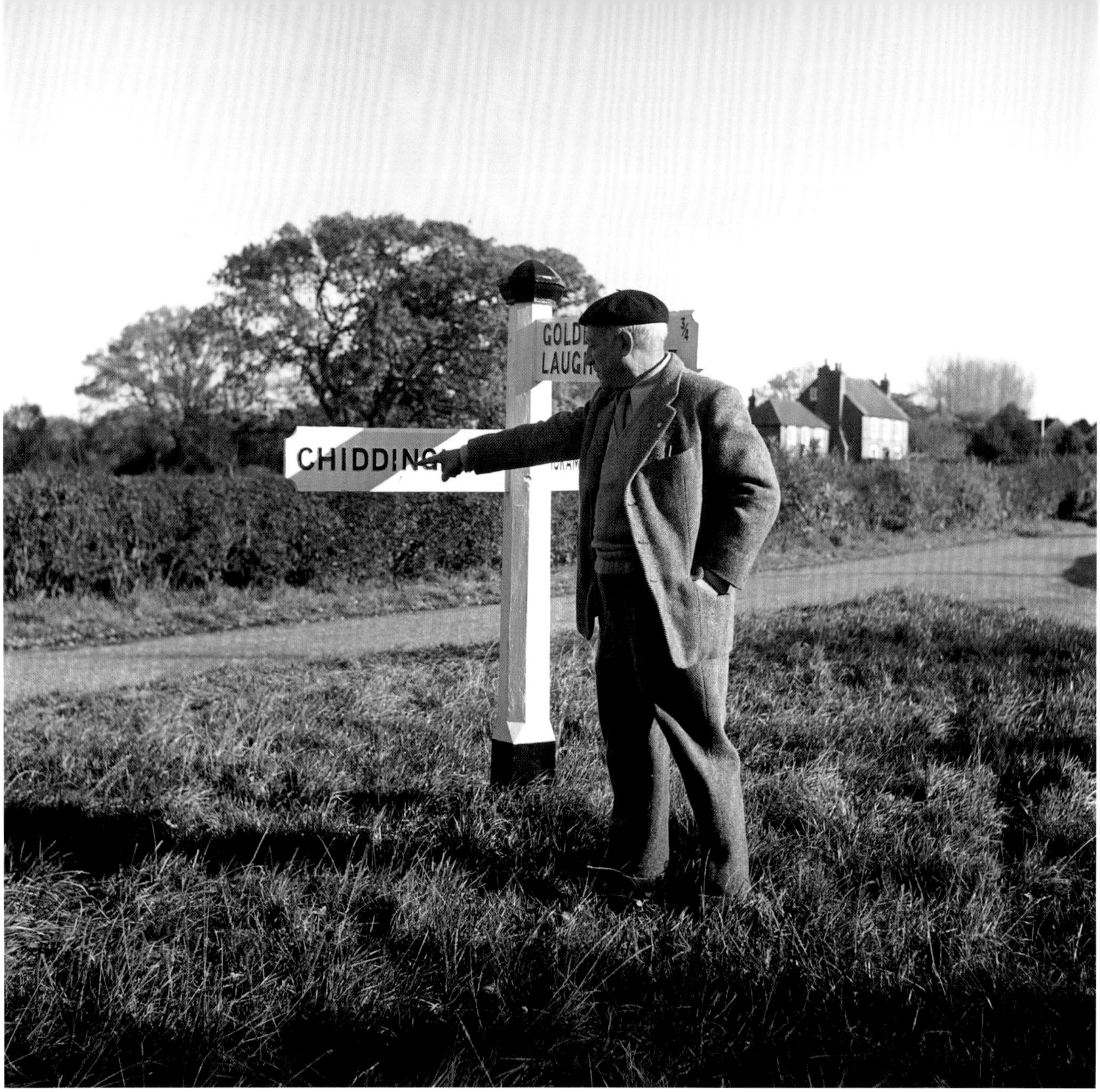

Picasso by the sign post, Chiddingly 1950

him I gave up in frustration. Then it seems I got a cunning idea. When he was not looking, I sneaked up and bit him, hard, on the wrist. With lightening reflexes, he turned and bit me right back, harder. Sometime later when my full-throated yells had subsided Lee heard Picasso say "Pensez, c'est le premier Anglais que j'ai jamais mordu".[1] ("To think, that's the first Englishman I have ever bitten".) From that day on I never bit another person. Sad, because given my parents circle of friends I could have had a serial career biting artists.

Lee does record Picasso's impressions of Farleys;

At the farm, Picasso found the world was very English; the landscape of the Downs with Constable clouds and transparent backlighting, the prudish Long Man of Wilmington, the driving on the left, the red and white Ayrshires, black and white Wessex pigs, open log fires, whiskey and soda nightcap, hot water bottles, cooked breakfast and tea. He could scarcely know that besides modern pictures, an English farmhouse does not have rows of French Sabots inside the back door, garlands of garlic, and furniture that lived it first hundred years in Gascony. But the tinned plum pudding on my tinned menu, holly wreathed and flaming was indeed English, VERY English and superb.[2]

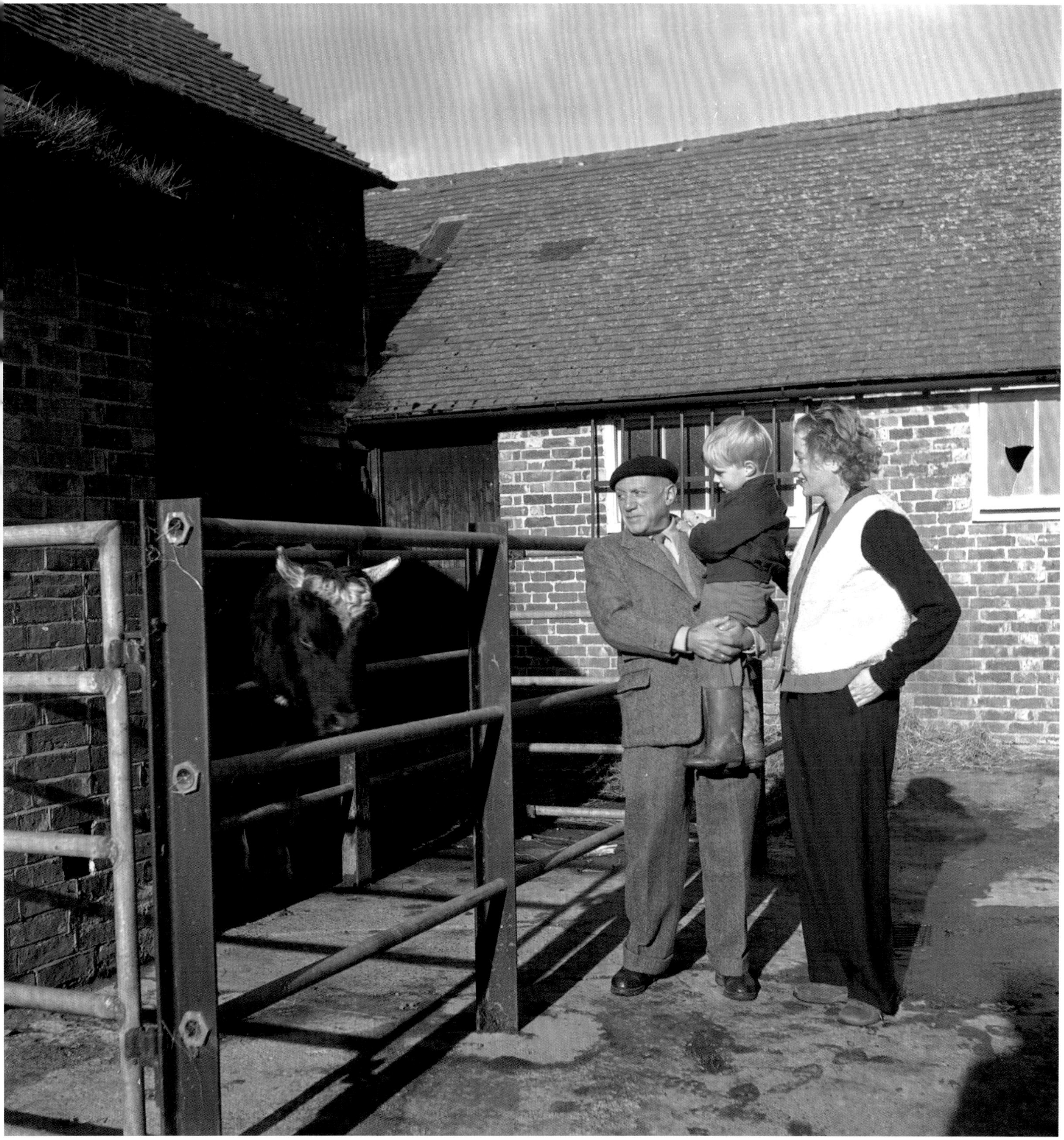

Picasso, Antony Penrose and Lee Miller, Farley Farm 1950 by Roland Penrose

The article was published with one photograph of Picasso and me. The flawless composition and technical perfection of this shot belies what photographers generally agree is the most difficult assignment they can land; photographing their own family. The one roll of film Lee took of Picasso in the setting of our home show us the woman who had, in extreme danger, unflinchingly photographed combat and scenes of utter depravity was clearly of this opinion. The film roll was cut before the negatives were numbered and they appear on the contact sheet out of their original sequence. The first shots are worthy of a 'Don't do it like this' sequence in a guide to photography. The composition is terrible and Lee's shadow invades the shot. She changes the angle to eliminate the shadow but the dog climbs in to the frame. Someone drags the dog away, but by then something far worse has happened and it shows clearly in my face. I have totally lost interest in being photographed and want to do something far more rewarding. Picasso saved the day. He whispered something in my ear. It was probably in French or Spanish but whatever he said the language did not matter as it did the trick and playing photos became fun again. In that moment Lee's shutter clicked on what photographers call 'The money shot', the one that made it into *Vogue* magazine. It is also the one shot that for me sums up the joy of that day in November 1950.

Ayrshire Cows going to be milked past Farleys House 1950

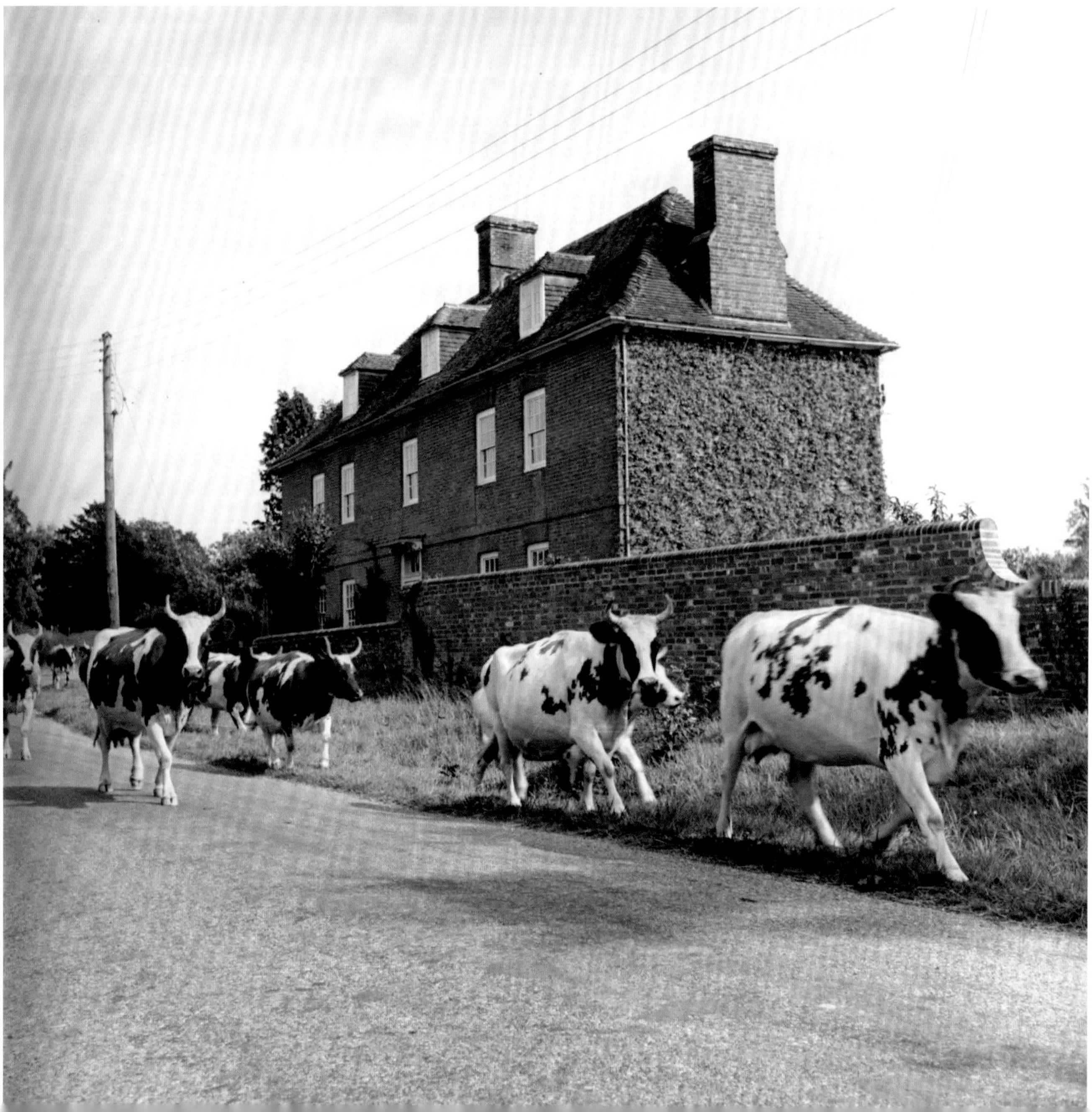

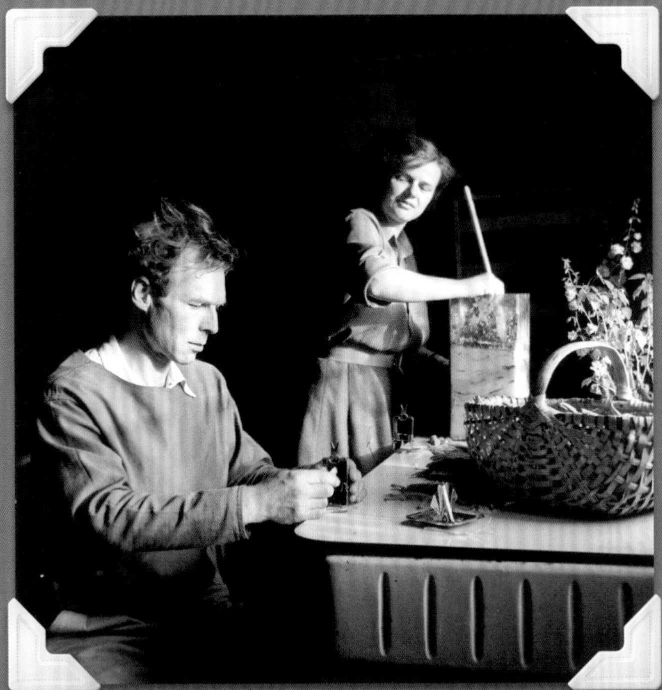

Reg Butler, prize winning sculptor and his wife Jo, slicing and salting beans for preserving, Farleys 1952

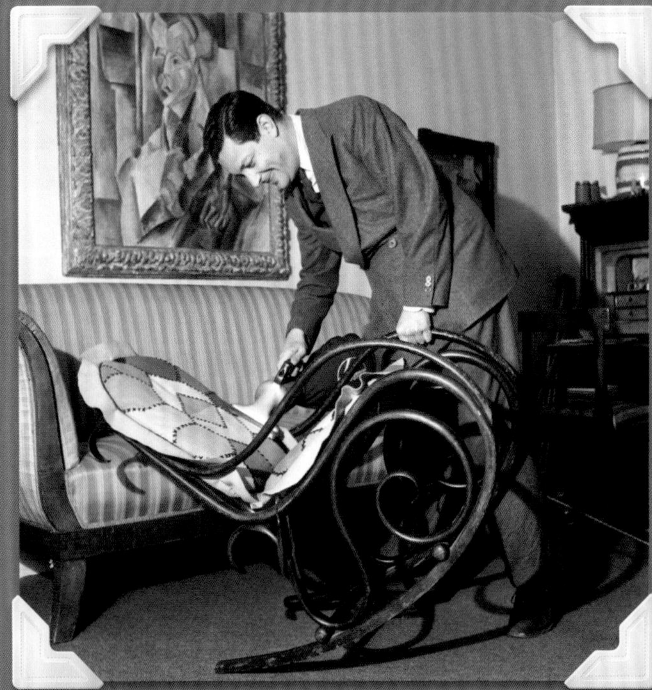

Georges Bernier (Humorist), Farleys House 1952

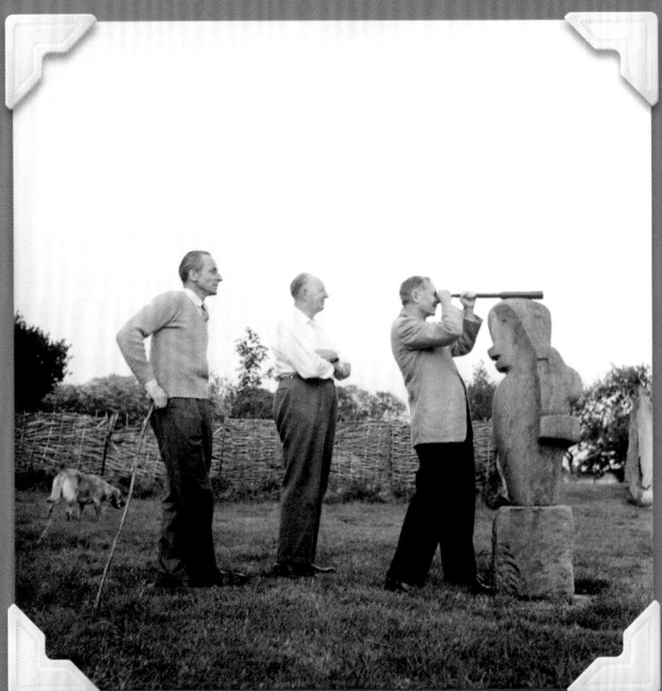

Jake Carter (Author), Peter Gregory (Publisher), Alfred Barr (Art Historian), Farleys garden 1952

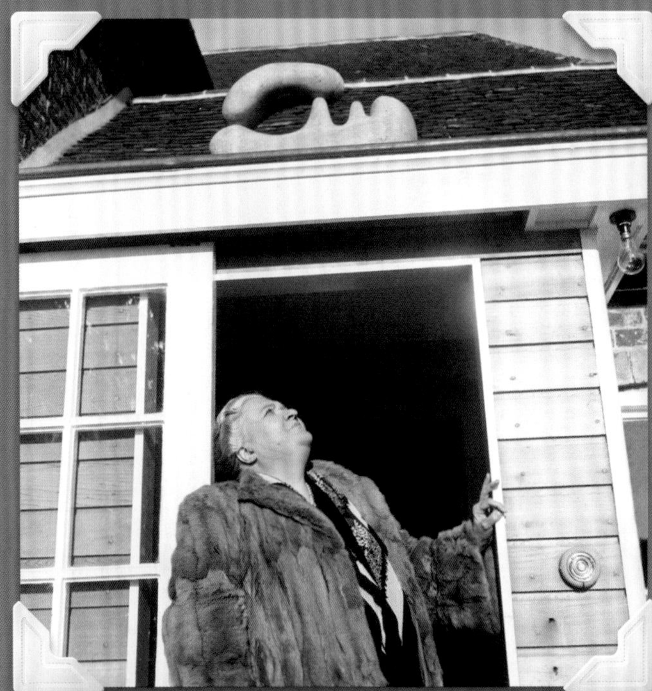

Moura Budberg (Baroness) Farleys 1952

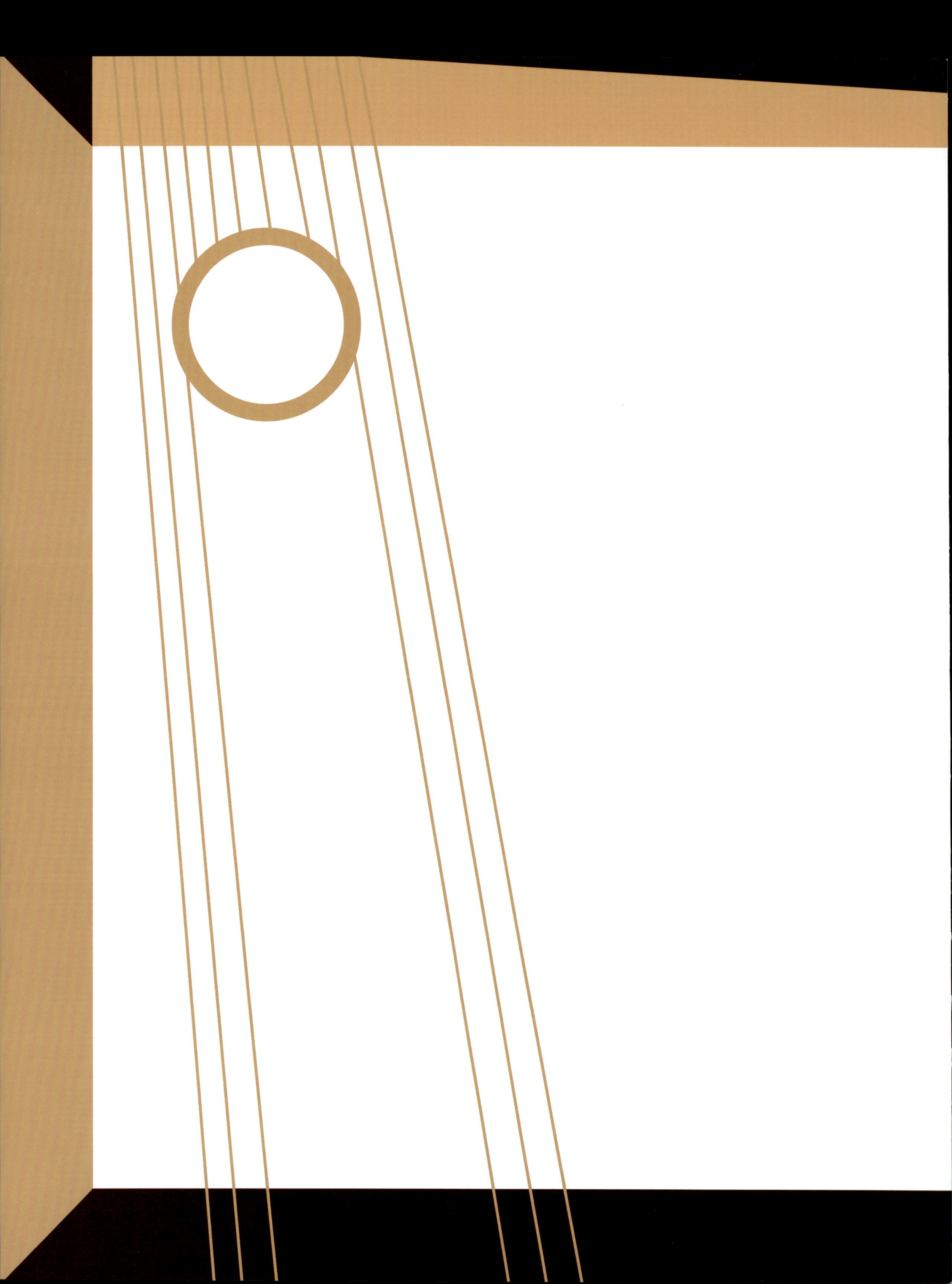

CHAPTER 02

CHRISTMAS AT FARLEYS

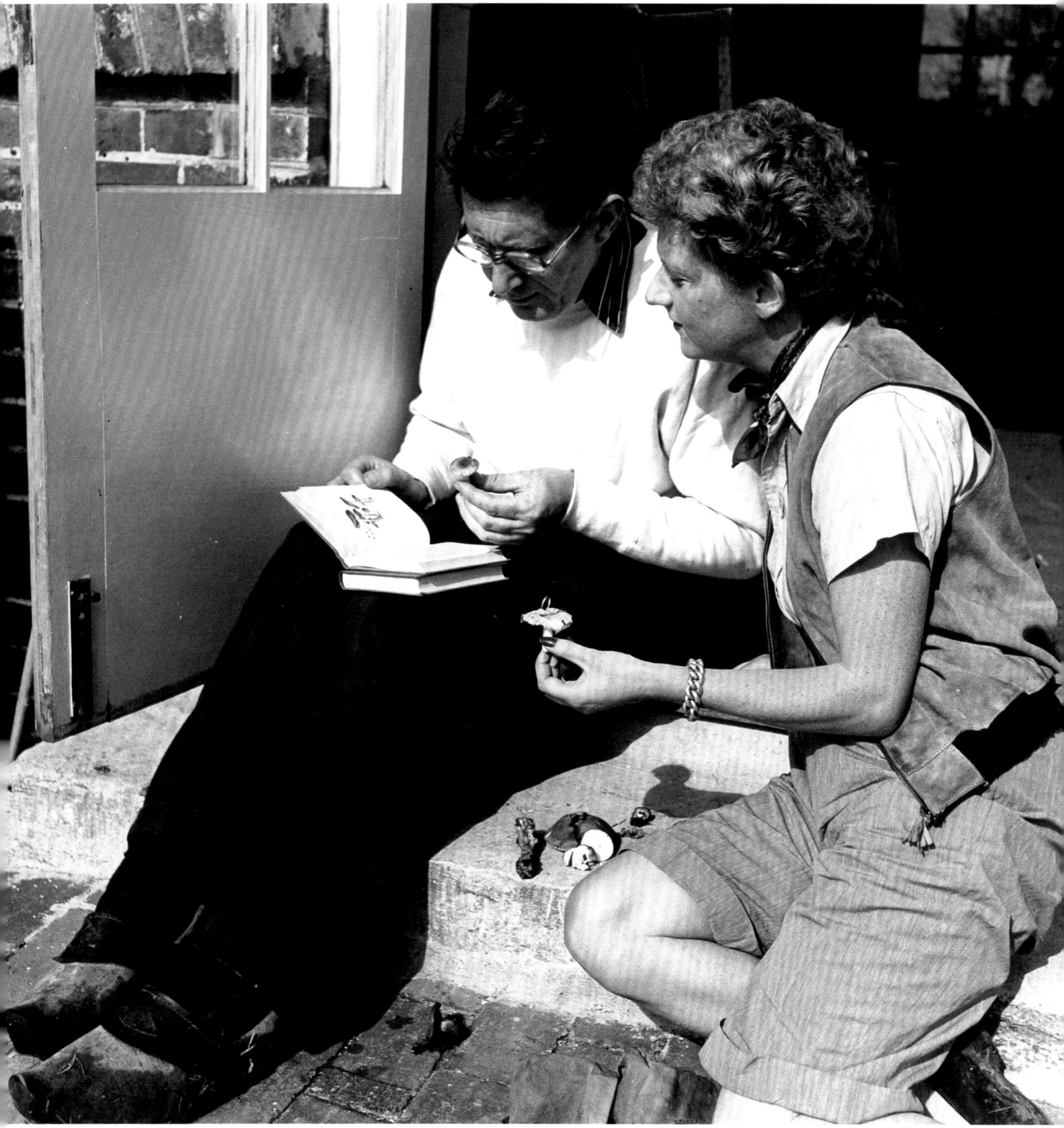

Roland Penrose and Timmie O'Brien, Farleys House 1951

The extreme weather at the end of 1949 was a rough introduction for my parents, Lee and Roland, to the hardships of living in the country. In an undated letter[1] to her parents Lee wrote;

> *... one of the biggest storms the country ever had. Tons of rain and a 50 mile (an hour) gale. The electricity held out but the telephone was cut off for three days. ... floods over the road so deep we were afraid of the ignition, cows marooned on islands.*

Their guests that weekend were Jeremy Hutchinson and his wife Peggy Ashcroft, the actress. Jeremy, later to be Baron Hutchinson of Lullington QC, met, my father, when Roland invited Jeremy, then a young lawyer, to defend him on a charge of 'obstructing the highway'. In 1948 the newly formed ICA (Institute of Contemporary Art) founded by Roland and Herbert Read, mounted the exhibition *40 Years of Modern Art* in the Academy Hall in Oxford Street. On the corner beside the hall, in an area cleared by a Luftwaffe bomb, they placed on a high plinth *Kneeling Woman*[2] by the Irish sculptor F.E. McWilliam. So many people stopped to admire this erotic and mysterious sculpture they blocked the street, stopping the traffic. The police charged Roland with obstruction and he was a summonsed to appear in court. Before proceedings began the senior magistrate spoke. "If – God forbid – my house was to catch fire and a crowd of people assembled to watch, blocking the street, would I then be charged with obstruction? This ridiculous case is dismissed". Jeremy was crestfallen. He relished using his already well-known cross examination skills. Among many other high profile cases Jeremy would later successfully defend Christine Keeler and Penguin Books in the *Lady Chatterley's Lover* trial. Much later he was to be the Chairman of *The Elephant Trust*, set up by Roland and Lee to fund projects by emerging artists that fell outside of the usual funding remits. I became a trustee in the late 1970's and being at meetings with Jeremy was for me a highly privileged tutorial in contemporary art and diplomacy.

But in 1949 Farleys despite is rustic crudeness was an intimate haven. Lee's letter continues about Jeremy and Peggy;

> *They are both very cosy and comfortable people, good conversationalists and love the country, though this time they did not see any of it. We sat around by roaring fires and read and gossiped. The house stayed pretty snug, no leaks in the main part though at one time we had to put the kitchen range out as the rain came down the chimney. The old bake oven kitchen isn't really water proof but we knew that and hadn't left anything in it for the winter which could come to harm. ... We got linoleum down on the nursery floor ... for Tony, because although they are beautiful old boards it's too cold and rough for Tony at his age especially as there is no heating except an electric fire.*

William 'Bill' Turnbull (Artist) and Terry O'Brien (Author) filling the pond, Farleys garden 1951

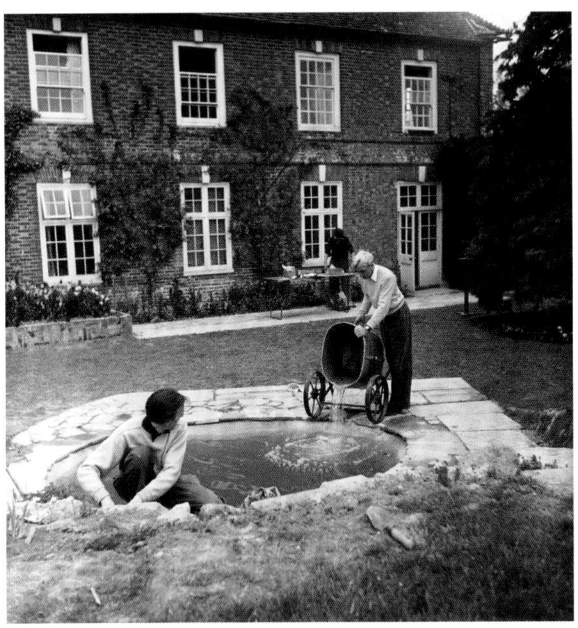

Antony Penrose, Farleys garden 1951

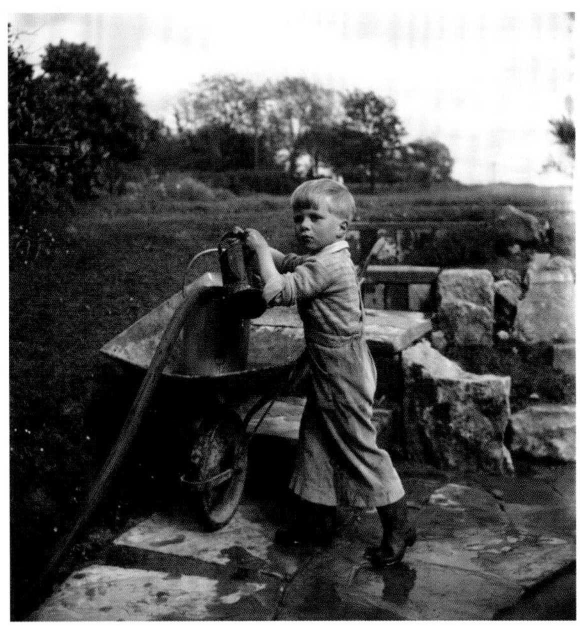

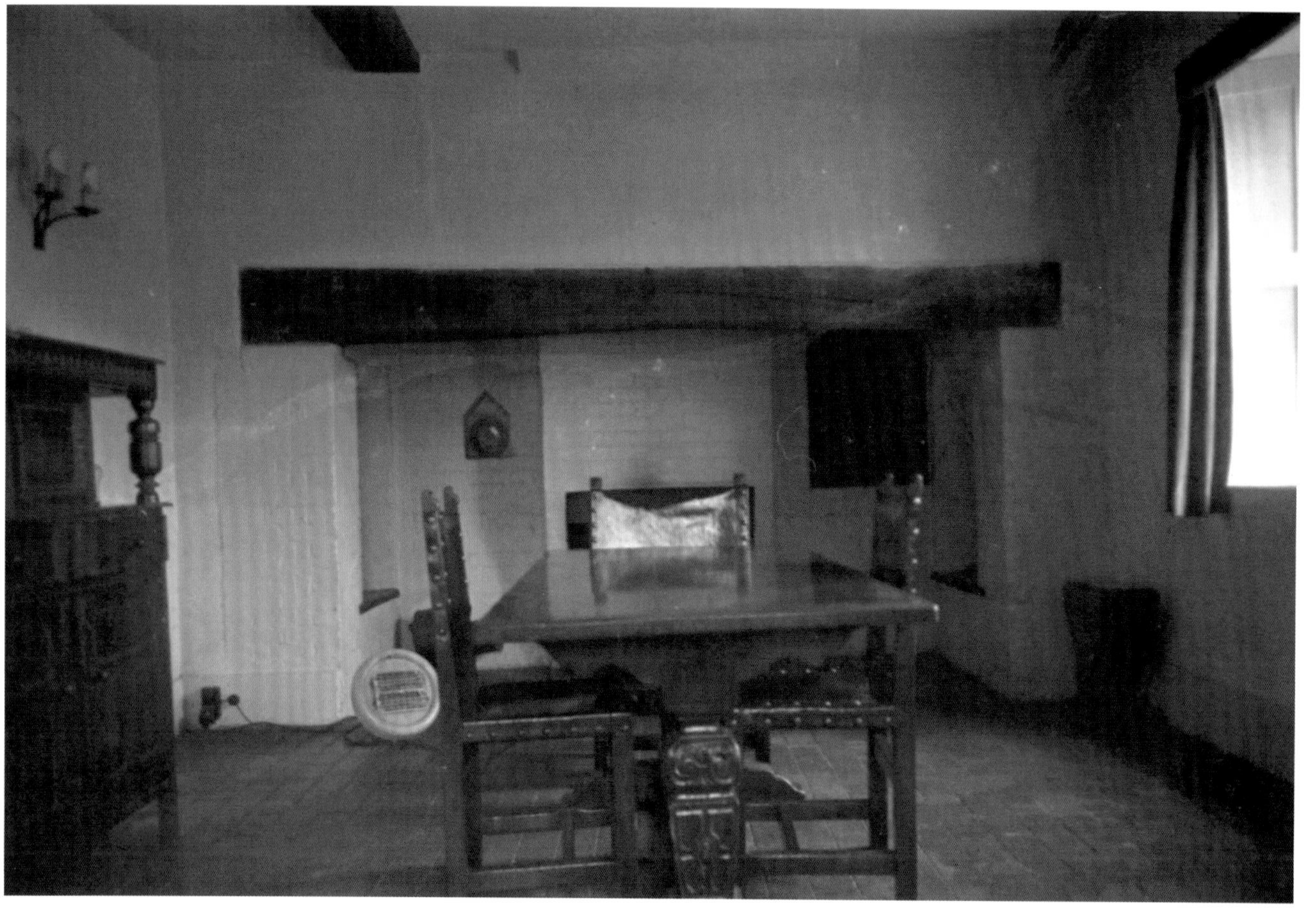

Dining Room, Farleys House 1949

The electric fire was a large sheet steel box with a vent heated by spirals of bare wire inside. A few years later it nearly cost us the house. My Plasticine was too cold and hard to work so I put it on the top of this heater to soften. The Plasticine melted and ran down inside the vent dripping onto the elements. It must have been close to the flash point of the linseed oil content by the time someone became aware, switched it off and dragged it outside.

Christmas 1949 was our first at Farleys, and we had a house full of guests. It was a courageous move by Lee because food rationing still applied and would be with us for another four years. The garden had not yet become the cornucopia it was in later years, but the dairy cows provided enough milk to allow Lee to experiment making soft cheeses. Lee and Roland were still feeling their way into farm life and it was still a year or so before we butchered our own pigs.

This background of improvisation called for carefully selected guests. Lee needed people who would pitch in and help with every task, who would laugh off discomfort and be jolly company. Those who had experienced the Blitz in London or served in the armed forces were particularly well suited and Jeremy had a distinguished war in the Royal Navy.

No records remain to give us an account of what they did for that first Christmas. Lee's lines about the Hutchinson visit give us a clue but she fails to mention she undoubtedly conjured a wonderfully startling series of dishes from our own produce augmented by foraging trips to our local towns. Cooking in a GI helmet over an open fire in sub-zero Alsace had been good training.

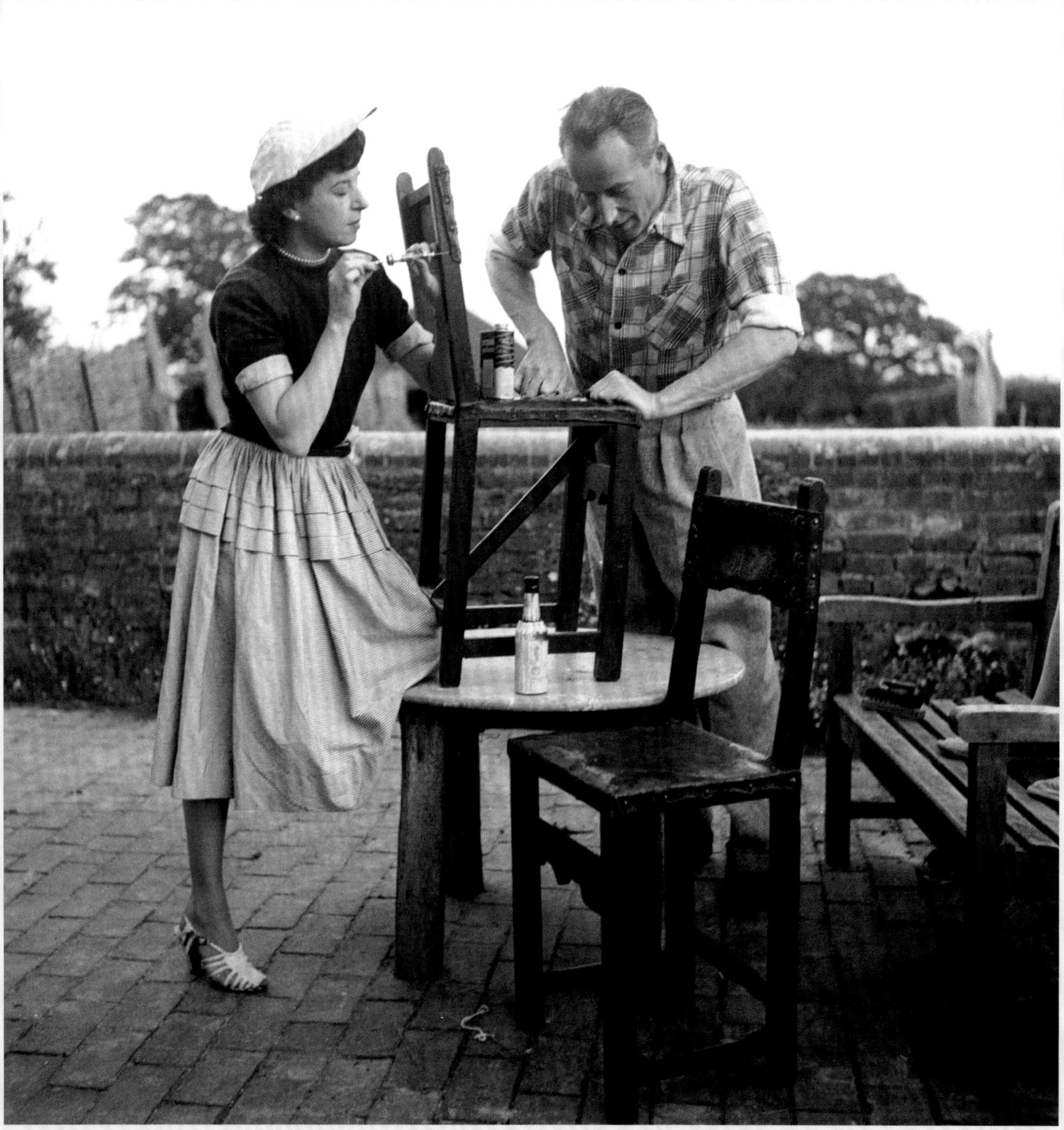

Ernestine (Fashion Editor) and Jake Carter (Author), Farleys garden 1952

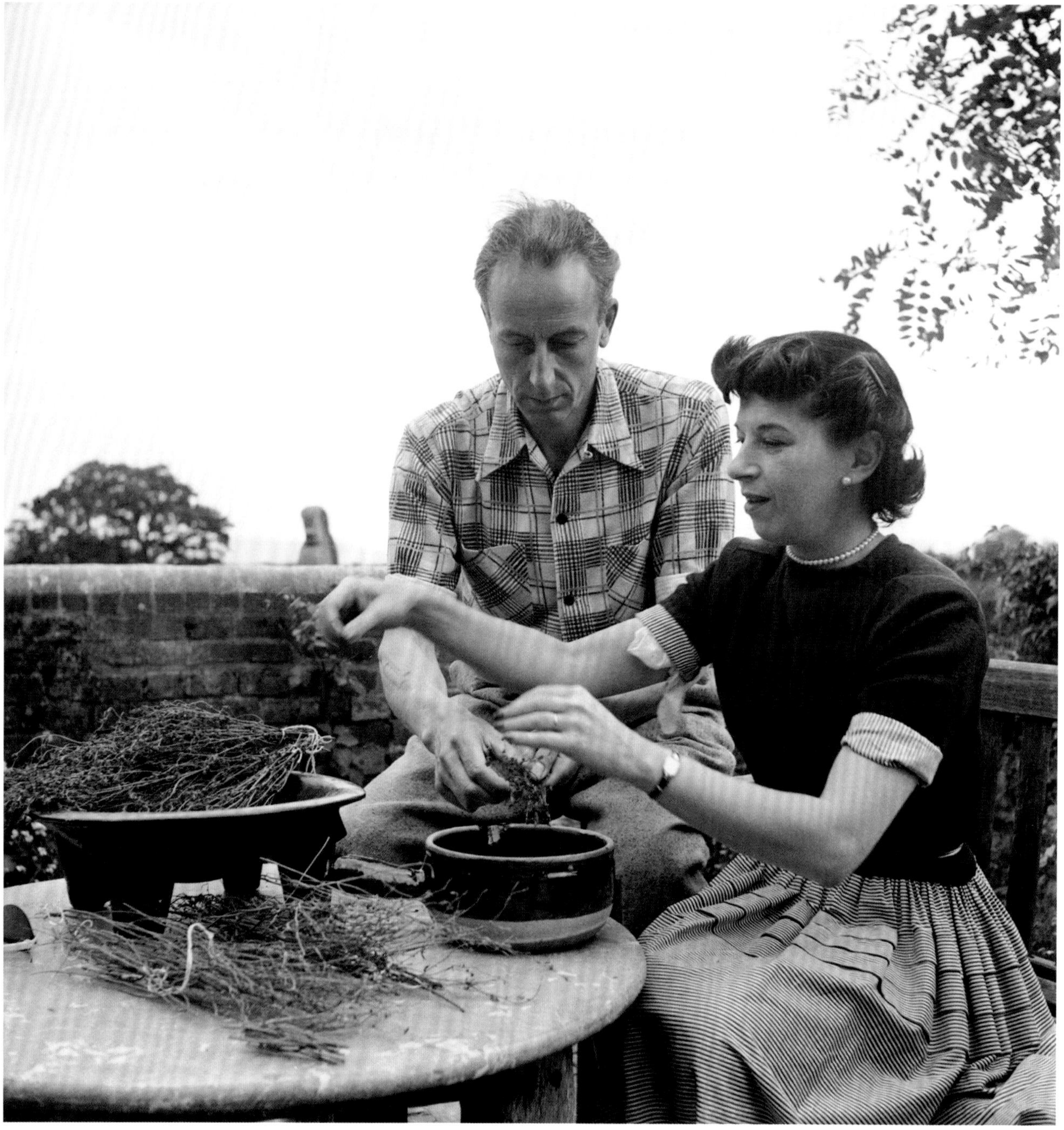

Ernestine and Jake Carter, Farleys garden 1952

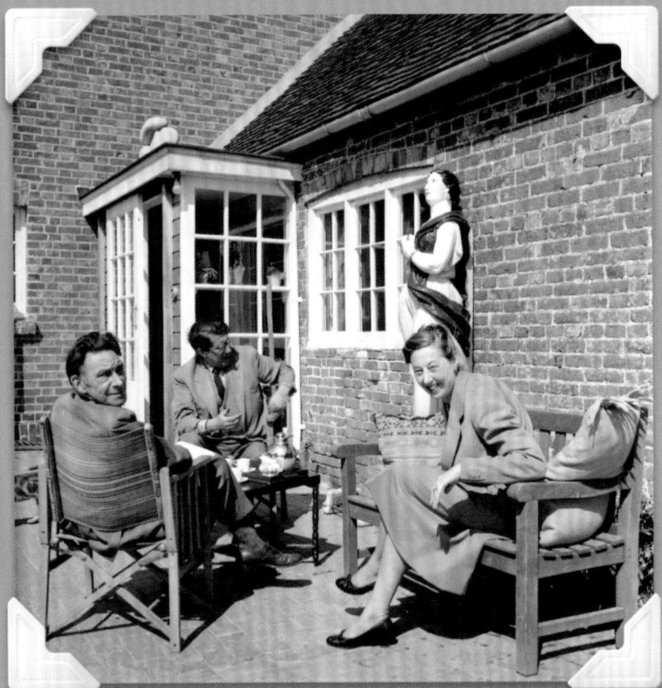

Eric Newton (Artist), Stella Newton (Fashion Designer) and Roland Penrose, Farleys 1953

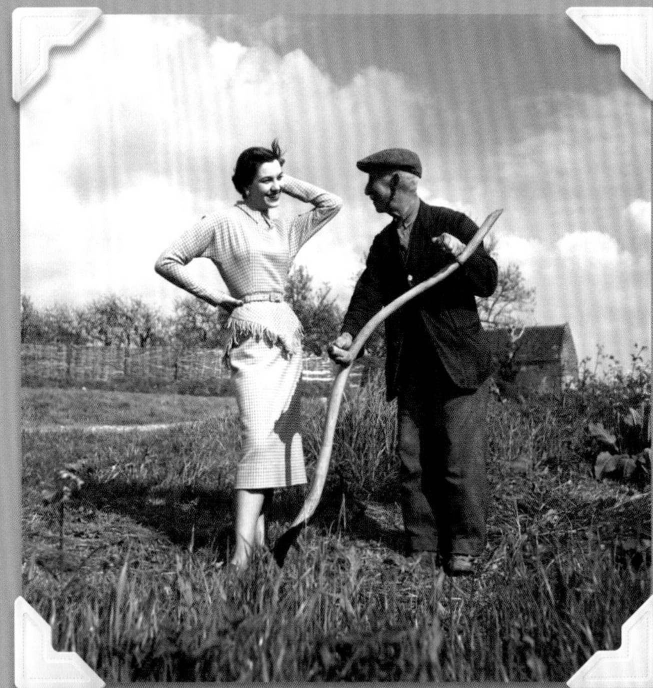

Model [Celia Thellusson] and Grandpa White, Farley Farm 1953

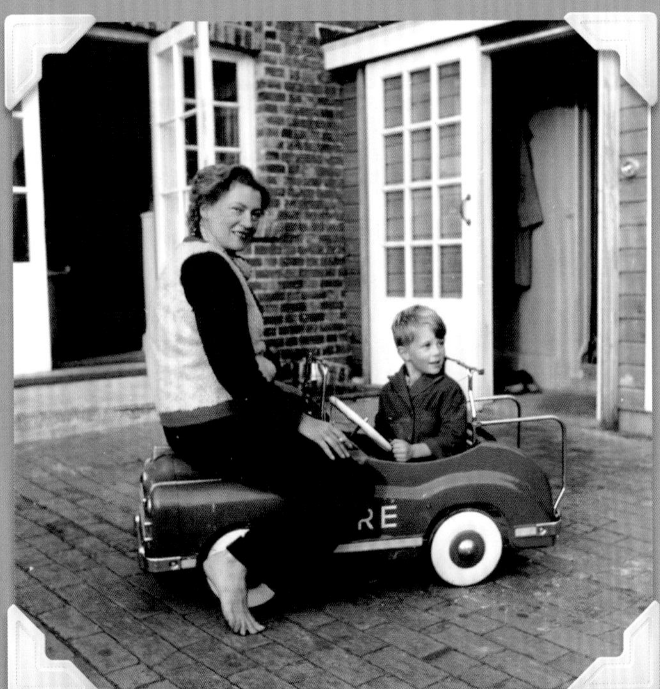

Lee Miller and Antony Penrose, Farleys garden 1953 by Roland Penrose

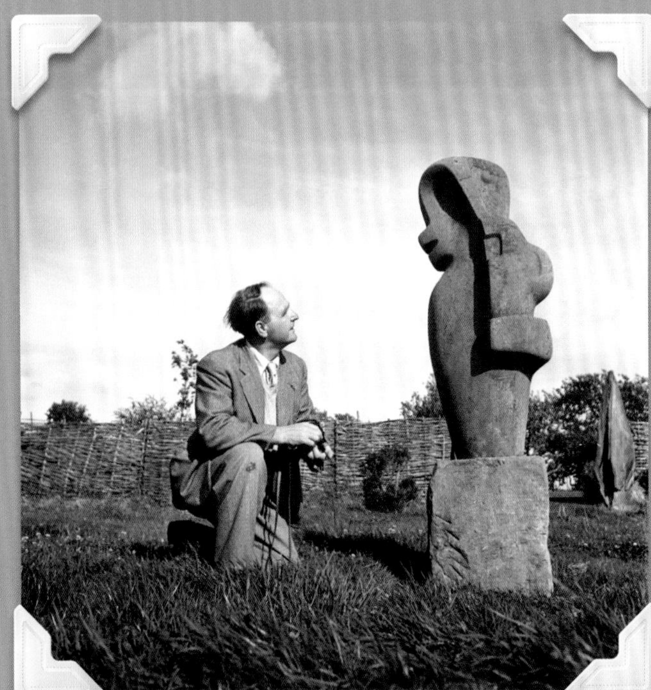

Henry Moore with his sculpture 'Mother and Child', Farleys garden 1953

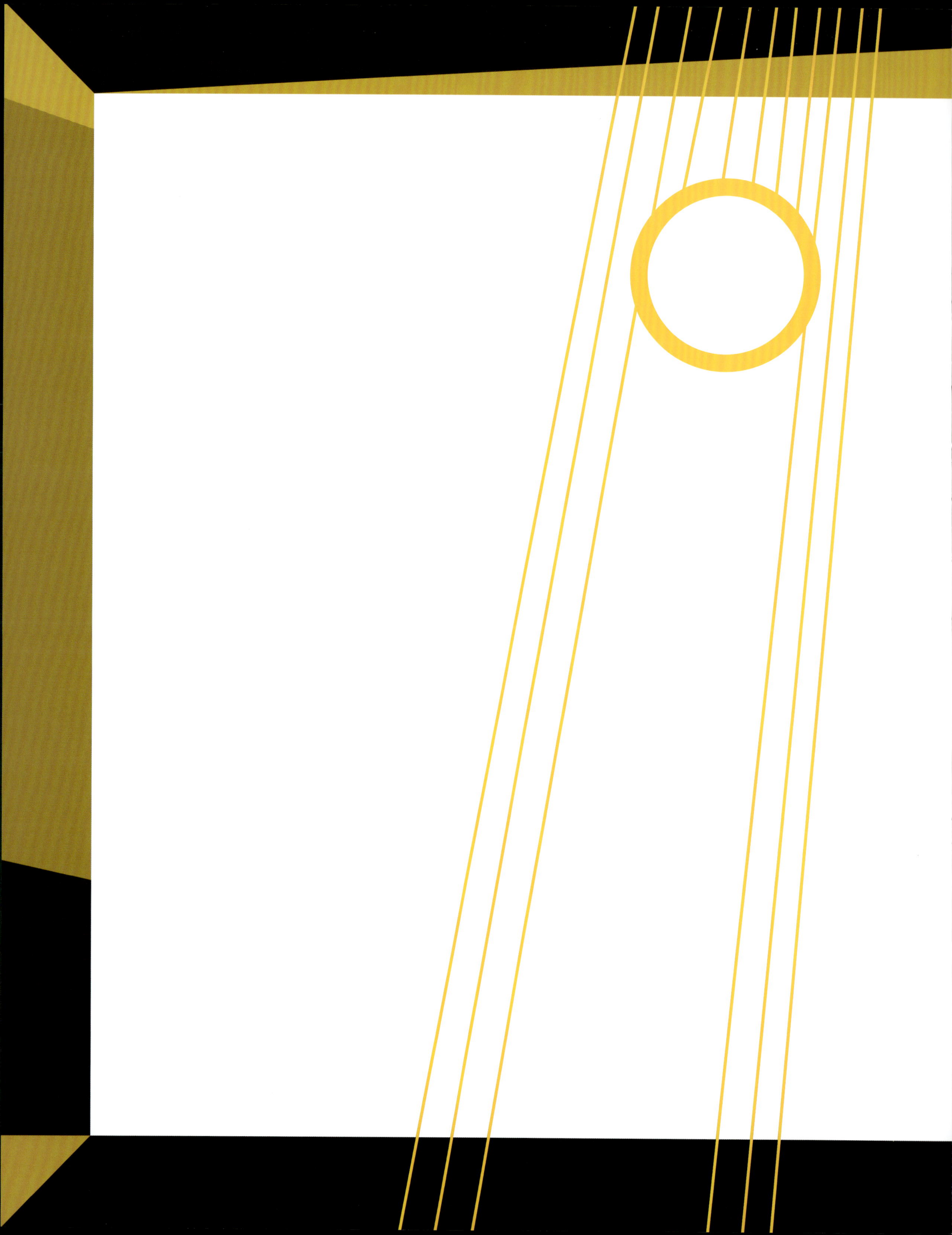

CHAPTER 03

TWO AVANT GARDE PHOTOGRAPHERS

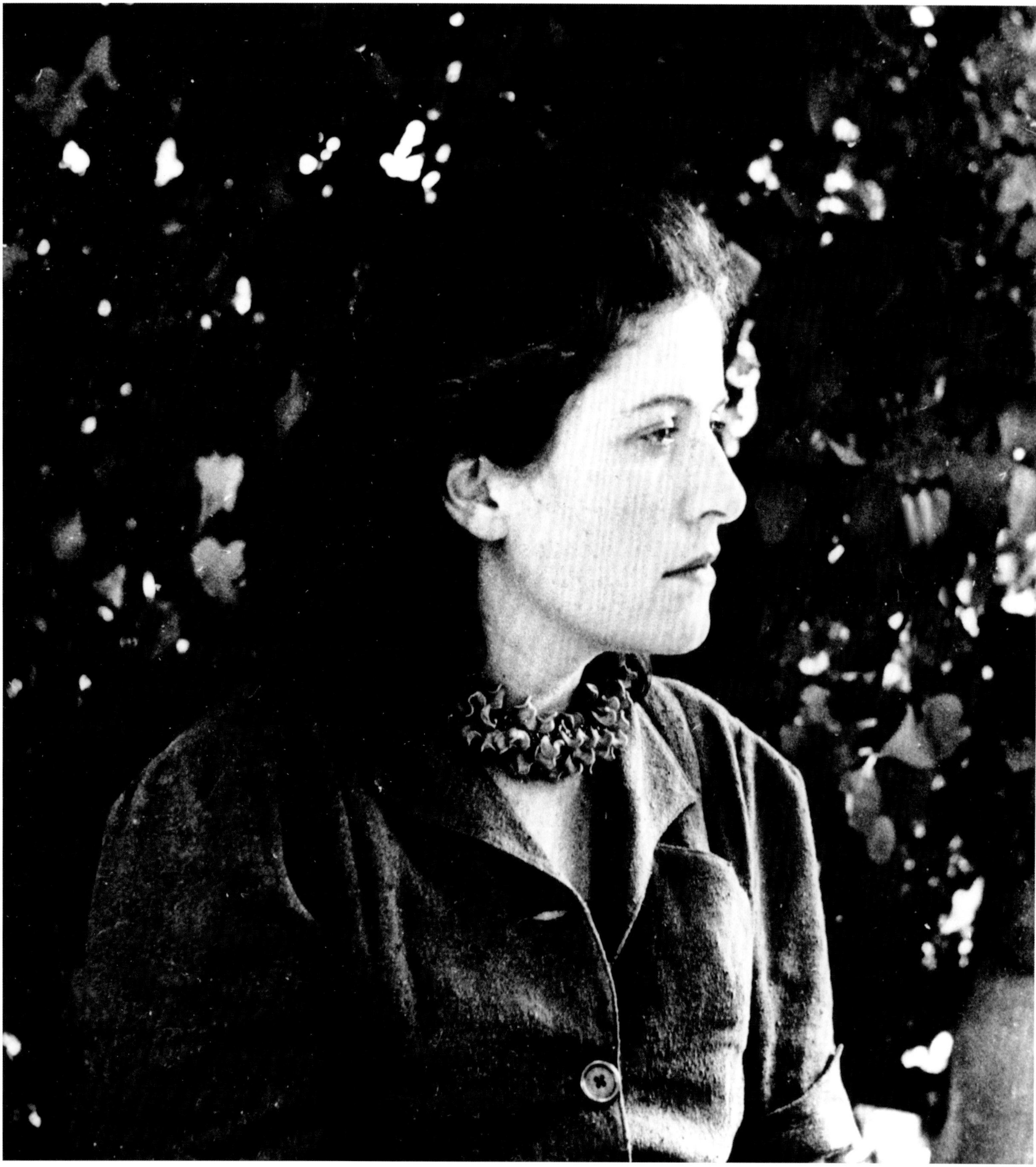

It is so desperately sad that neither of my parents kept journals of their lives. We are left with trying to piece together their time at Farleys from the sparse details found in the Visitors' Book, a few letters, Lee's photos and my memory.

I don't recall Dora Maar coming in January 1950, but her return in September 1956 remains firmly in my memory. She informed us in advance she would only come if she could be assured that she could go to mass. This caused an immediate problem. My father Roland was a Quaker and Lee an atheist with strong Quaker principles. None of us had any idea where the nearest Catholic church might be. Asking our neighbours found us St Pancras Roman Catholic Church in Lewes, not too far away for Roland to drive Dora there and back. She returned seemingly satisfied with the arrangement.

How the rest of the visit passed is guess work. What was the weather like – winters were colder then, so did Dora find the old house uncomfortable? Did they walk in the woods? The conversation, based on a long friendship, would have been well founded. When Lee lived in Paris 1928-32, she met Dora whose photographic studio in rue Campagne-Première was in the same street as Man Ray's which she frequented. Dora had become successful as a commercial photographer and well known to the surrealists for her wonderful dream like images. Three of her best known photographs, including her enigmatic shot of a baby armadillo titled *Pere Ubu*, were shown in Roland's 1936 International Surrealism Exhibition in London. In 1937 they met again when Lee and Roland joined a surrealist holiday on the Cote d'Azur staying in the small town of Mougins in the hills behind Cannes. Man Ray and Ady Fidelin were there, with Paul and Nusch Eluard, Eileen Agar and Joseph Bard, and Picasso. He had met Dora the year before, attracted to her wild recklessness as, in a café, he watched her repeatedly stabbing her pen knife into the gaps between her spread fingers. Her volatile character was evident in the blistering rows between her and Picasso, as occurred on the morning they were all planning to go to Ilse de Sainte Marguerite, in the Bay of Cannes. Dora and Picasso stayed behind to cool off thus missing inclusion in Lee's famous *'Picnic'* photograph. But Dora was never excluded from Lee's life.

Lee had an intimate understanding of the sufferings endured by creative women struggling in a male dominated world. We might expect the surrealists to have celebrated the importance of equal rights and recognition for women artists but this was far from the reality. This movement, so wonderfully iconoclastic in many other ways, remained stuck in the dark pre-feminism ages in a rigidly unenlightened way. Perhaps it was the bond of adversity, a love of photography or maybe Lee's recognition of some of the torments of Dora's soul that connected the two.

During the Cote d'Azur holiday Lee photographed Dora with Picasso, a powerful, self-determined and serious looking woman. In 1956 Lee photographed Dora in her Paris apartment looking utterly crushed, seated under her portraits by Picasso. The down swing of Dora's life was established by now. She and Picasso had finally parted in 1946 and the trauma had made her seek the help of a prominent psychiatrist. She endured the shattering effect of electro-convulsive therapy and sought solace in the Catholic church.

Being a devout Catholic is a direct contradiction to being a Surrealist. For the surrealists there was little difference in the harm they perceived done by the church and by the state. They held a relentlessly hostile attitude to both, rooted in their rebellion against control by authority. This begs the question as to how and why Dora, a surrealist photographer of outstanding brilliance should cross to the side of state sponsored religion as a fervent convert. Perhaps by contrast she was looking for something reassuringly conventional.

Picasso bought her a house in Ménerbes, where rejecting photography and her previous cubist style, she painted abstract works, some inspired by her surroundings. Among Dora's works in Lee and Roland's collection were two landscapes, small, bold, slightly brooding but wonderfully alive, although my favourite is a gouache of a glass of red wine and the broken off *'bec'* of a baguette. It is so evocative I feel I can smell the wine and the bread.

From Dora's 1956 visit I remember her as distant and not child friendly. She clearly liked the solitude of the house and the beauty of the surrounding landscape because she made three very lovely drawings. A pencil sketch looks west across the farm to the Oast Houses on Burgh Hill beyond. Using a slightly different angle of the same

Dora Maar, Mougins, France 1937

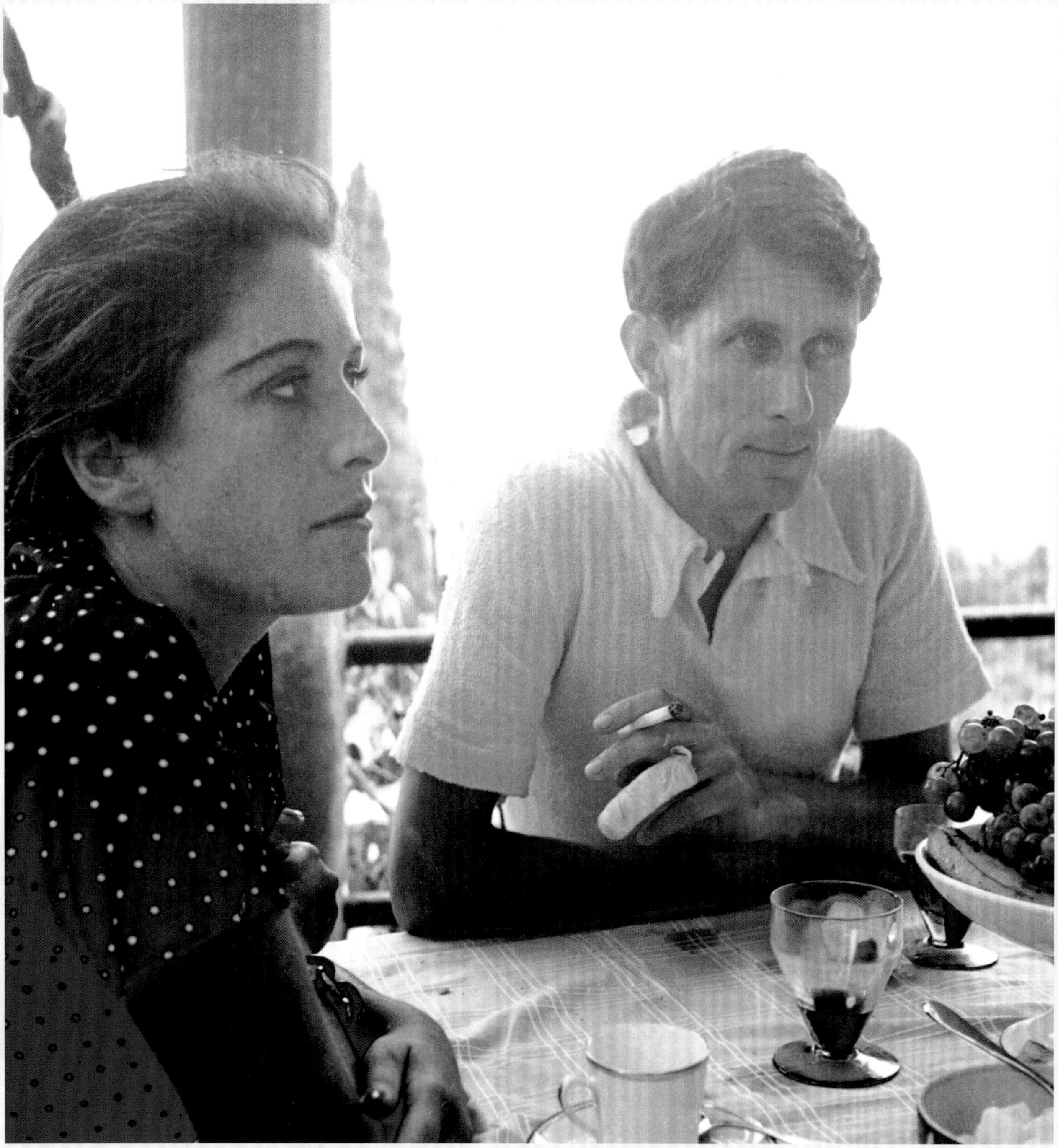

Dora Maar and Roland Penrose, Mougins, France 1937

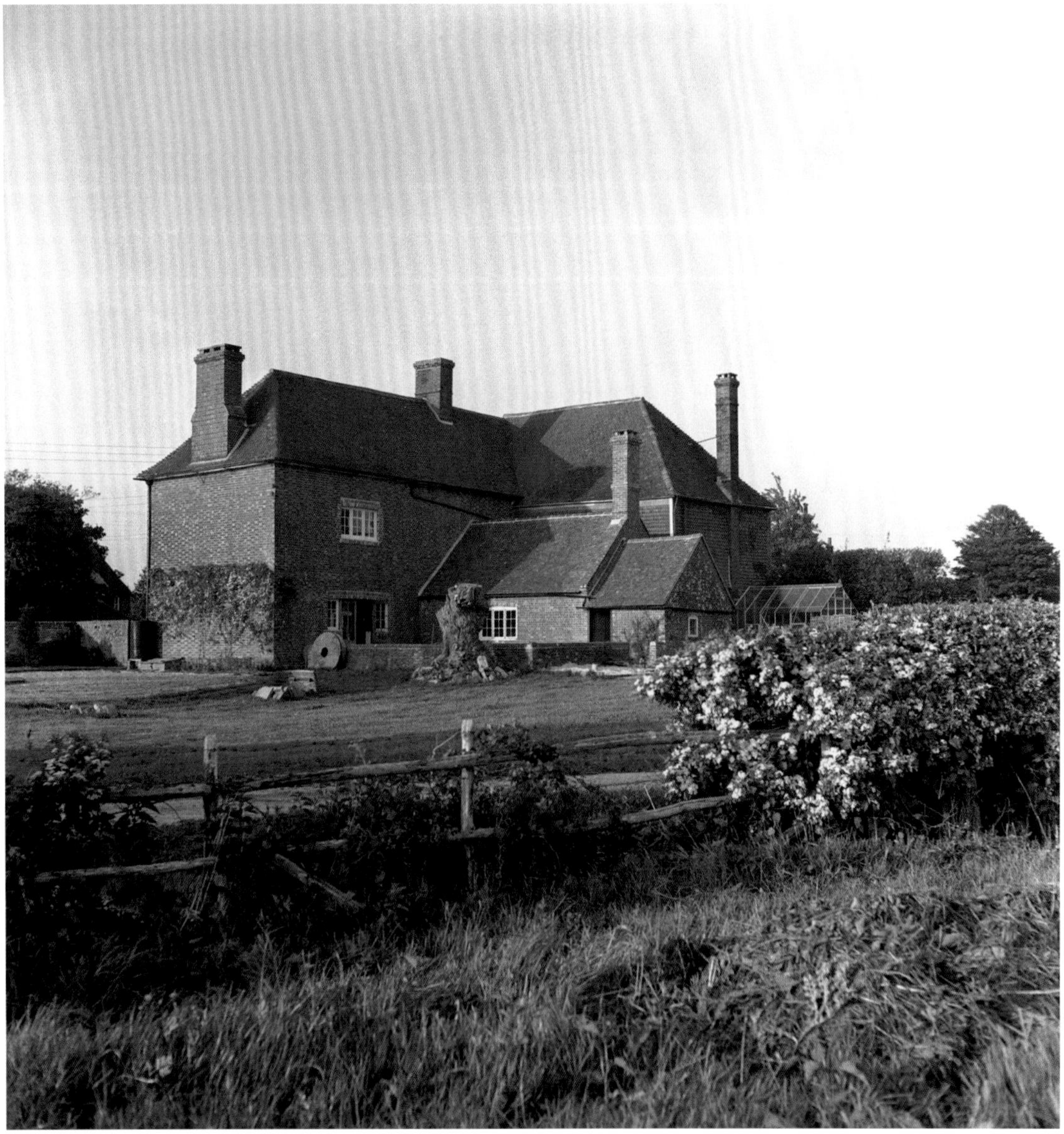

Farleys House 1951

view she made an ink pointillist drawing and then turned south to draw the tiled roof of a farm building in the same manner. Maybe there were showers that day as it seems she worked from inside the house. Lee photographed[1] her drawing from the window of the parlour, a room added by Roland in 1954. Dora returned Lee's compliment by making a deeply sympathetic pointillist portrait of Lee. Dora, who re-met Lee at the Liberation of Paris, had through her own experience a clear understanding of the acute emotional pain Lee was suffering as a result of her war work. In the years that followed Dora became increasingly reclusive. Lee stayed in touch as best she could, but sadly in Lee's final years these two women saw little of each other.

Our other visitors in January 1950 were Oscar Dominguez, the painter who originated from Tenerife and came with his wife, the painter Maud Bonneaud. Oscar, afflicted with a disease that distorted the shape of his face could have been a little scary but clearly his charm must have won through as I recall not a trace of trauma. He gave me a little painting of a fantastic car sprouting flowers, dated 1948. Sadly, the wonderful works by him that Roland owned are no longer part of our collection but the car still rolls along.

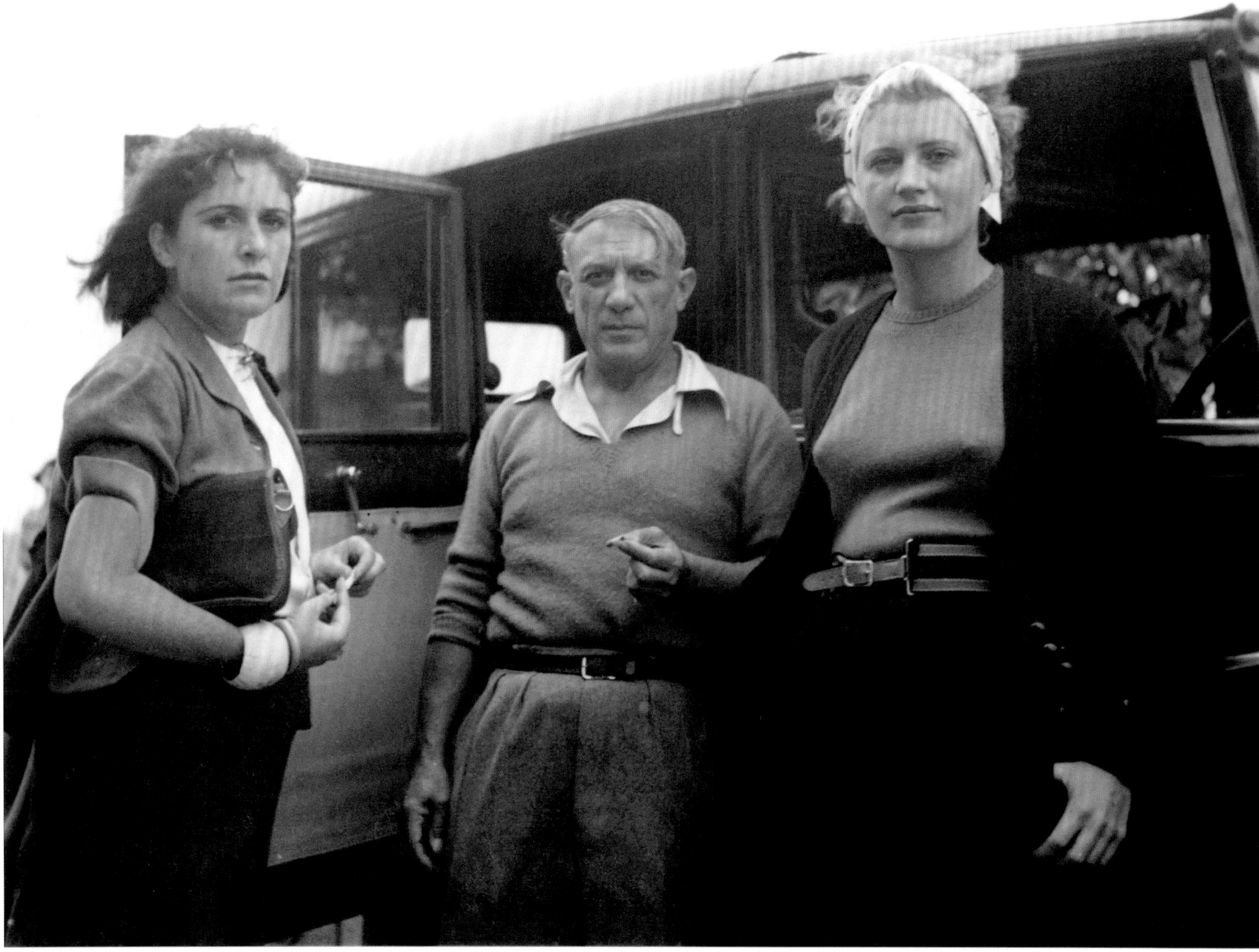

Dora Maar, Picasso and Lee Miller, Mougins, France 1937 by Roland Penrose

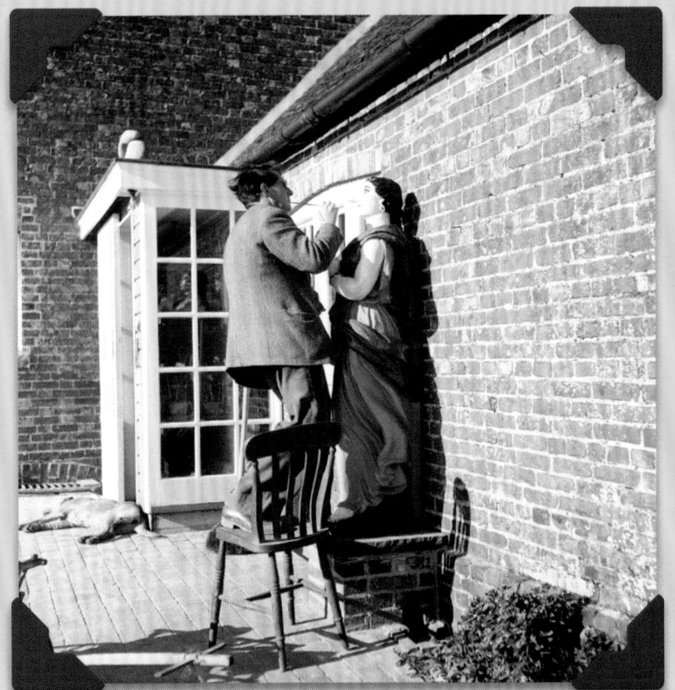

Roland Penrose, Farleys House 1954

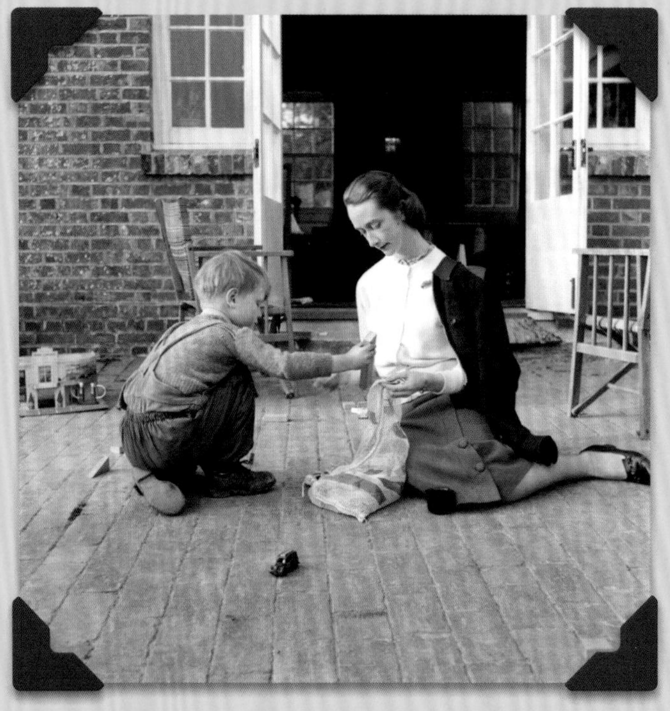

Antony Penrose and Jane Samuel, Farleys 1954

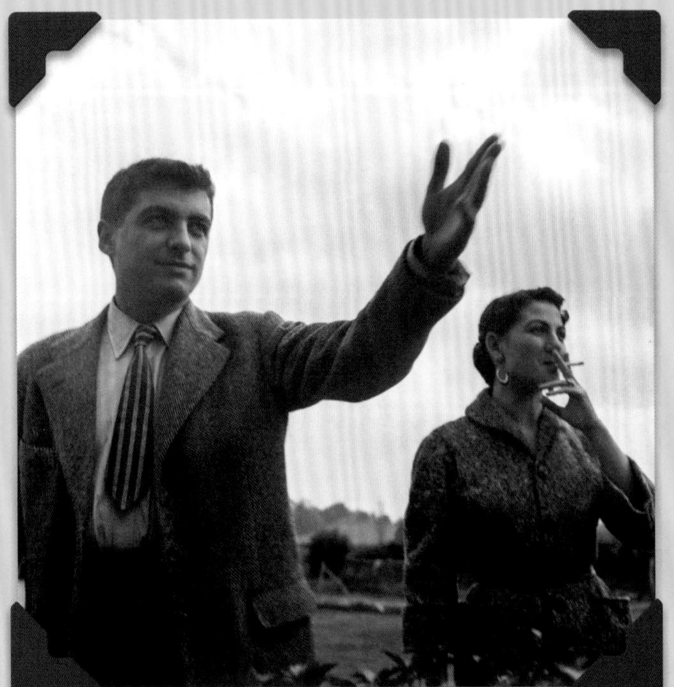

Alain Gheerbrant (Author), Farleys garden 1954

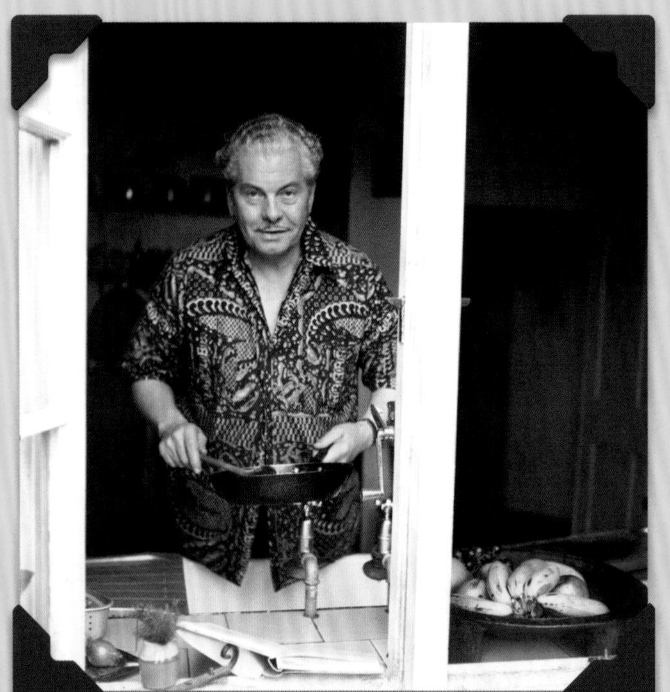

Wells Coates (Architect), Farleys kitchen 1954

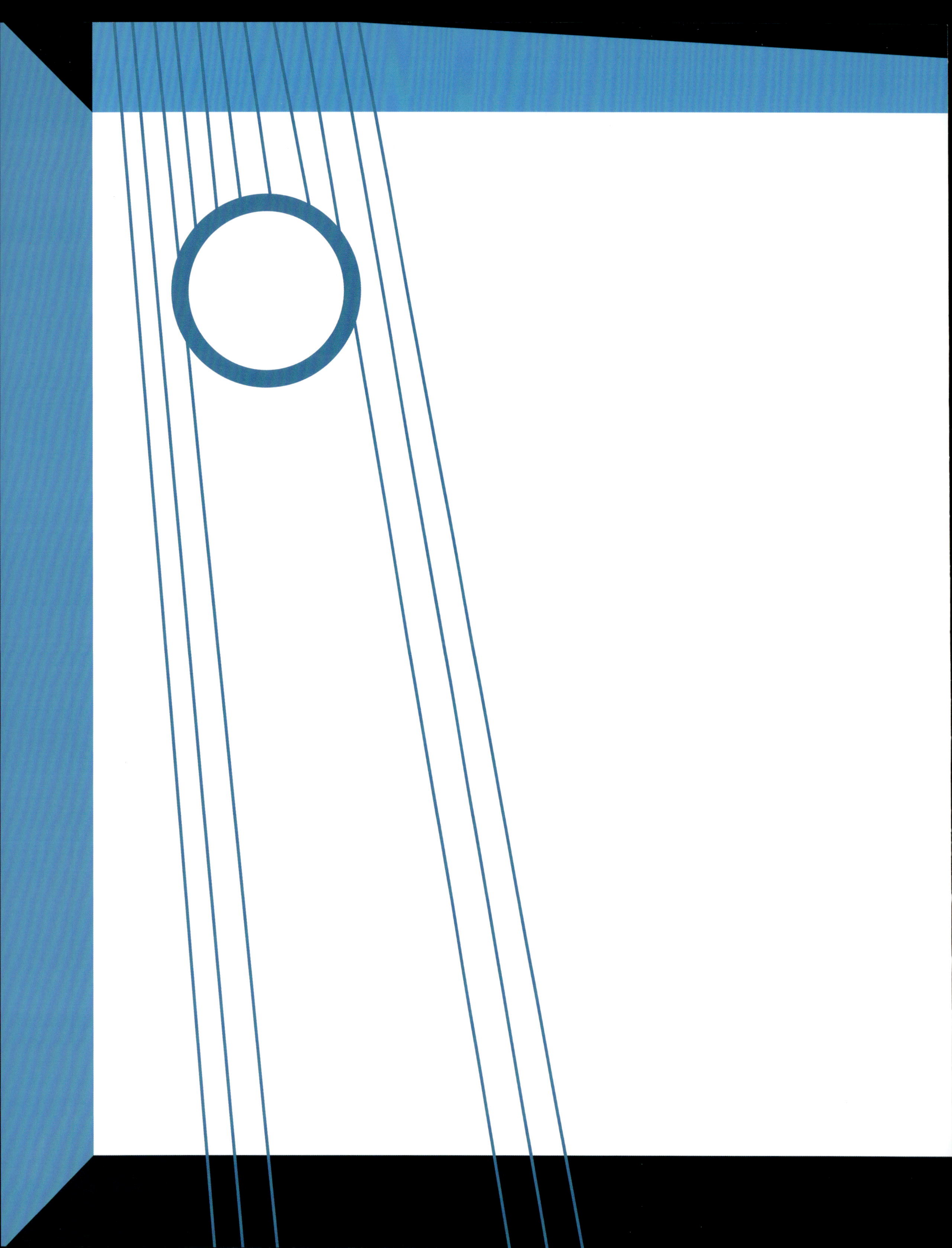

CHAPTER 04

FEEDING FELIX

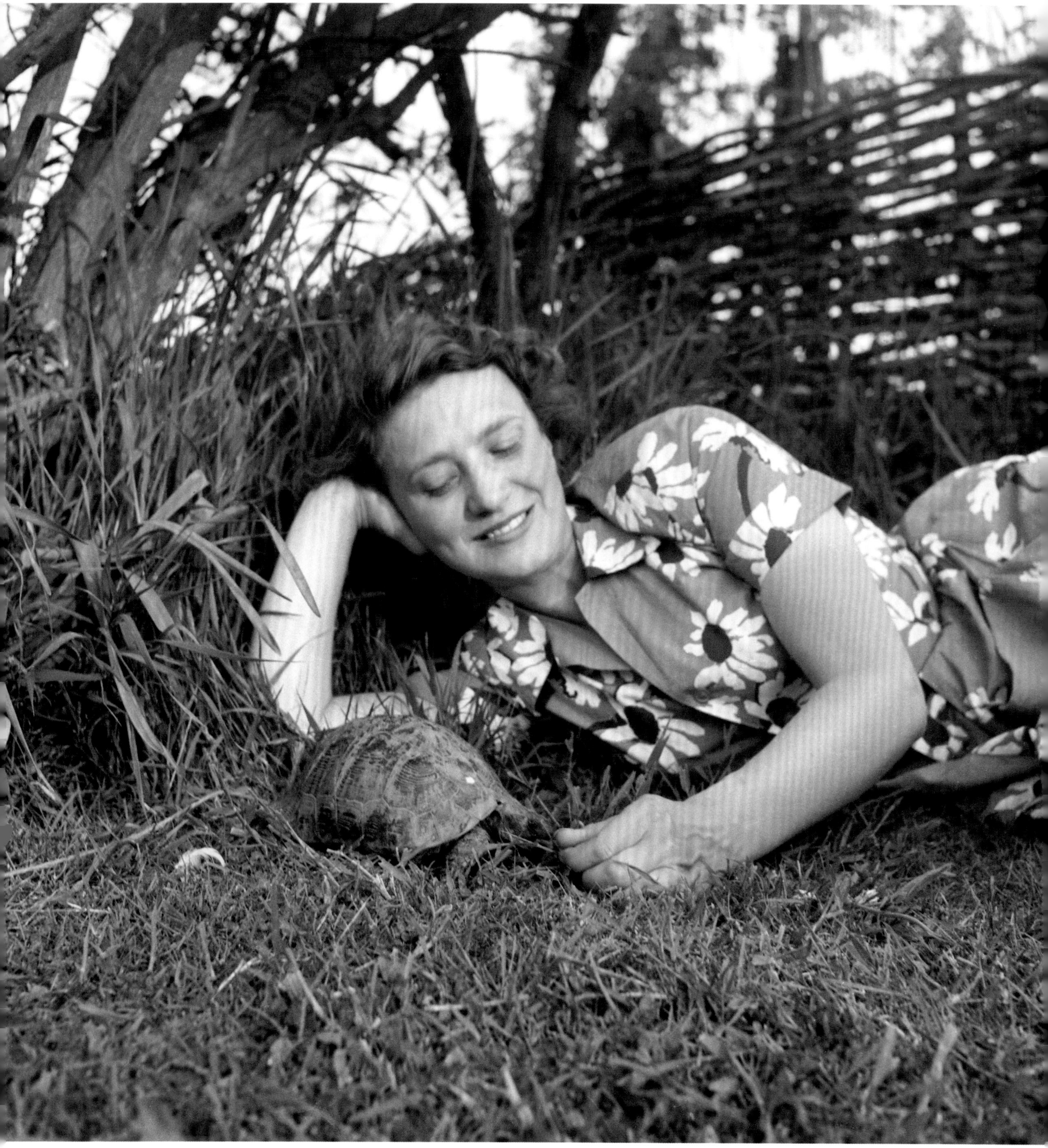

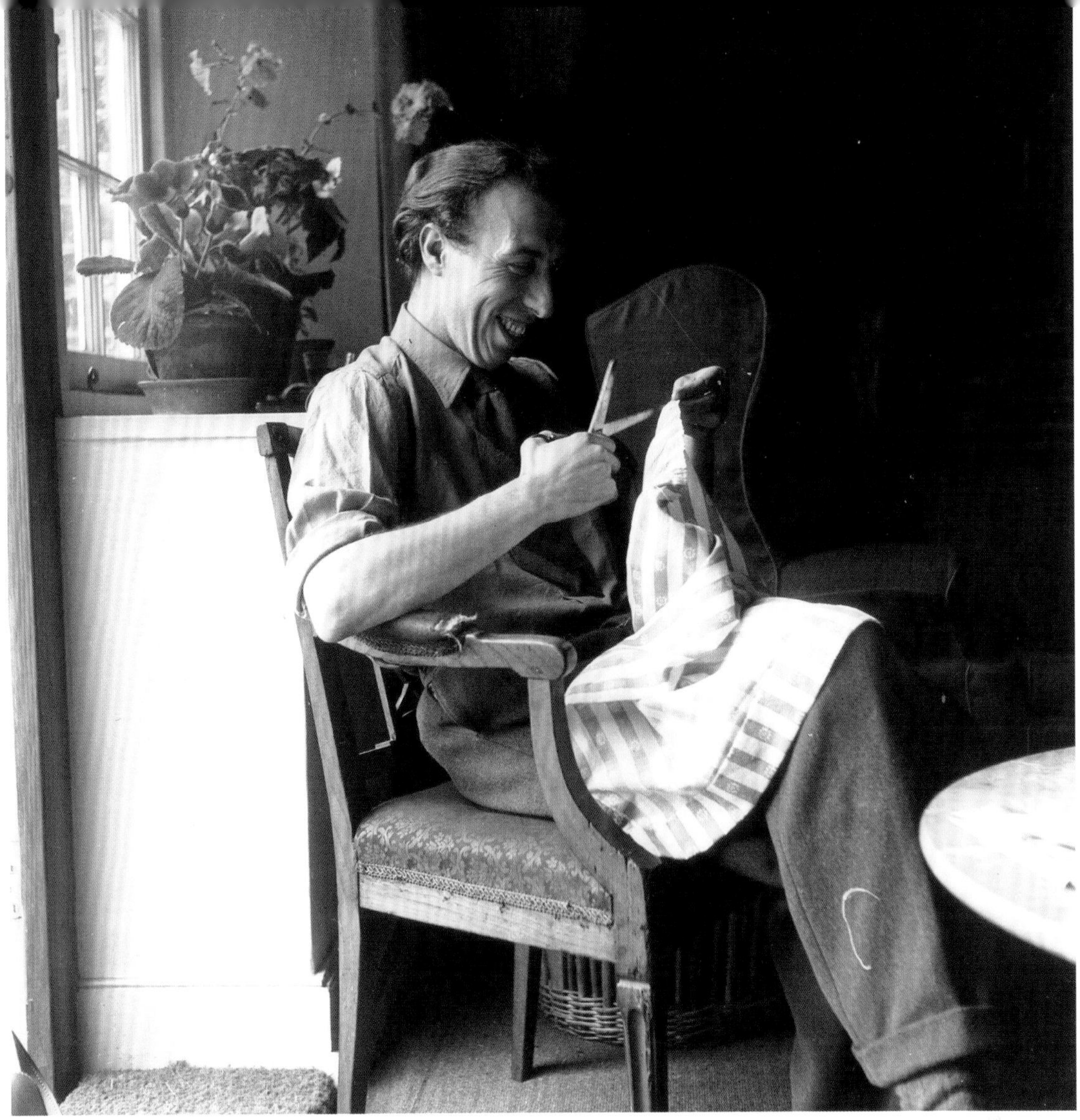

Richard Hamilton (Artist), Farleys sitting room 1951

Cynthia Thompson has rolled up the sleeves on her checked shirt. Hair tied back in a ponytail and wearing denims, she looks every bit the practical, resourceful and cheerfully helpful person she always was. Her first visit to Farleys had been with her husband John in February 1950 but in the photograph, it is September 1st of the following year. She knew her weekend would be spent helping my parents make Farleys more habitable. Lee stands in the doorway to the sitting room, supervising the workforce which also comprises the artist Richard Hamilton and his wife Terry.

Richard Hamilton had recently completed his *'Reaper'* series of lithographs and would have felt a familiarity with our reaper and binder as it gathered in our wheat harvest.

With the sculptor William (Bill) Turnbull he had just mounted the ground-breaking exhibition *Growth and Form*, 1951 at the ICA, becoming firm friends with my parents in the process. Later he was to design the *Wonder and Horror of the Human Head* exhibition, 1953, the only joint curatorial collaboration Lee and Roland ever made. It was at Farleys in 1954 that Hamilton met Jean Dubuffet, the French founder of the Art Brut movement which is said to have been a significant influence in Hamilton's contribution to Pop Art.

Lee was on what she called her "Upholstery Jag". Furnishing Farleys in the years of post war austerity required her to become instantly knowledgeable about renovating the pieces she scavenged. She had a good eye for finding things that were well made and would come to life with her choice of bright and bold fabrics. She assembled an impressive tool kit and for labour inveigled her friends help.

Cynthia Thompson, Farleys garden 1953

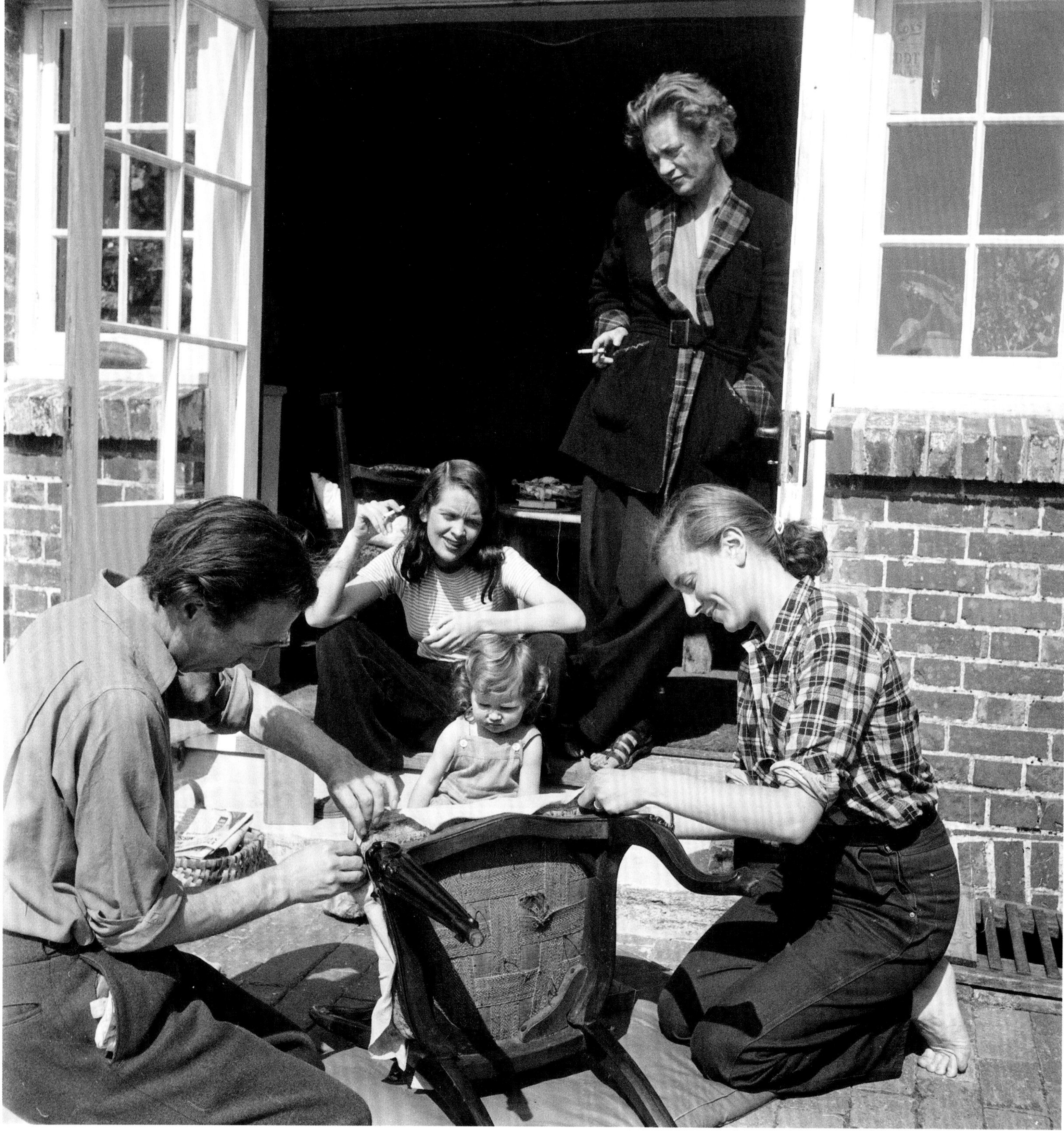

Outside Farleys sitting room, Lee Miller, Richard and Terry Hamilton, Cynthia Thompson and child, 1951

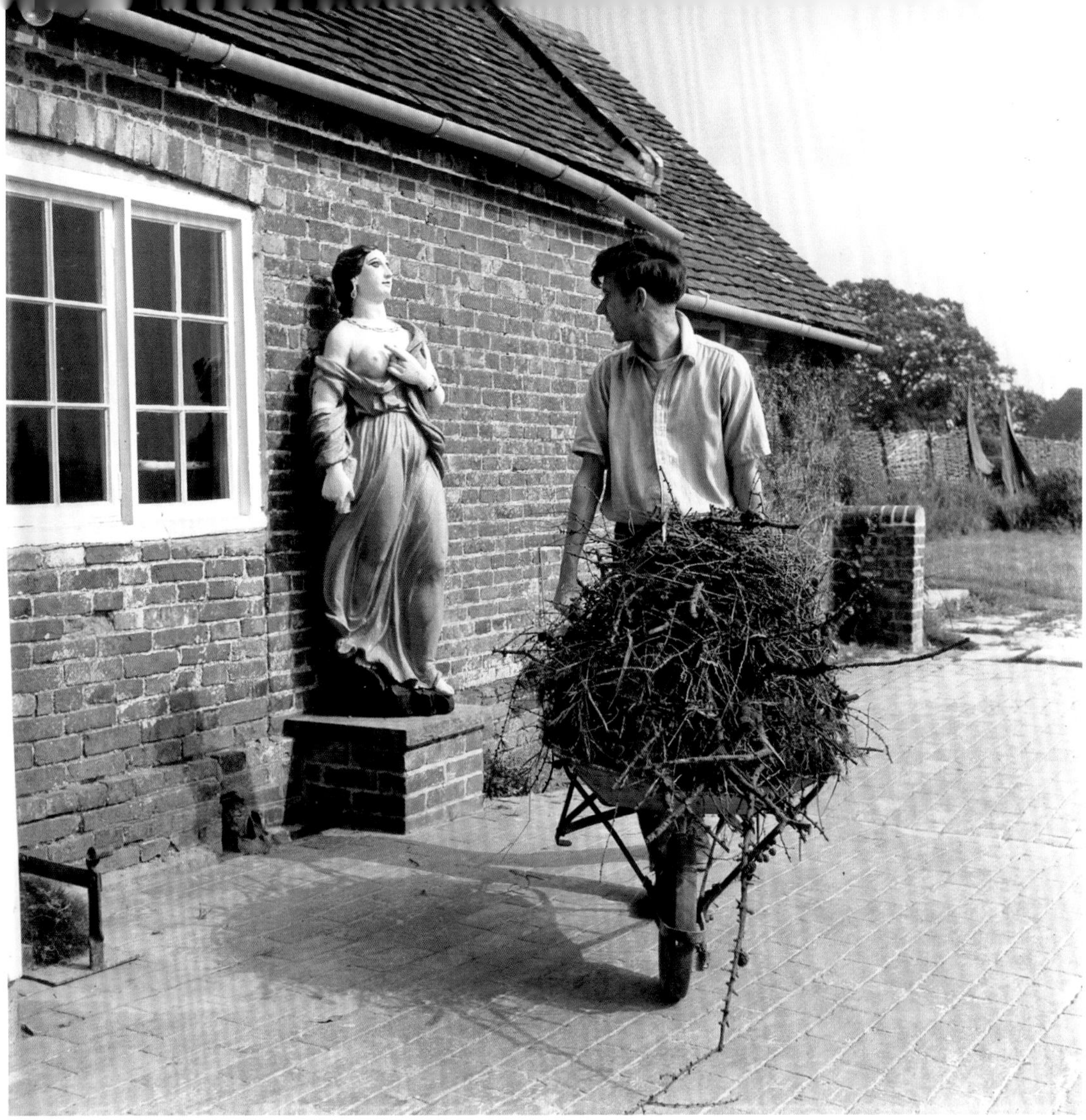

John Craxton (Painter), Farleys House 1951

John Craxton preferred helping in the garden to upholstery. He trimmed trees and cleared up the debris from a recent storm. He and I drew and painted together. We felt the bird needed a caterpillar to eat so Lee added the paper band from around her 120 film as its dinner.

Bill Turnbull heroically struggled to dig the pond and his wife Kathy painted the lower panels on the greenhouse. Alfred Barr, the Director of the Museum of Modern Art who scandalised New York in 1939 by exhibiting Picasso's painting Demoiselles d'Avignon, helped feed the pigs in the farmyard. It was agreed he was accustomed to casting pearls before swine.

Early on Lee recognised the photographic possibilities in these industrious weekend gatherings and began to gather material for what was to be her swan song after thirteen years as a contributor to British and American *Vogue*. It was a witty photo essay titled *Working Guests* for the July 1953 issue of the British edition, featuring a host of friends, mainly artists and curators fixing up Farleys. Lee wrote;

... I've devoted four years of research and practice to getting all my friends to do all the work. There is scarcely a thing in or out of sight, from the wood-pile to the attic water tank, from the chair coverings to the brined pork and the contents of the deep freeze, without the signature of a working guest.

Since most visitors sleep all morning, and I'm siesta minded after lunch, it takes dove-tailed planning to keep industry on its feet. The visitors' book is flanked by an album of grim significance: in it are no 'happy hols' snaps of leisured groups wearing sun glasses and sniffing Pimm's cup. It could easily be taken for a set of stills in a Soviet workers' propaganda film. Everyone busy doing a job: Joy through Work.[1]

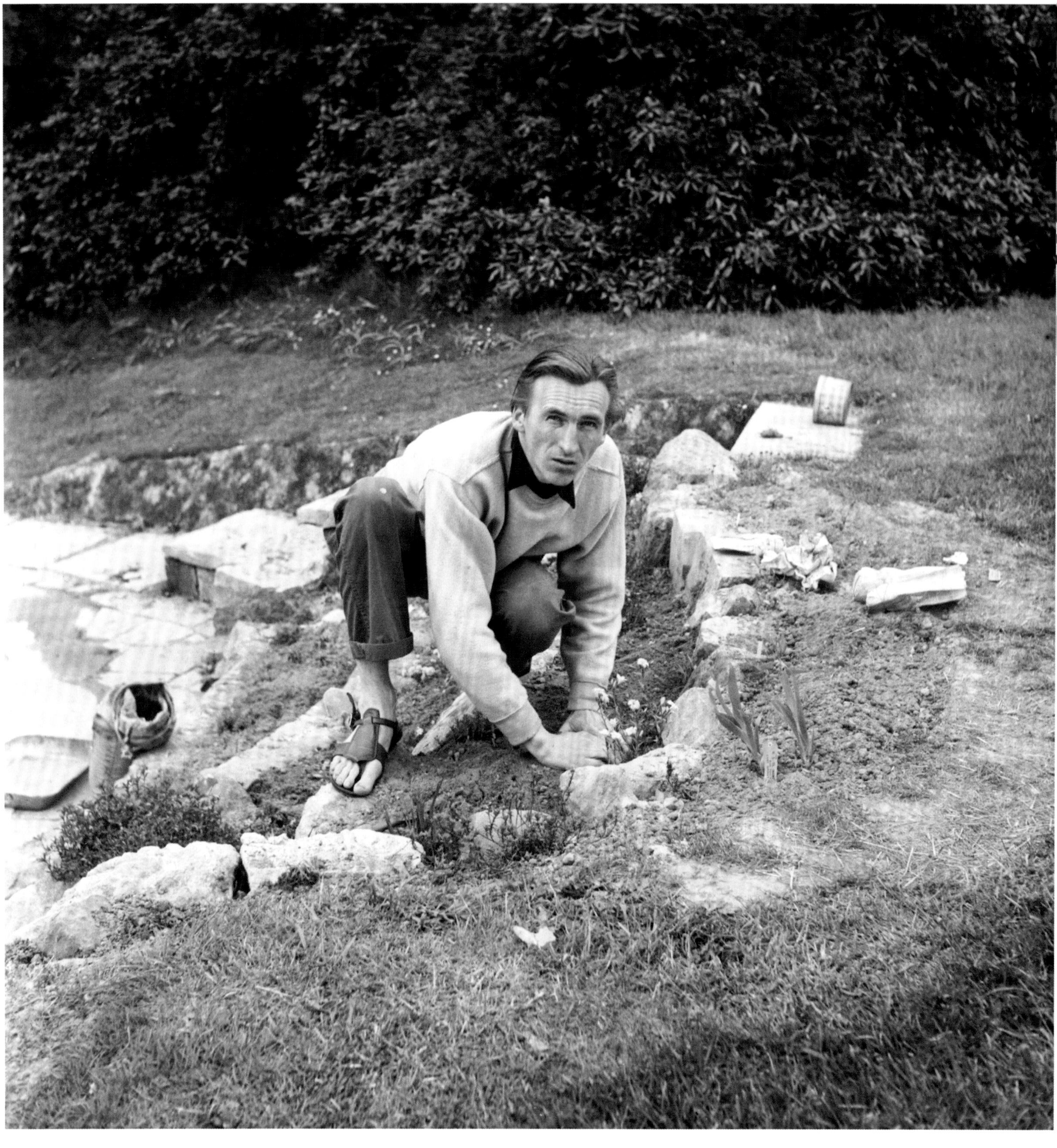

William 'Bill' Turnbull (Artist), Farleys garden 1953

'Learning on the job' was not new to Cynthia Thompson. When the war began, she falsified her age and joined the WRAF, quickly earning a place among the radar operators tracking aircraft during the Battle of Britain. Later she joined the staff of *Time Life* in London as a researcher but soon became a reporter among some of the superstar journalists of that day. One of them, already distinguished for his photographic coverage of the sinking of the passenger ship Zam Zam by a German raider, was David (Davie) E. Scherman. He and Lee, as two Yanks in London became 'buddies', with Davie moving in with her and Roland in Roland's house in Downshire Hill, Hampstead. Through Davie, Cynthia in turn also became close friends with Lee and Roland, a friendship that endured for their lifetimes.

The most wonderfully crazy movie *Hellzapoppin* had its debut in 1941. Amid this romp of high-spirited jazz and the sort of action in which surrealists delighted there was a well-known running gag set in a cinema with announcements imploring an unfortunate member of the audience named Stinky Miller to GO HOME. Davie and others applied the sobriquet to Lee who became 'Stinky' and Cynthia could not avoid becoming 'Stinkthia'.

Despite this and the long separation, while Lee and Davie covered the war in Europe after D Day, the friendship with Cynthia endured. It was at a party at Lee and Roland's in 1947 that Cynthia met her husband, John Thompson. A measure of their clear-sightedness was that they were married three months later. John was a journalist on

David E. Scherman (Photojournalist), London, England 1942

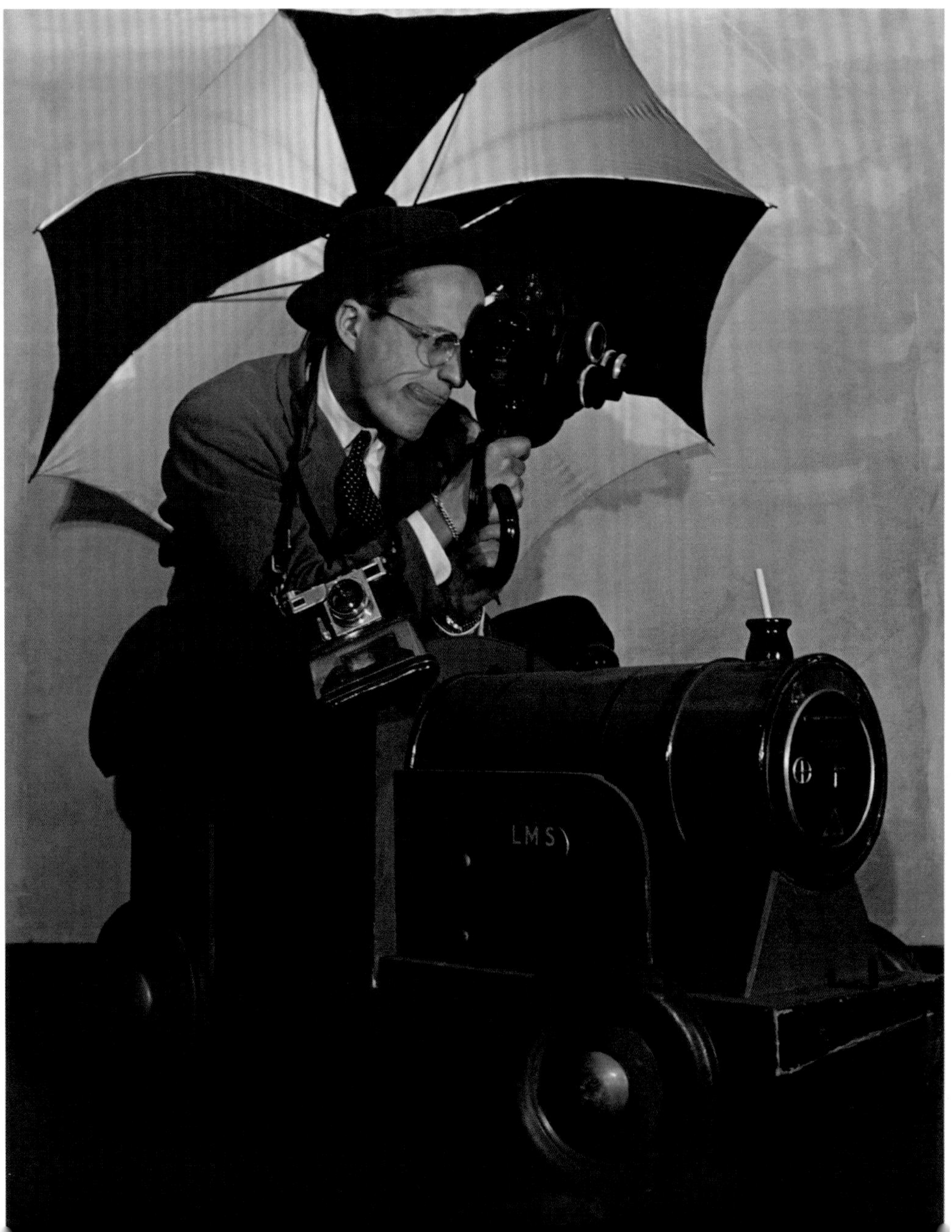

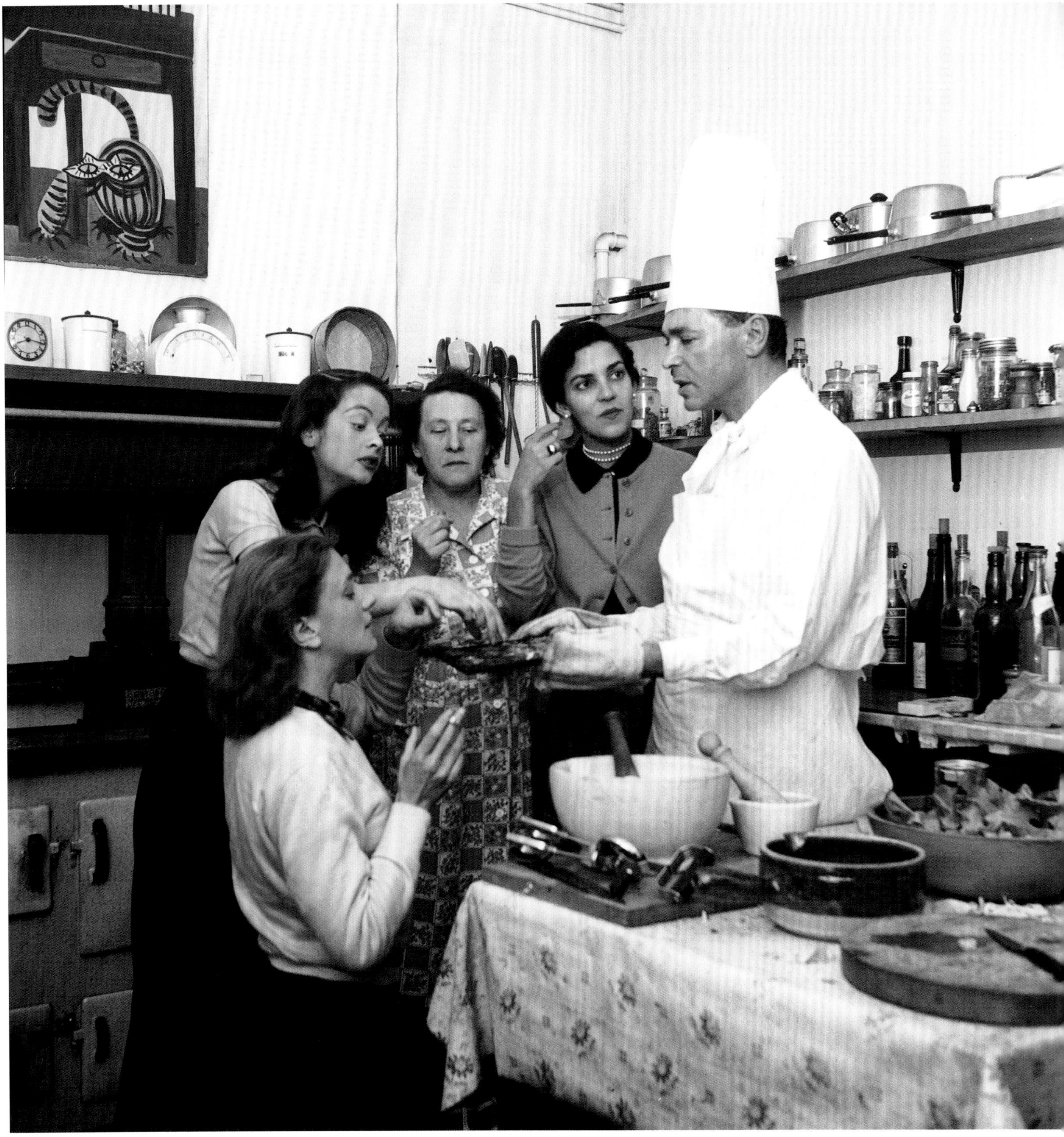

The Evening Standard, later becoming the editor of the *Sunday Telegraph*. This wonderfully erudite and witty man was to need every bit of his well-hidden steely determination to succeed in publishing the paper despite the print unions who were wreaking havoc with the news-paper industry at that time. This strife torn time did not prevent him from bringing the paper's circulation to unprecedented heights.

It is always interesting to speculate where the glue lies that binds an elective affinity. At that time, they were all left wing, loved the arts and held a passion for peace, freedom and justice. Apart from their preferences one thing in common with them all is they were all self-taught. Davie, as a teenager, bought a camera and taught himself to use it to such good effect that he was hired by *Life* magazine as junior and finished his career as their book editor. Cynthia was thought to be too delicate for school and whilst kept at home read encyclopaedias incessantly. When her *Time Life* career ended, she was offered the editorship of a prominent woman's magazine but turned it down to be a mum. John left school and began as a very junior reporter on a paper in Driffield, moving on to the *Yorkshire Evening News*. Lee was thrown out of every school she attended for unruly behaviour. Roland was severely dyslexic but in his day the condition did not have a name so he never let it concern him. They were all unqualified for the work they did but they all succeeded absolutely in their roles. In no way did they disparage the academics, it was just that they found their own paths to excellence through the pages of countless books and gutsy personal experience.

A couple more years had to pass before I grew old enough to retain Cynthia and John in my memory. John remains in my mind as a warm, quiet, thoughtful figure, usually in conversation with my father, with whom he shared a love of the country and all forms of wildlife. Cynthia remains as the sort of friend of the family I loved best. Colourful, endlessly patient and kind, and entirely happy to lie on the ground to play with me or find dandelion leaves for Felix, my tortoise.

When Cynthia and John's own family arrived with Matthew in 1954 and Sarah in 1958 their weekend visits to Farleys stopped. Living as they were in Much Hadham made Farleys too long a journey but we kept in touch exchanging news of Davie, and with John reminding me he was with Roland on the Golden Arrow platform at Victoria Station to welcome Picasso in November 1950. Cynthia was always enthusiastic about our efforts to make Lee's work more widely known. The last time I saw her was at the opening of Hilary Robert's 2015 landmark exhibition at the Imperial War Museum, *Lee Miller, a Woman's War*. Sarah tells me it was one of the last times Cynthia felt up to travelling from her home in Burnham Norton on the north Norfolk coast to stay with her in London. We did not have much time to talk that evening, but I felt deeply grateful she had made the huge effort to come, so typical of her supportive nature.

John died on 24th November 2013 aged 93 and Cynthia on 31st March 2020 a month short of 96. Their inspiration remains.

Eliot Elisofon (Photographer) with Cynthia Thompson, Terry Hamilton, Marion (Paula) Paul and Joan Elisofon, Farleys kitchen 1951

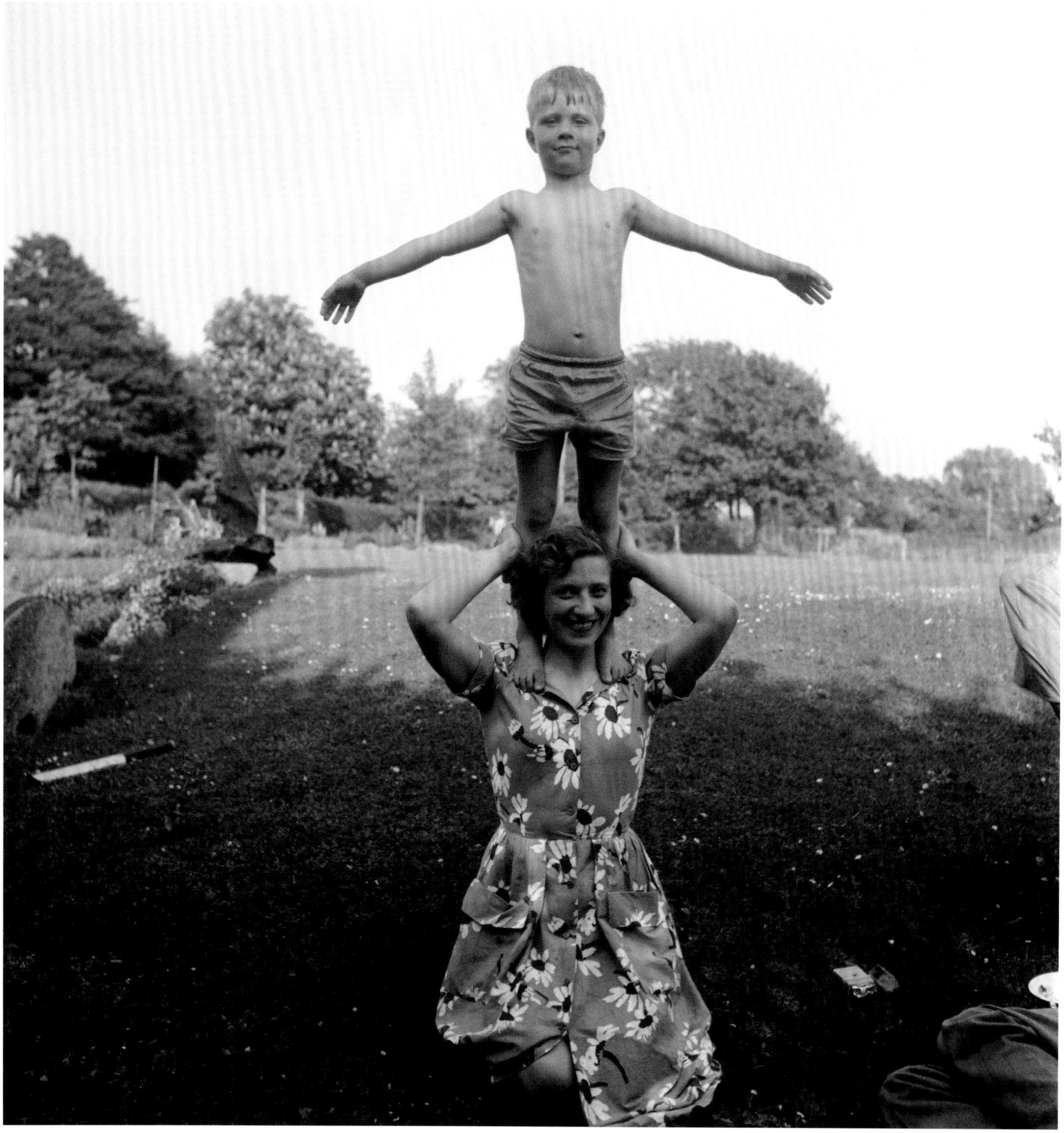

Cynthia Thompson and Antony Penrose, Farleys garden 1953

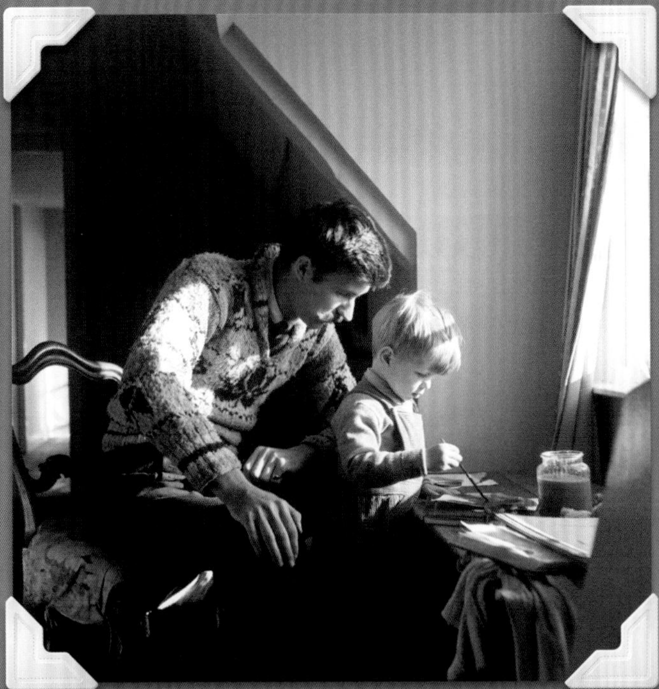

John Craxton (Painter) and Antony Penrose,
Farleys House 1951

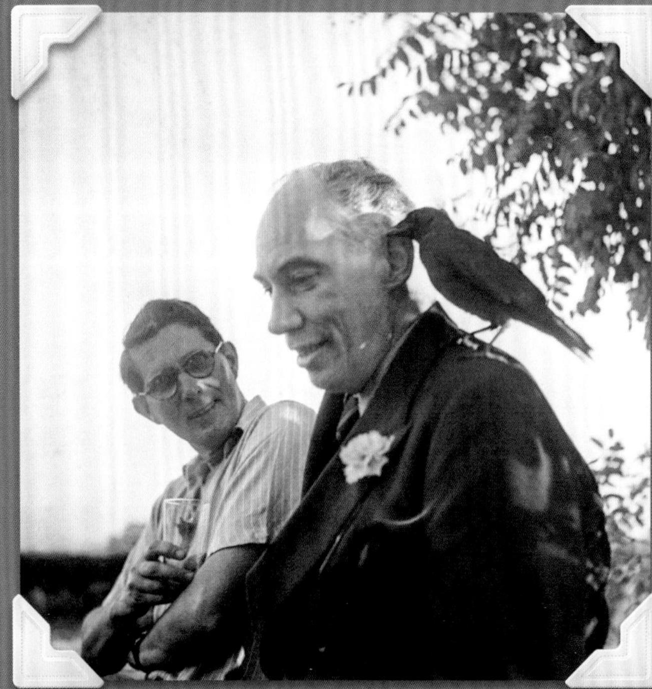

James Johnson Sweeney (Curator) and Roland Penrose,
Farleys garden c1952

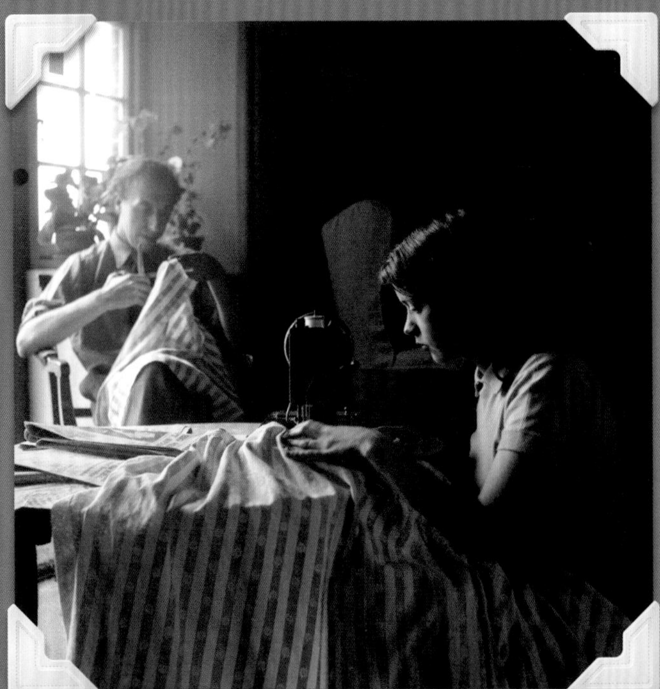

Richard (Artist) and Terry Hamilton, Farleys House 1951

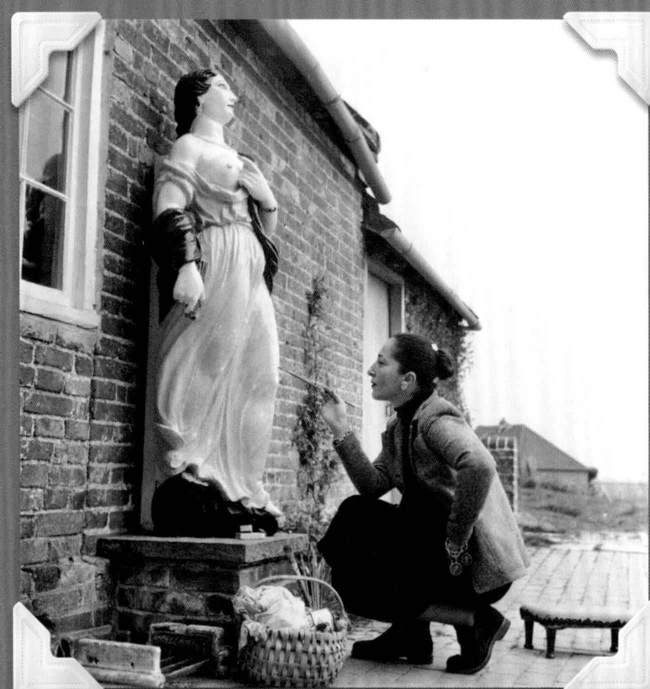

Susana Gamboa (Registrar), Farleys House 1953

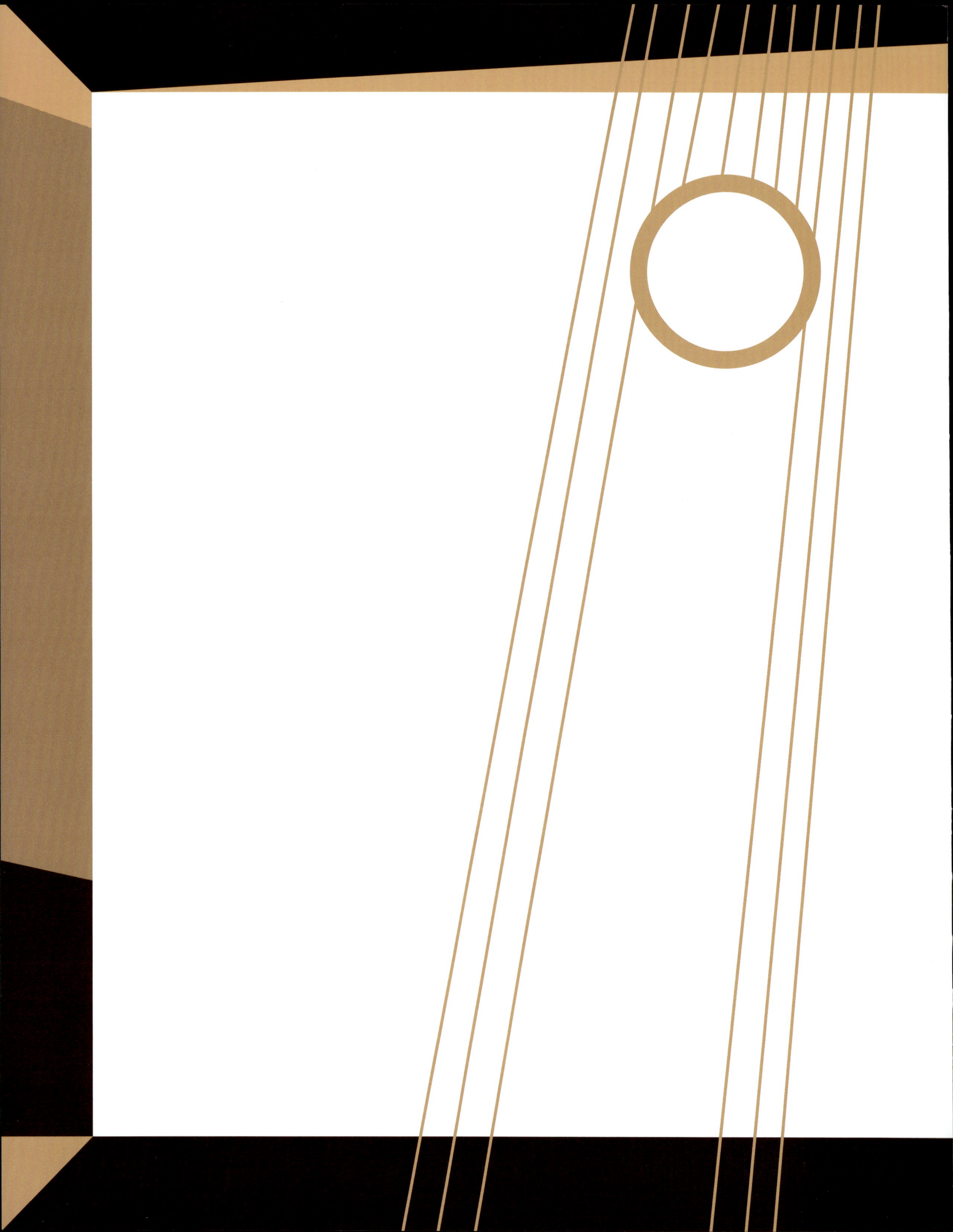

CHAPTER 05

BY THE POWER OF A WORD

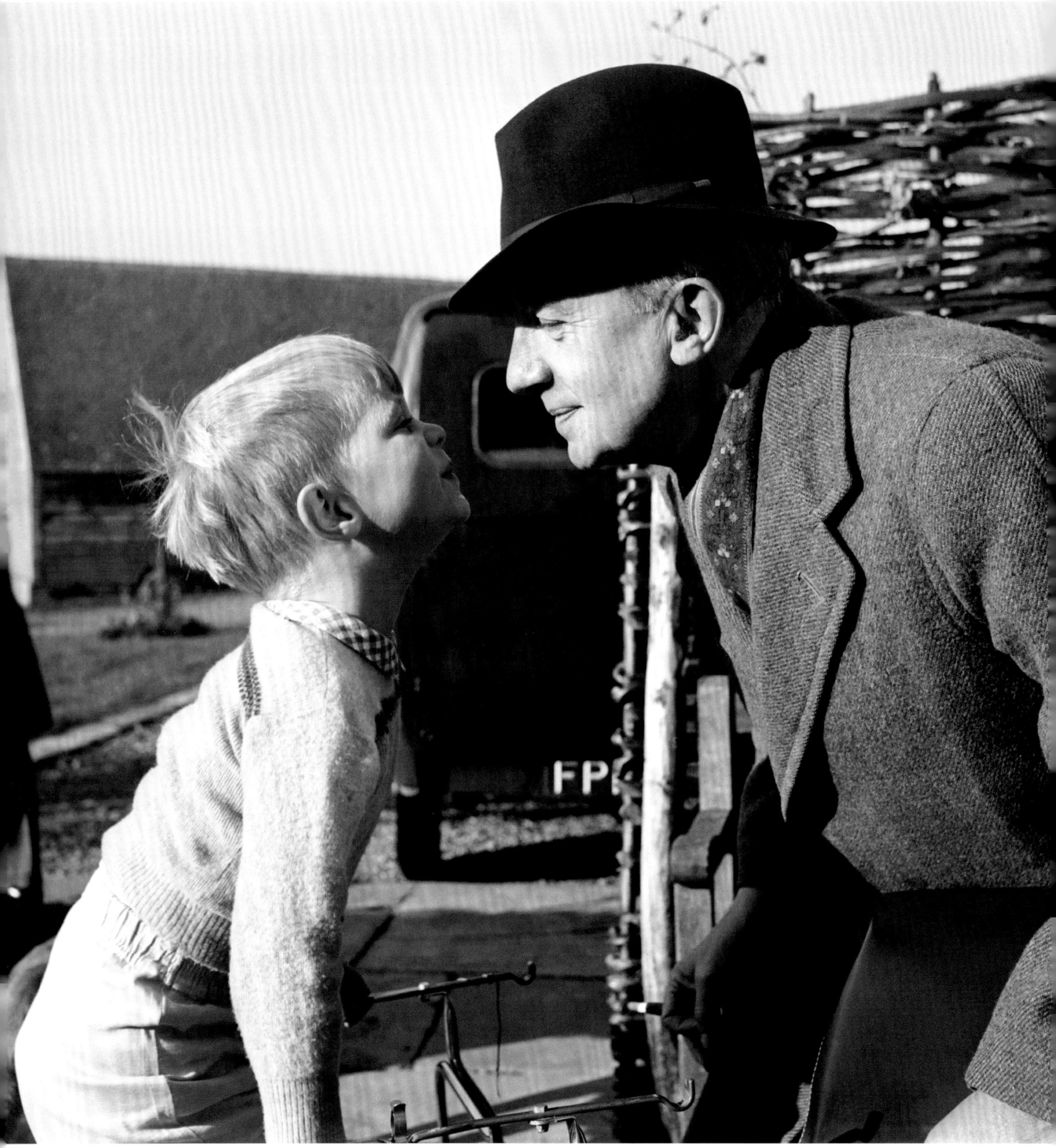
FP

Lee had almost certainly met Paul Eluard when she was in Paris with Man Ray from 1929 – 32 but Roland knew him earlier, probably in 1924, when they were introduced by his first wife, the French surrealist poet Valentine Boué. Roland stated his fascination with surrealism began with Paul and was later expanded by Max Ernst and Joan Miró.

In 1934 Paul married Nusch (Maria Benz) whose grace and beauty was captured by Man Ray, Picasso and Lee herself. It was Paul and Nusch Lee sought out during the liberation of Paris, overwhelmed at finding them still alive and now free. Paul's resistance activities had forced them to be on the run from the Gestapo for the duration of the Nazi occupation, and the effect on their health was catastrophic.

Paul's signature in the visitors' book is undated. It is also upside down on the page indicating he opened the wrong end of the book, and had to turn through about five pages of full plate heavy duty sepia photos of dull but worthy tourist sites, originally a record of my great aunt's travels.

He wrote;

A la suite de ces merveilles, j'invite les professionels du paysage irlandais ou frivolais, à me prouver leur gentilesse en nous montant ce qu'ils voient par la fenêtre – ou sans fenêtre, avec le jour qu'on a en soi. Merci![1]

Paul Eluard.

'At the end of these wonders, I invite the professionals of the country of Ireland or frivolous to prove their kindness to me in showing us what they see through the window, or without the window with the light we have in itself. Thank you!'

These lines hint at Paul's deep understanding of Roland, who was a Quaker. "… the Quaker belief in the supreme guidance that comes from the 'inner light' seemed to me to find a legitimate comparison with the importance given to the subconscious by Freud and Jung"[2]. He wrote more than thirty years later. With his phrase *the light we have within ourselves* Paul could be signalling how he well understood Roland's inner drives.

Under Paul's signature there is an undulating line that suggests the profile of the South Downs seen through the window of the house. Roland is unlikely to have missed the opportunity of taking Paul to see *The Long Man of Wilmington*, the Neolithic figure drawn on the hillside and visible from Farleys.

The charming lines in our visitors' book came from the foremost surrealist poet whose poem *Liberté j'ecris ton nom* was published in France secretly and became a rallying cry for the French Resistance. It caused Paul and his wife Nusch to be hunted mercilessly by the Gestapo. A copy of the poem was smuggled to Roland in London by the Brazilian artist and diplomat Cicero Dias and his wife. Roland translated and published the poem. It gained the attention of the Ministry of Information who made it into a leaflet dropped by the allied aircraft over occupied France. It was included in a booklet distributed to the French Resistance fighters. The Gestapo redoubled their efforts. At the Liberation of Paris Lee found Paul and Nusch hiding in a friend's apartment. Roland soon arrived for a reunion where the joy was tinged with grief in the knowledge that so many of their friends who had been taken by the Nazis had been brutally murdered.

Antony Penrose and Paul Eluard (Poet), Farley Farm 1950

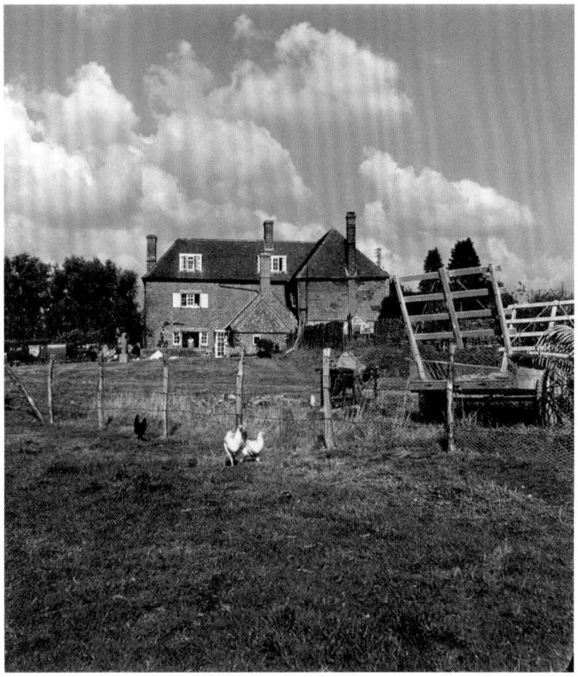

Farleys House 1951

Roland asked Paul if he could forgive him for putting Nusch and him in mortal danger by publishing *Liberté* … and being instrumental to the leaflet drops. To his relief Paul told Roland he had done exactly what he had hoped for when he entrusted the poems to Cicero Dias, adding that he and Nusch regarded the liberty of France as being of far greater importance than their own lives.

None of this was evident to me as a child when Paul visited Farleys. Little remains in my memory of the visit other than a contribution to a feeling reinforced later that Paul was good and kind and my parents were very happy when he was around. He had come alone. Nusch, so much adored by all for her warmth and wit, died suddenly in the street in Paris in 1946. Her health had been destroyed by the suffering she endured whilst on the run from the Gestapo.

Lee wrote that as a four-year-old I elevated Paul Eluard to hero status. Later we were in St Tropez and Roland, was working and 'very busy'. Work seemed a good idea if the endless high-spirited sessions he passed in cafes with Picasso and Françoise Gilot were defined as work and classed as 'very busy'. Clearly this was something for me to look forward to as an adult. The purpose of our visit was to celebrate Paul's marriage to Dominique Laure, a warm and friendly woman.

I knew there was something important going on that I didn't understand and it seemed the whole town was part of this marvellous event. The *Bravade* parade filled the streets of the citadel. Processions of men in sailor uniforms marched and fired blunderbusses, leaving soot marks on the ground and the heavy white smoke of gun powder in the air. Women in beautiful costumes were everywhere and massive effigies of Saint Tropez and his friends, including, to my delight a cat, were borne shoulder high on poles.

I was sure Paul was in among them somewhere with his good friend Picasso who I also held in hero status. Mythically they were everywhere. The floating crane working in the port must have been theirs. Beside the quay the spherical copper helmet of a diver burst through the surface in a shower of spray. He grabbed a crowbar and vanished again. The glass port in the helmet was too small to identify Paul but I was sure it was him.

Later we sat in a small damp-smelling room around a table presided over by a grumpy man in a suit who shuffled a lot of papers. It was 15th June 1951 and Paul and Dominique had married with Picasso and Françoise Gilot as their witnesses. Later we had a wonderful lunch on a terrace shaded by trellised vines. The contrast to Britain with post war food rationing was total. We had wonderful fish, fresh baguette, followed by peaches and figs, with an abundance of particularly delicious patisseries with which Françoise earned my undying love by feeding me indulgently.

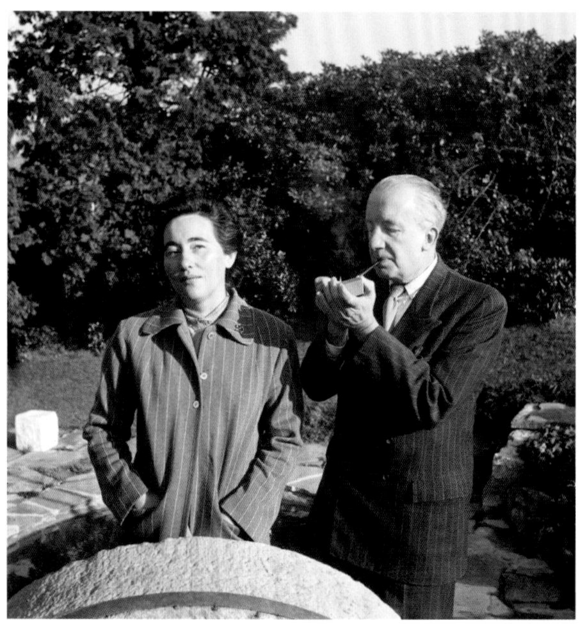

Dominique and Paul Eluard 1951

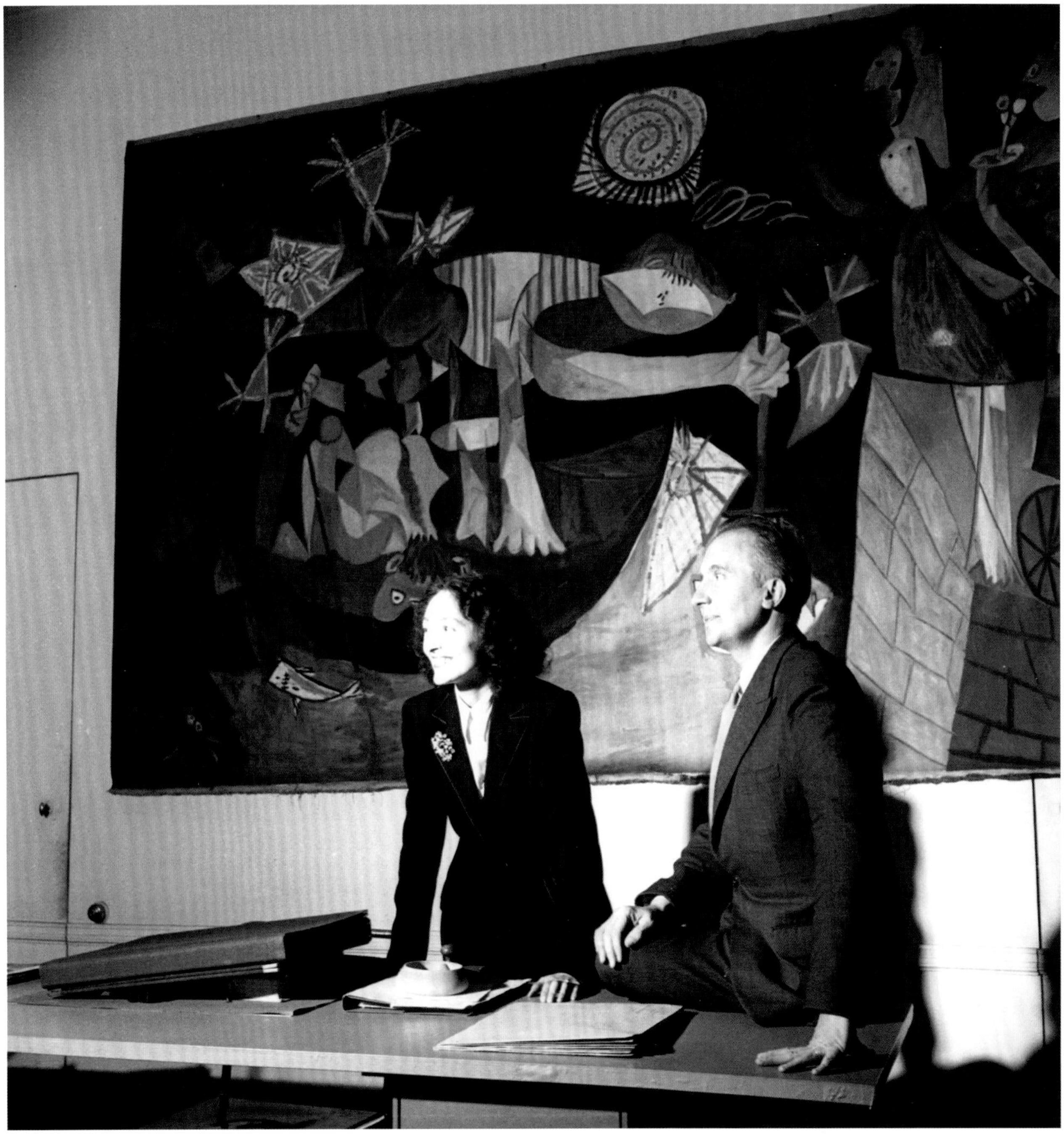

Nusch and Paul Eluard in Christian Zervos' apartment, Paris, France 1944

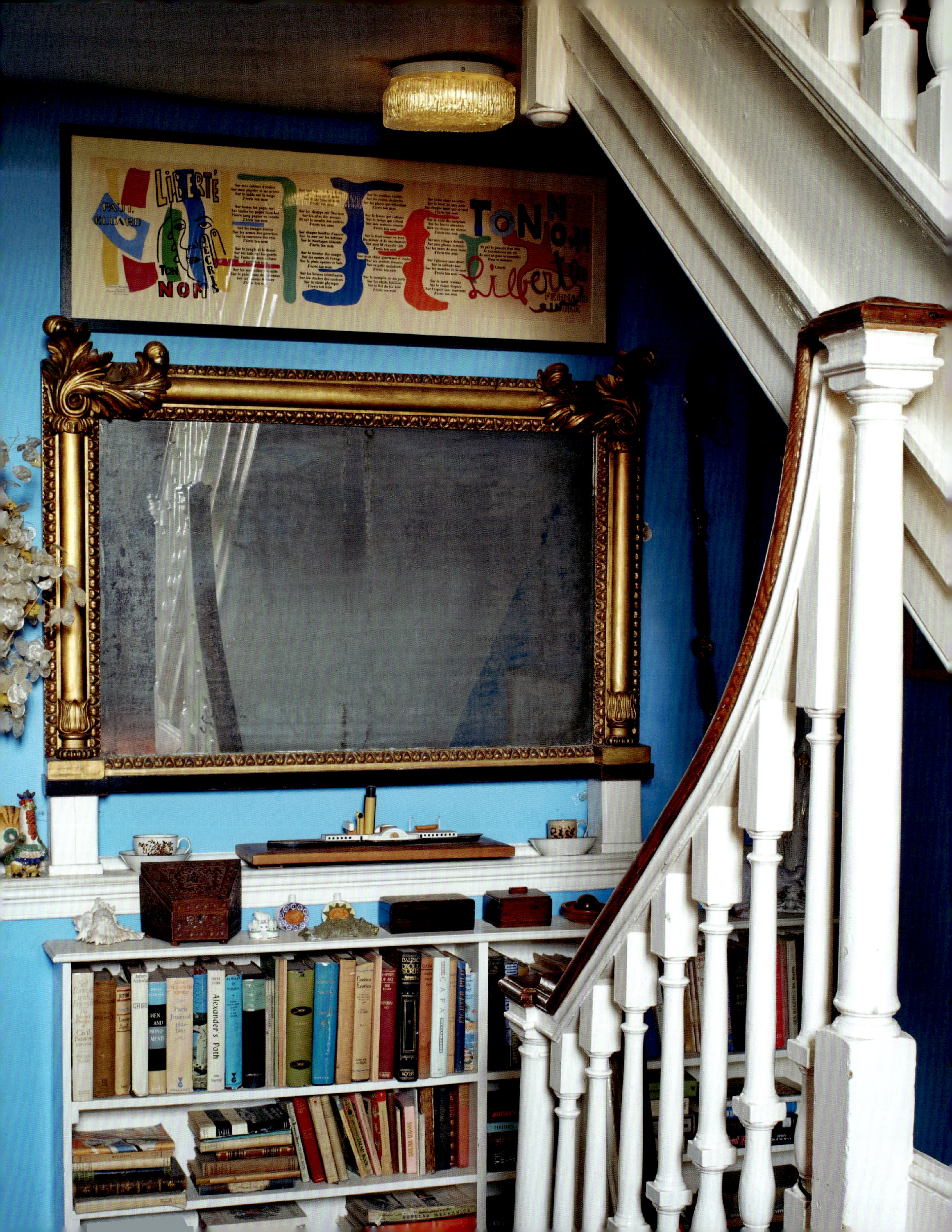

Paul and Dominique came to Farleys in October of that same year. Paul's health, never robust after TB in his youth and badly damaged by his wartime suffering, was failing fast.

A month later Valentine, Roland's ex-wife, a poet and close friend of Paul, wrote from Paris;

Dear Roland and Lee,

What a terrible day! Yesterday Paul was doing better; I had phoned him. Dominique had told him you sent your love and had embraced him from you. And that was it… he died this morning at 8:30, after reading the newspapers. It didn't take long—it was over in 30 seconds. Snow was falling in huge flakes, the way he loved it. …

It was 18th November 1952. Paul will never be absent from the lives of our family. Today a framed copy of *Liberté j'ecris ton nom*, illustrated by Fernand Leger, hangs where Roland placed it on the stairs at Farleys. *Liberté…* remains one of the most emotively powerful poems ever written, yet in literal terms it makes no sense at all for that is the manner of surrealism. It ends;

And by the power of a word
I recommence my life
I was born to know you
To name you
Liberty.

Stairway in Farleys House
by Tony Tree

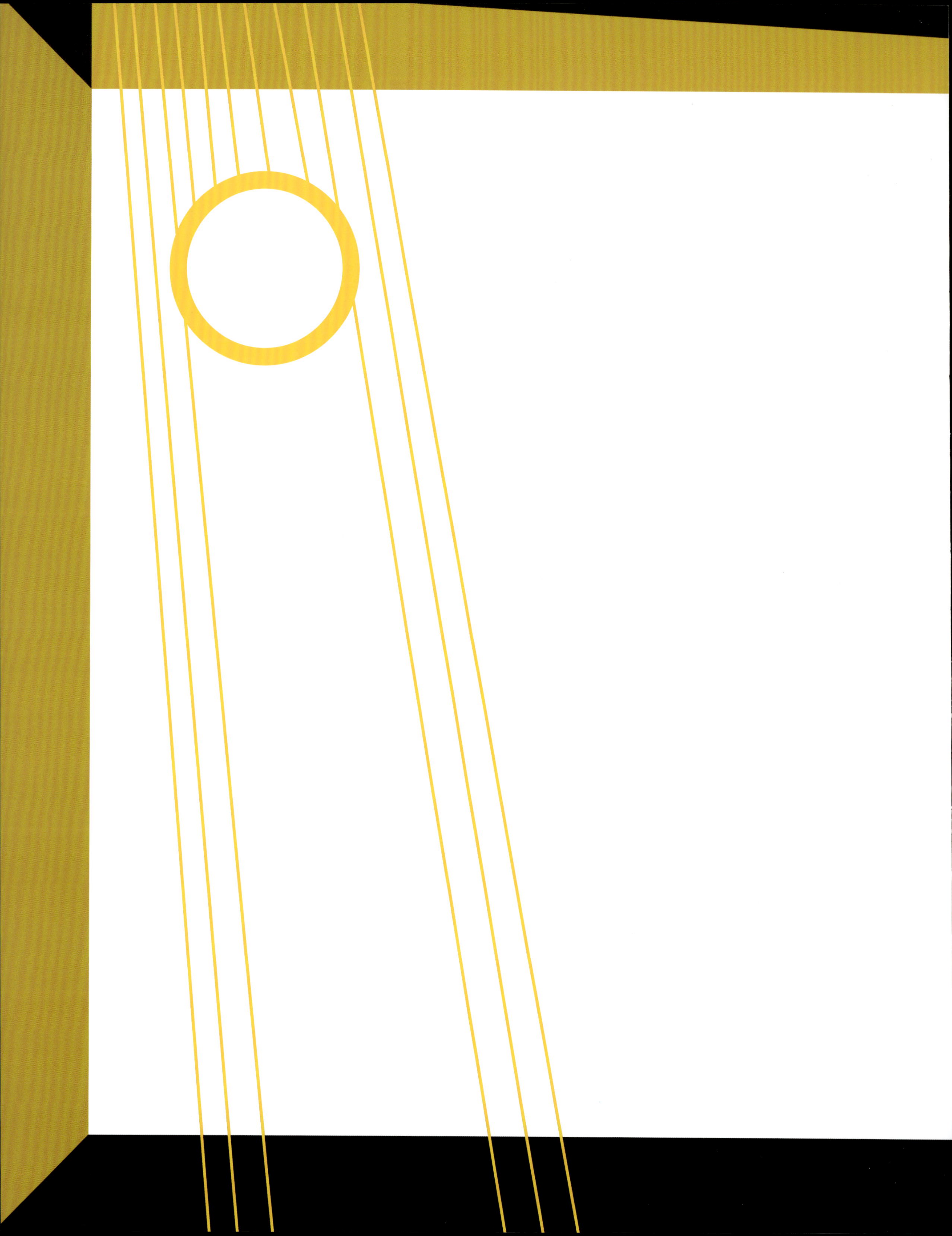

CHAPTER 06

'AFTER EASTER CAME MANY HAPPY DAYS'

DOROTHEA TANNING

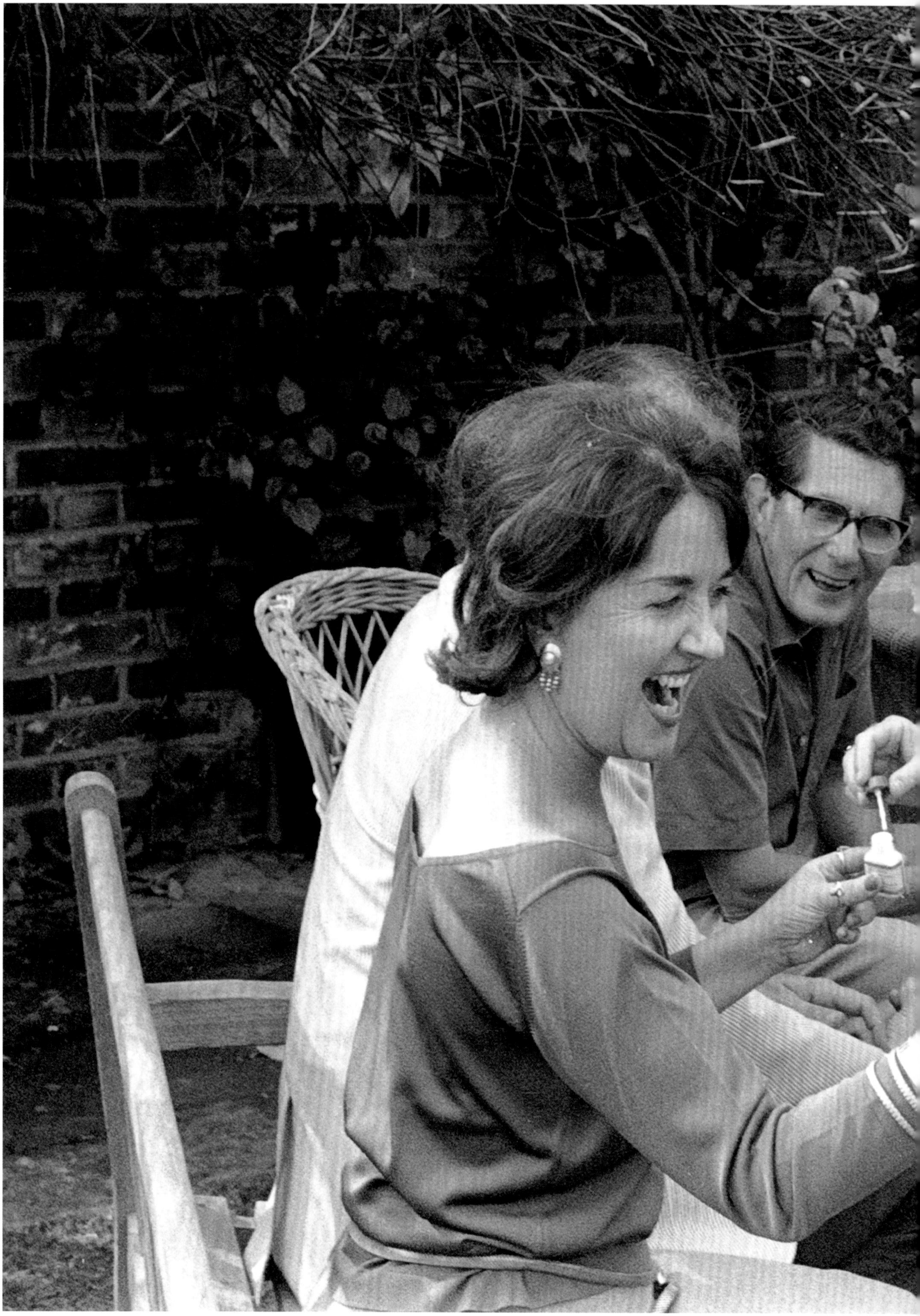

Garden Party (Dorothea Tanning (Artist), Roland Penrose, Max Ernst (Artist) and others), Farleys garden 1958

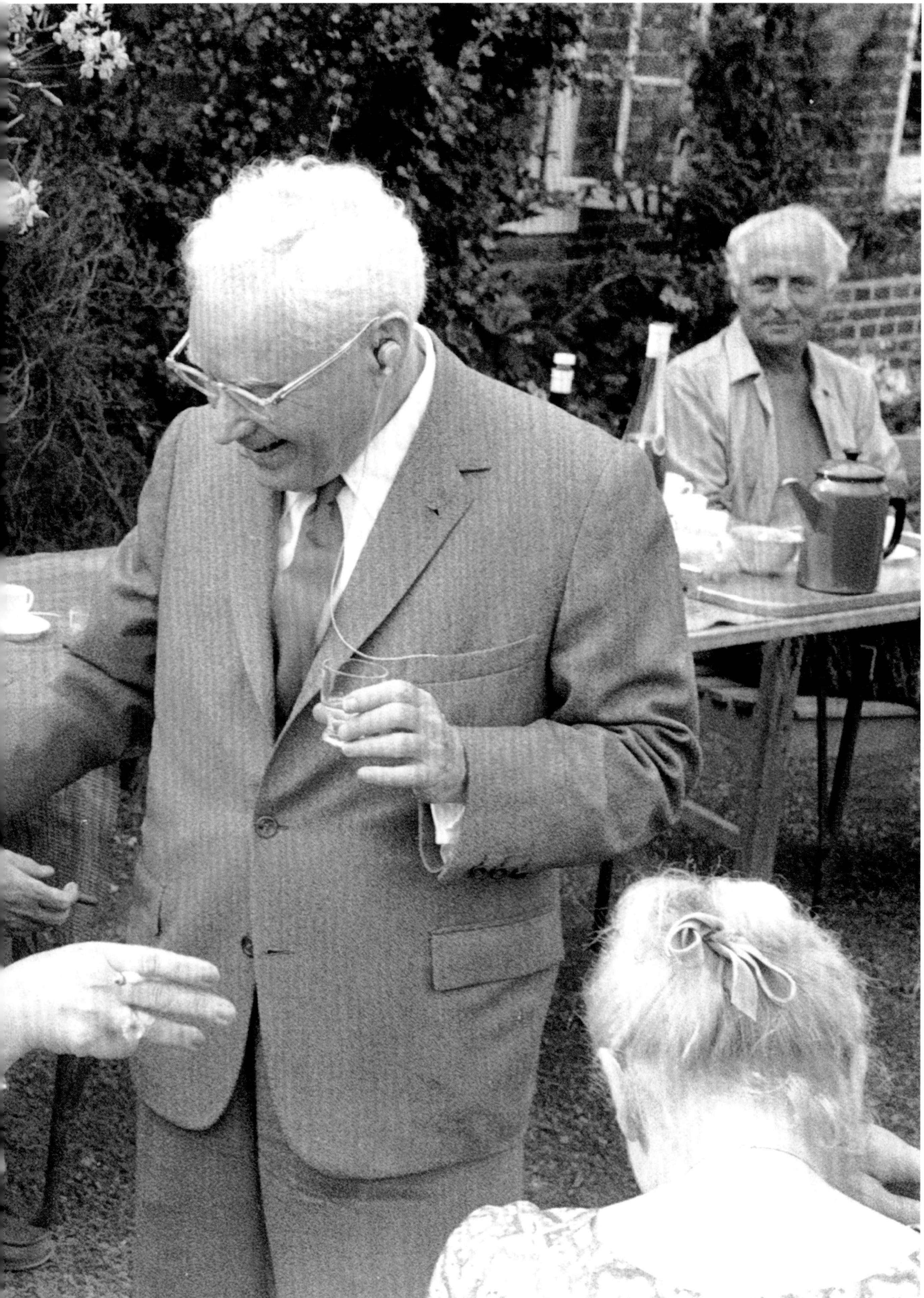

'After Easter came many happy days ending with the glorious 23rd: Date of birth of Lee Miller, afterwards Penrose – otherwise Lithospermum out of Difusuum (Heavenly Blue)'[1] (sic)

Thus, Dorothea Tanning signed the Farleys visitors' book for herself and Max Ernst after their Easter at Farleys in 1950. These few lines, illustrated with a tiny sketch in ink of a bunch of flowers, contain a wealth of information.

Dorothea tells us she was impressed with the rich purple flowers of the Lithospermum and that in turn shows that my parents had been quick off the mark. They had been at Farleys almost exactly a year and had begun to establish a rockery around a corner of the courtyard on the south-west of the house. It is hard to establish a rockery in a region devoid of rocks but they used anything they could lay hands on including leftover stone from friends who were sculptors, quickly providing a home for the *Lithospermum diffusa, 'Grace Ward'.*

Was it the colour of the flowers, their early appearance or the curious name that intrigued Dorothea? We will never know but she certainly shared Lee and Roland's love of the garden and of cooking. At Farleys the two went together as with post war food shortages the garden was a valuable source of good things to eat. No doubt when Dorothea returned later in the year she was delighted to find the abundance of American sweetcorn grown from the seed Lee's parent had sent her.

This brief inscription also hints at the deep affection between Dorothea and Lee that began in 1946. Lee and Roland had been in New York with Lee the guest of *Vogue* magazine to celebrate her achievements as their war correspondent. When the formal events ended, they flew on to Arizona to visit Max Ernst who had secluded himself there in Sedona following his fraught breakup with Peggy Guggenheim. With him in the cabin he was building was Dorothea, sharing the studio for her own fabulous works. Times were hard for them. Fearing the wrath of Guggenheim most dealers shunned Max causing difficulty in selling his work. Dorothea, although established as an artist in her own right and exhibited by Lee's old friend Julien Levy still struggled against the widely held perception that the work of women artists was for some undefined reason inferior to that of men.

It is easy to assume the affinity between Dorothea and Lee came from them both being women artists, both from modest backgrounds and both feisty avant garde Americans. Few details remain to give us a deeper understanding but for the rest of their lives it was one of their friendships they valued most highly.

By 1949 Dorothea and Max had moved to Paris, first settling in Huismes in the Loire valley and later in Seillans in Provence. Living in France allowed Dorothea and Max to visit Farleys three times in 1950. Lee and Roland later visited their home in Huismes but Dorothea's visits to Britain ended when she could not bear to be parted from her dogs. Her letters to Lee lamented that the UK regulations against rabies denied entry to her dogs without a lengthy quarantine period she would not inflict on her pets.

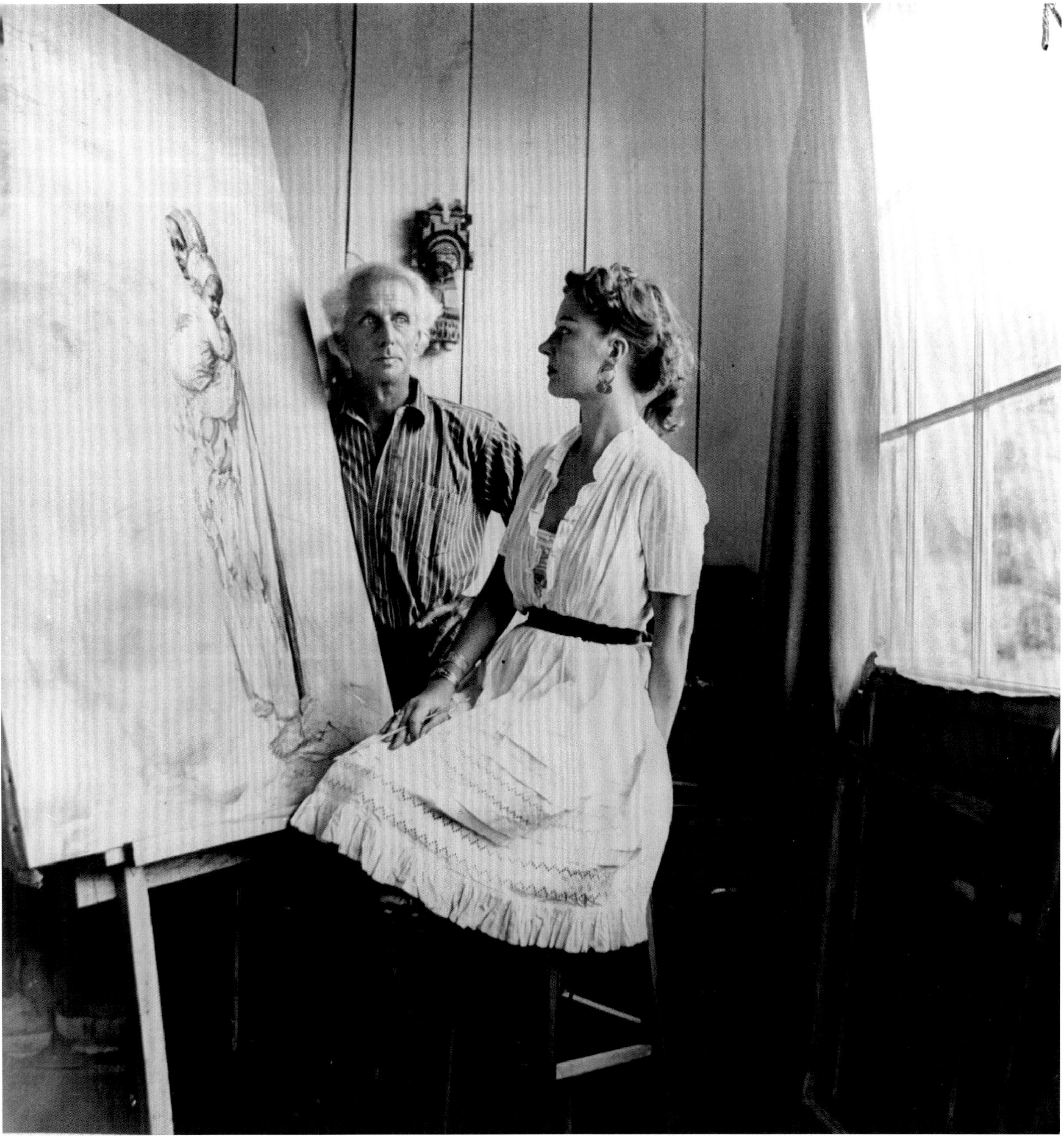

Max Ernst and Dorothea Tanning, Sedona, Arizona 1946

It is possible the early visits to Farleys helped set the style for their life in Huismes where there was plenty of space for both of them to work, and a huge vegetable garden for Max to tend. Max, a city person, was intensely practical and had built their home in Sedona, as recorded by Lee during their visit. It was too arid there to grow much so at Farleys Max was keen to help and learn what could be coaxed from the soil of a more equable land.

A succession of witty collages and delightful small drawings by Dorothea for Christmas and Lee's birthday chart the continuation of the friendship. Two more visits to Farleys followed. In September 1961 they were back for the opening of the Max Ernst retrospective Roland had organised at the Tate Gallery. It was a fleeting visit as the opening made many demands on their time but Max found time to paint a design of two birds for me in my workshop. Dorothea's final visit was 22nd February 1976 which she noted *'George Washington's Birthday – Sumptuous Souvenirs'*. The light-hearted and affectionate words hide a looming grief. Max was ill and would die six days later. It must have been a time for reminiscing and for seizing on moments of optimism and when Dorothea met my late wife Suzanna she seemed to delight in her youth and vitality.

The following year our first daughter Ami was born to Suzanna and I. A tiny pair of jeans arrived in the post from Dorothea, with a note saying she had bought them in the store where all the best cowboys buy their jeans. As Ami arrived, Lee left, dying at Farleys on 22nd July of that year.

It was several weeks before the news caught up with Dorothea who was in the process of moving back to America. She wrote to Roland:

Max Ernst and Dorothea Tanning, Farleys garden 1950

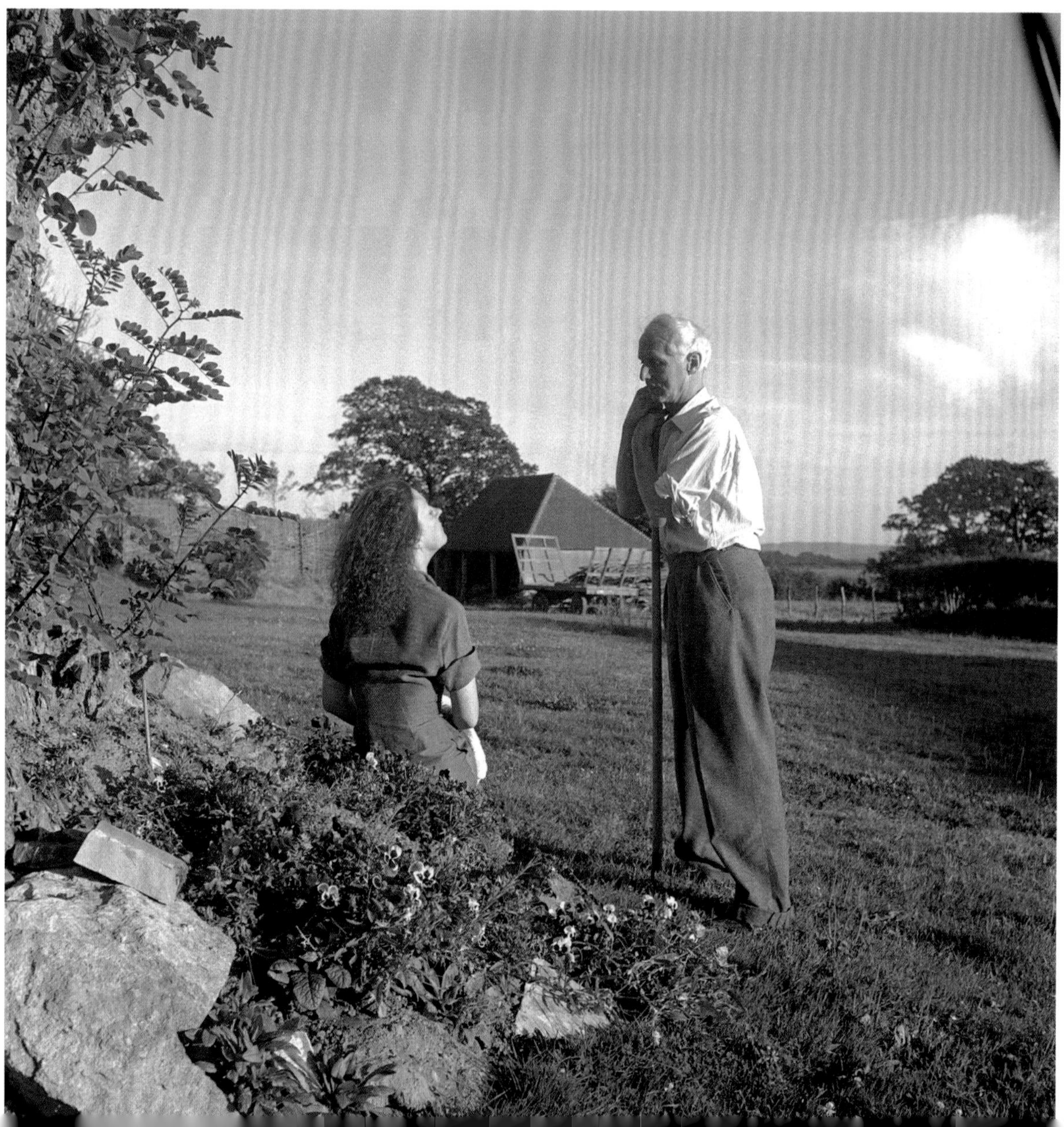

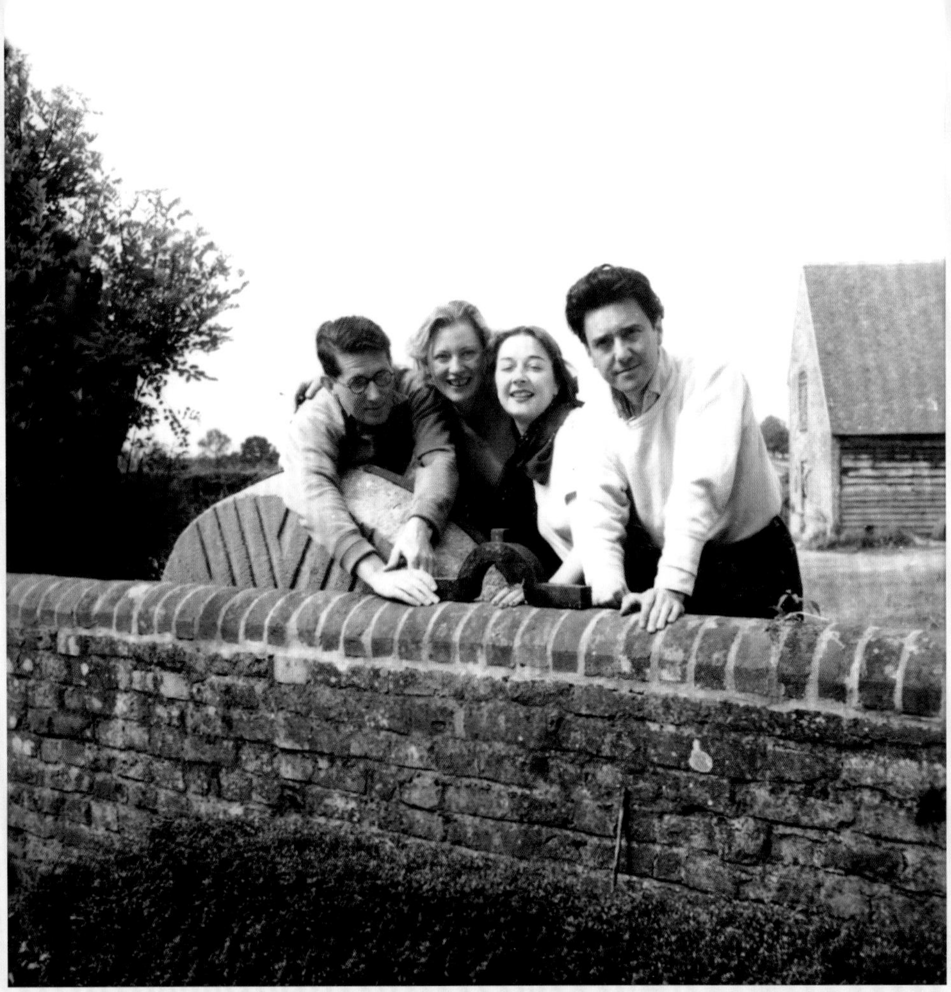

Roland Penrose, Lee Miller, Dorothea Tanning and Roberto Matta (Painter), Farleys garden 1950

Whatever happened, I know now that it was shattering. A letter from John Russell met me on my return from Seillans yesterday. He spoke of "Lee's last days" and how Peggy had been there. And there were the times I tried to phone from Seillans, and once she took the phone and spoke to me, Lee did, in a flat dry way not at all as we always talked. Of course I knew she was awfully sick - you had let me understand so much. But from that to hearing, only now, that she is gone, gone, is unbelievable and a thousand questions rise up and then what it all comes down to is that Lee isn't there any more and that you have lost your best pal and believe me, my darling friend, I know how hard that is. Please, Roland, please know that I loved her too.

And you, Roland, are you going to be OK? Please say yes.

With a heartful of love

Dorothea 8 Sept. 1977[2]

In 1985 we had our first exhibition of Lee Miller's work in New York at the Staley-Wise Gallery. Dorothea came to the opening, greeting me with great warmth and affection. She loved the show, astonished by so much work completely new to her. Then she saw Lee's shot of Max towering over her at Sedona. "It gives the wrong impression", she said, "we were just experimenting with the perspective".

There was no need for Lee to experiment. She knew exactly what she was doing and had used the technique in Egypt nearly nine years earlier. In time to come when Lee's career as a photographer became subordinated to Roland's work, she could have changed places with Dorothea in that image. Lee knew all too well how the work of a woman is sidelined when she is associated with a male partner of conspicuous talent. Dorothea's objection to the image did not fade over time. Fiercely loyal to Ernst, she always denied that he had suppressed her career. It is interesting to note that after she returned alone to New York her work took on a new vitality with wonderfully original explorations of three-dimensional works made of fabric and large-scale three-sided installations, born out by her fabulous 2019 show at Tate Modern.

Dorothea continued to work until close to her death in Manhattan on 21st January 2012 at the age of 101.

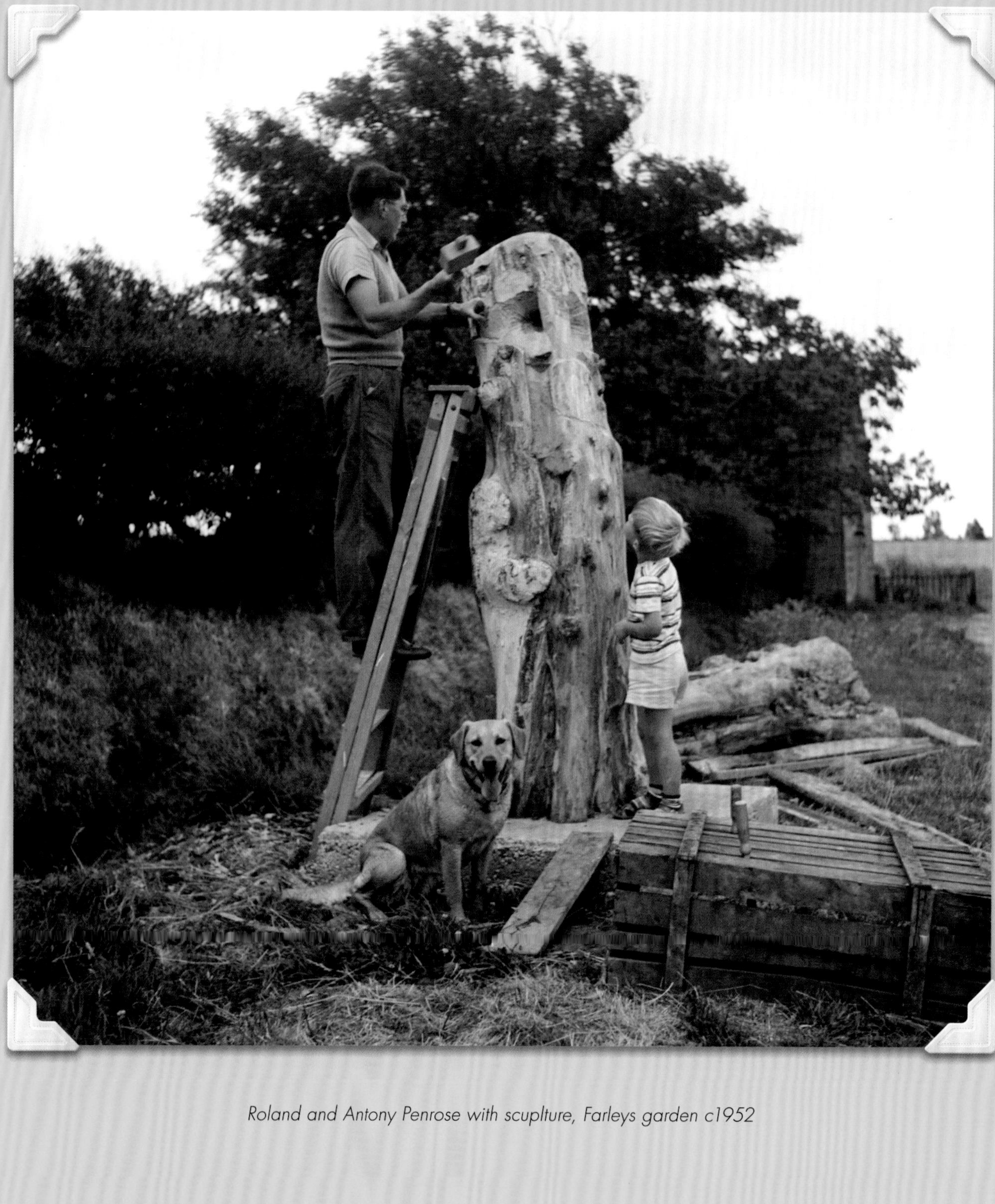

Roland and Antony Penrose with scuplture, Farleys garden c1952

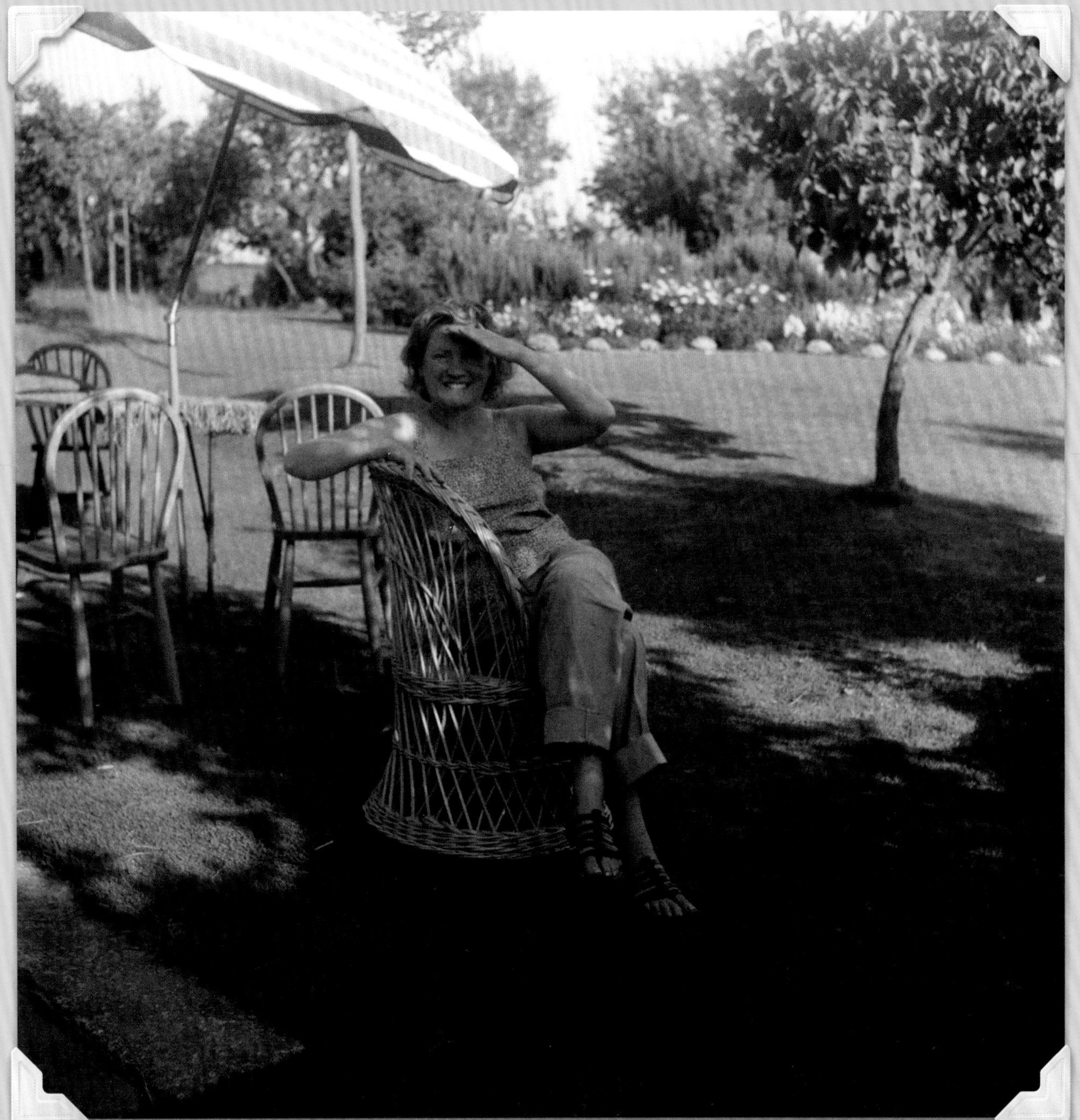

Lee Miller, Farleys garden c1958 by Roland Penrose

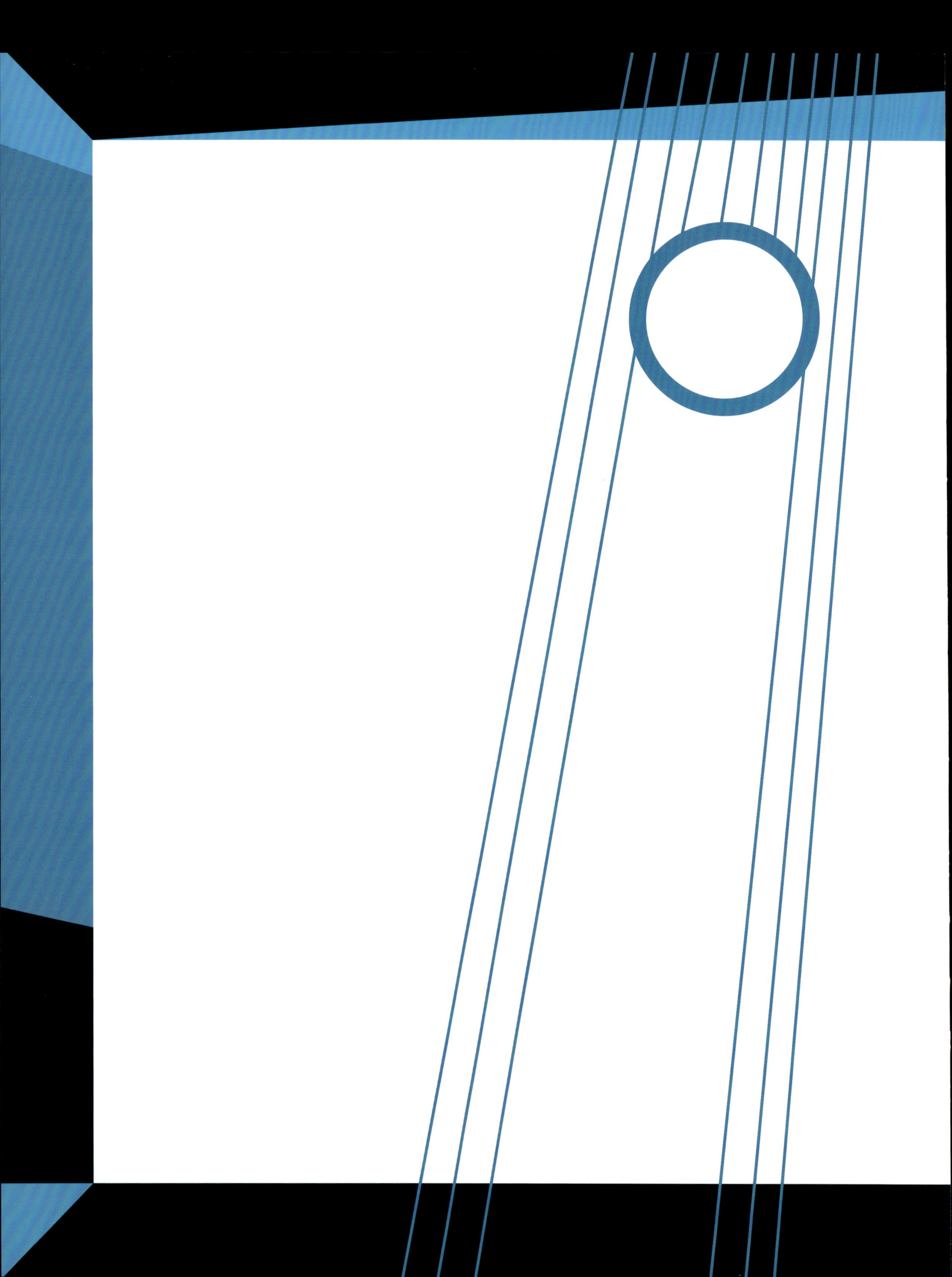

CHAPTER 07

JOYCE REEVES - SLIPWARE POTTER

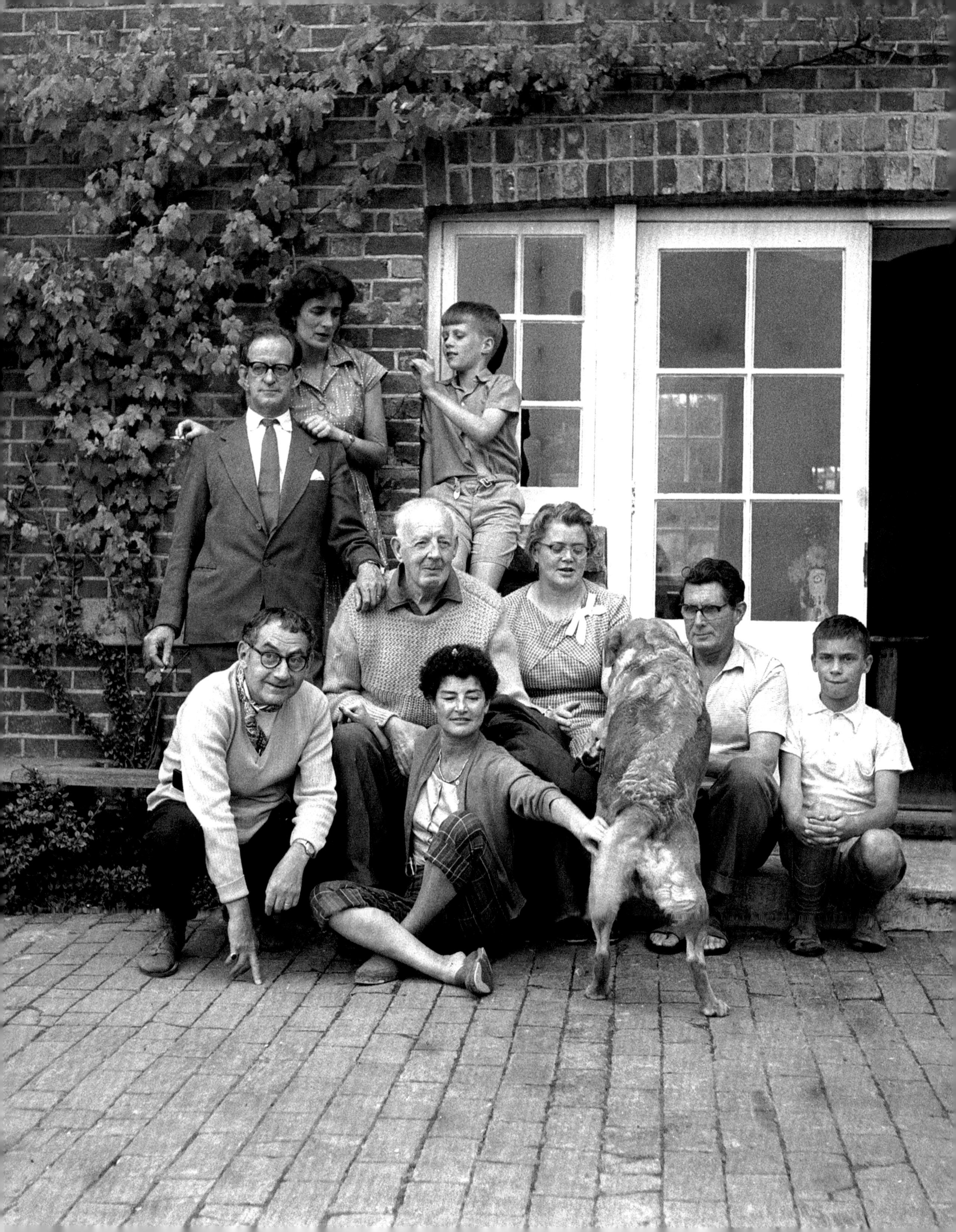

When I first knew her, Joyce Reeves was a potter. Her studio in Newhaven was small, cramped, filled with fascinating things and interesting smells. She had a small electric kiln, a piece of equipment that was both boring and exciting at the same time.

Joyce would carefully place the glazed unfired works in the kiln and clamp the door shut. Next was the boring part but with a sense of anticipation. "Firing takes a long time," she said, adding "When you come back next week everything we have put in the kiln will look very different". And it did. The kindly, sensual, matt beige surfaces emerged with the highest gloss imaginable, transformed into wonderful colours.

Joyce mixed her own slip wear glazes with great effect. Glass sweet jars standing in a row were filled with coloured powders. Joyce had labelled them, writing their names in heavy pencil on the brown paper tape. I don't know what influenced her but I recall her talking about Bernard Leech. Some of her slip wear designs were inspired by tabby cats. Our home at Farleys, to which Joyce was a frequent visitor, was the home of two tabbies named Mrs De Valera and Deli Cat and their descendants. For me it was as if the cats' markings were magically echoed in the glazes.

When the background glaze was air dry, Joyce would take a device that looked disturbingly medical. It was a long black pipette with a huge red rubber bulb like an old-fashioned car horn fastened to the end. She would use this to squirt a stream of glaze on to the plain surface of the dish in the form of a decorative pattern of dots or parallel lines which she modified by stroking them with a comb or a feather.

Joyce did have a traditional potters' wheel but most of her work was moulded. She made concave moulds in a slab of plaster and pressed a sheet of soft clay into the shape. If it was to be a serving dish it was deep, and sometimes with a divider across the middle. The edges were often decorated with light scallops.

Lee loved using them. She enthusiastically spurned the use of fine china and used Joyce's work to showcase her often theatrical dishes.

Joyce's moulding skills extended to taking casts of her friends' hands and feet. She cast a mould in plaster and then to get a faithful impression pressed a softer than usual clay into the cavity. As the clay dried it shrank so her casts of Lee's hands and mine are both significantly smaller than they were in reality but the proportions remain the same. Lee's have a pale blue tint, but Joyce glazed my hands black as with my fondness for the outdoor life on our farm that was their normal colour.

Being an artisan potter, even one with Joyce's considerable talent, was not sustainable and she left the pottery in the late 1950s and went to live in Blackheath. This was the time that Roland needed some help to cope with the work on his biography of Picasso, and she became his secretary for many years, doing his typing and proof correcting. It was demanding, and luckily Joyce had a strong rectitude for grammar and spelling as Roland wrote longhand in a not-so-legible style and was dyslexic. She was competent and unflappable and it was she who was at his elbow when he was curating the 1960 Picasso retrospective at the Tate.

Not much has been recorded about Joyce – sadly, as she was an interesting person. I don't know how she became friends with my parents, but her brother the writer and poet John Reeves lived in Lewes, and she may have come into contact with Roland through him. Born in 1911, she had been in New York In 1938 where Georges Hugnet, also a friend of Roland's, introduced her to Hans Bellmer and they became lovers. When talking to us about Bellmer she said she did not like him much, so none of us could understand why that should be the basis of a love affair. Moving in these circles gave her an innate understanding of artists and the art world. She had also been a teacher and a literary agent; all these experiences were very useful when helping Roland with his work.

Although as a youngster I found her work as a potter fascinating, I was not fond of her as a person. Try as she might on occasion, she was not child friendly. She had a disturbingly high-pitched querulous voice and was bossy – and greedy. She would slip into the larder and gobble up the left overs which annoyed Lee who had been saving them for later but on the whole she got on well with everyone and in later years I developed an affection for her.

Man Ray (Artist), Juliet Browner (Dancer), Heather the dog, Peter Gregory, Joyce Reeves (Potter), Roland Penrose and John Funnell, Maxwell Fry (Architect), Patsy Murray and Antony Penrose, Farleys House 1957

Her work for Roland was only part time so she began to write. Strangely for someone who seemed to have an aversion to children, she became a successful author of children's fantasy books writing as Joyce Gard and getting at least eight titles published. Among the best known are *The Snow Firing* (Gollancz 1963) about a boy who revives a derelict country pottery and *The Mermaid's Daughter* (Gollancz 1969). It was failing eyesight that defeated her – I don't know the name of her condition but she had several sessions of painful surgery which sadly did not improve anything. She found travel much harder and we saw little of her. She died in 1993.

In the photo we see Joyce surrounded by friends at Farleys among whom are Man Ray and his wife Juliette. About this time Man Ray gave us one of his *Abat Jour* – a lampshade made from a spiral of heavy paper about 1.4 metres tall. It hung in a spiral from a thread in the dining room at Farleys softly twirling in the air currents. It was there for years, and then one day without warning the thread broke and it fell to the ground. Lee picked it up, and threw it away. "It's covered in fly shit and I will ask Man Ray to give us another one," she said. He did not give us another and the whole thing was forgotten by everyone except me because I loved it and missed it. Many years later I found that Joyce had written a poem titled *Abat Jour* of which this is a short extract;

Wreath of bonfire smoke
On a still day in autumn
Silk smooth
Birch bark peel
Ribbon of white deal from a plane blade

Abat Jour, Joyce Reeves Feb 7th 1958

In its collection of spirals, the poem references Farleys in many ways;

Birch bark peel – Roland had planted three Birch trees in the garden.

Ribbon of white deal from a plane blade - There were often carpenters at Farleys using smoothing planes that made big curly shavings.

She gave a copy to Man Ray who drew a design of the *Abat Jour* on the page and wrote *What a birthday present!*

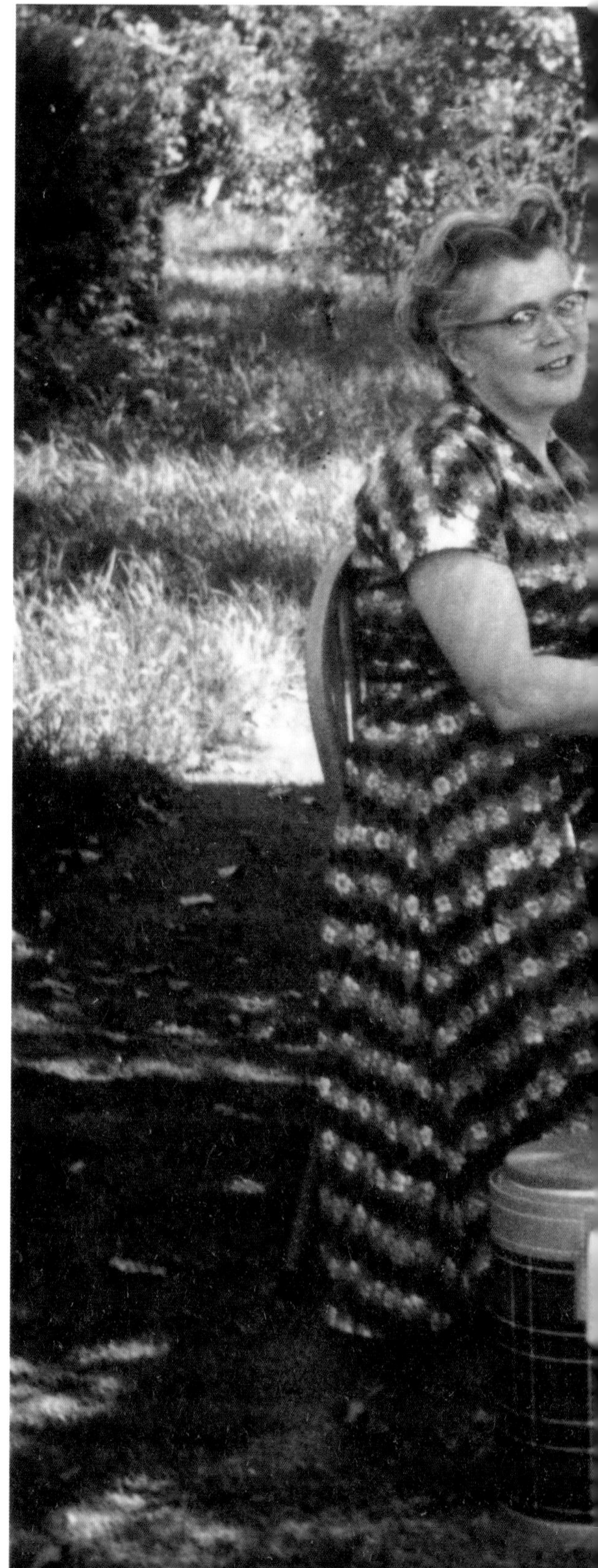

Joyce Reeves, Nick Benden, Antony Penrose, Patsy Murray, Roland Penrose and Madge Benden, Farleys garden c1954

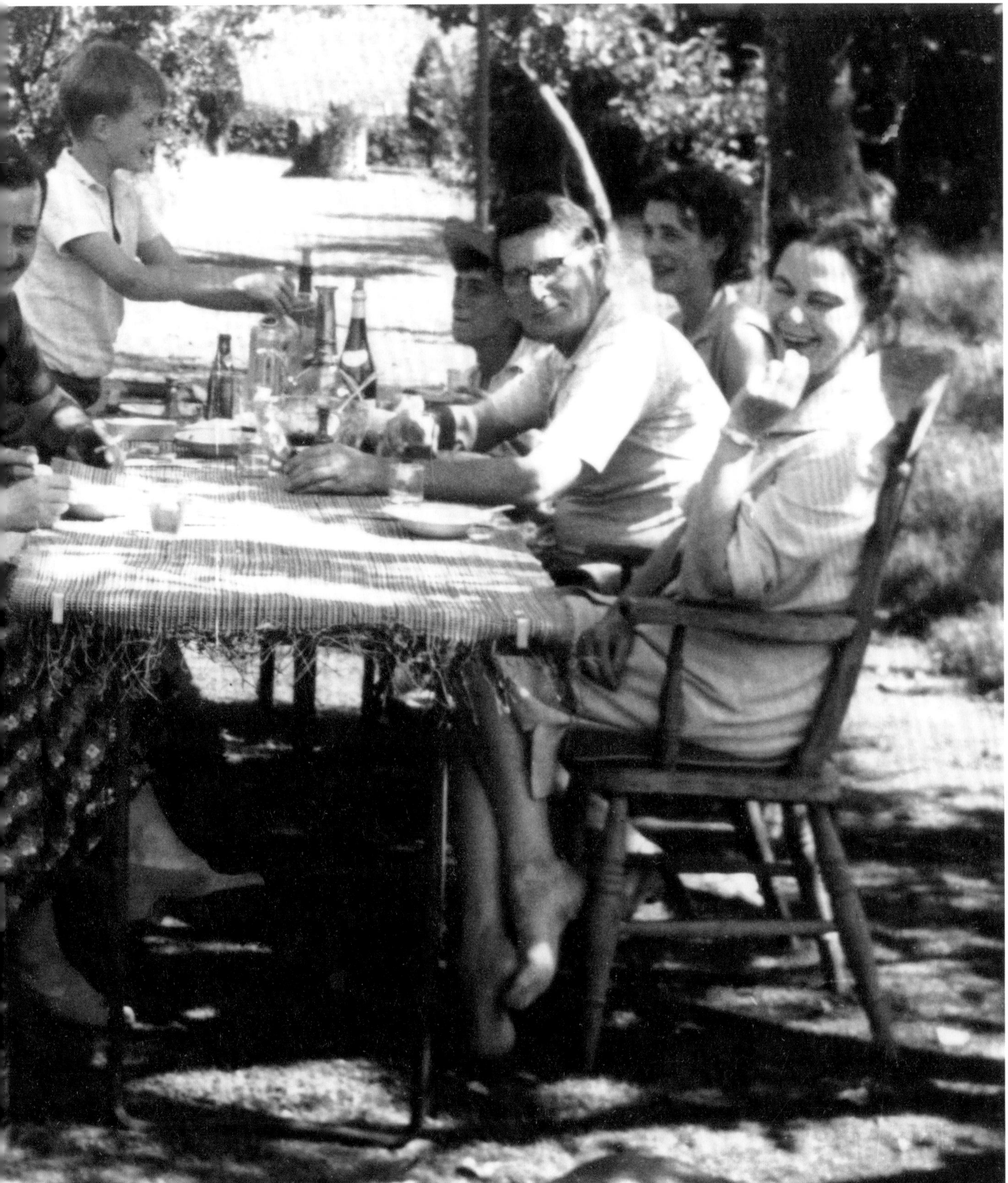

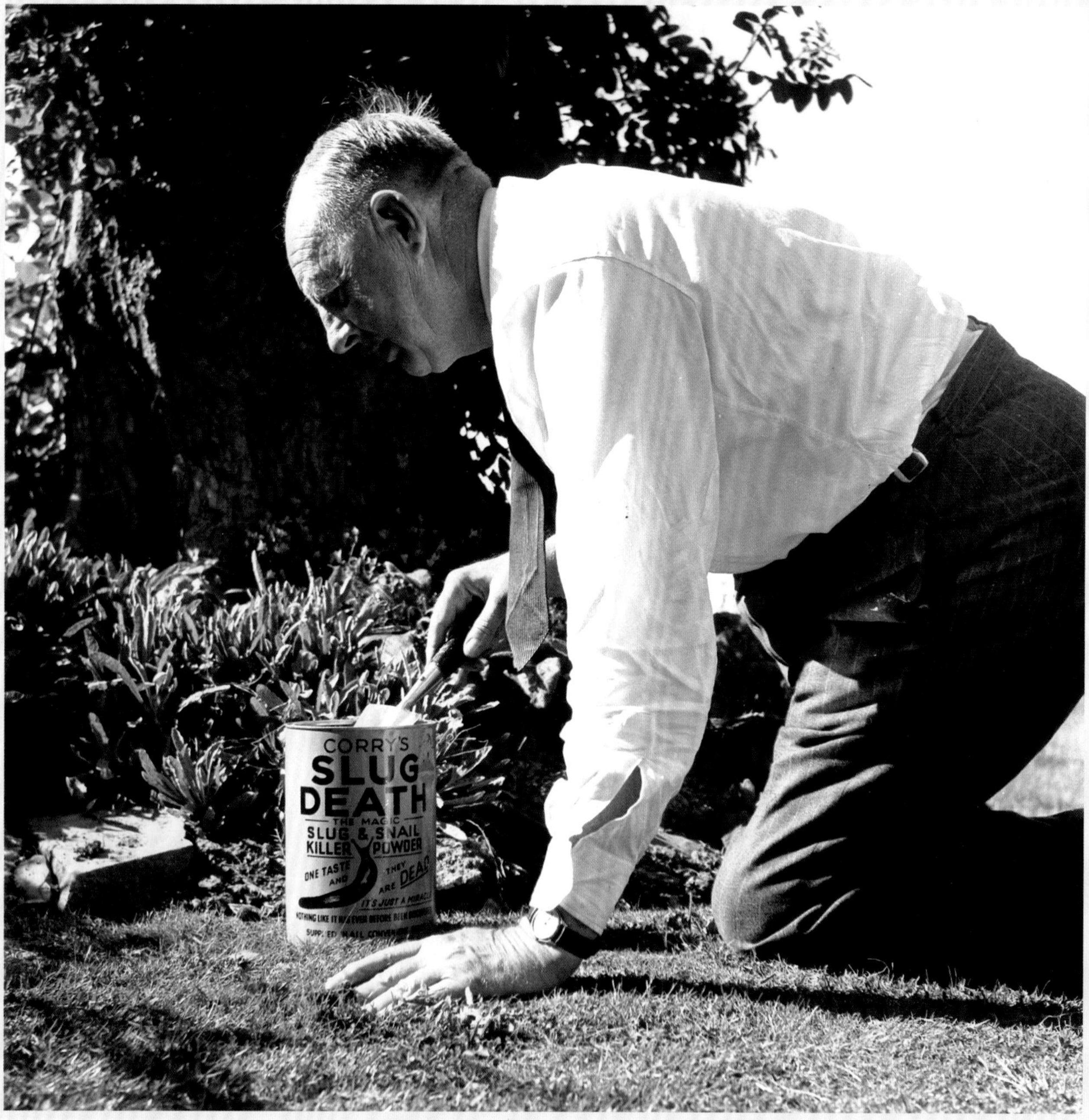

Peter (Eric Craven) Gregory (Publisher), Farleys garden c1952

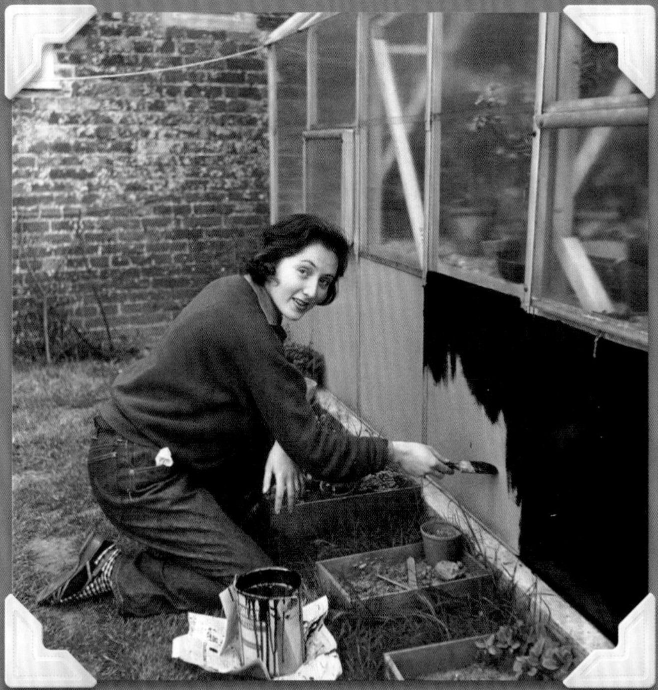

Katherina Turnbull (Pianist), Farleys garden 1951

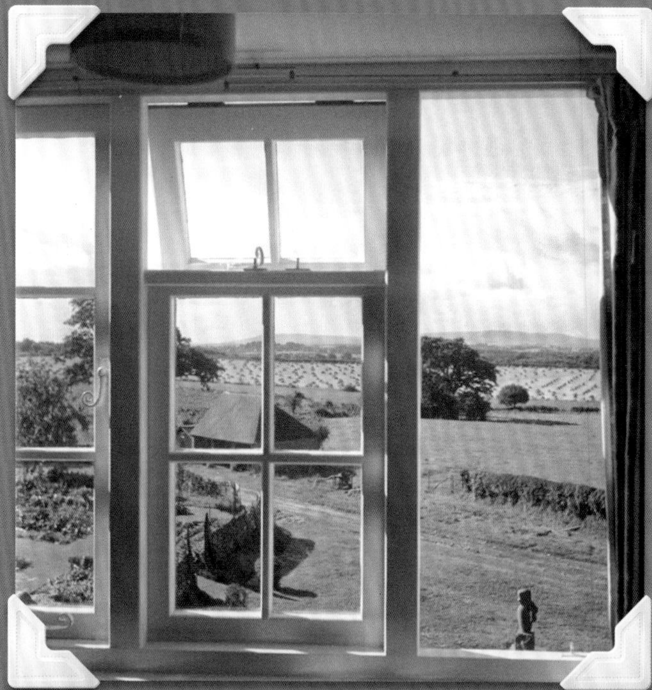

View from Farleys, Farleys House 1952

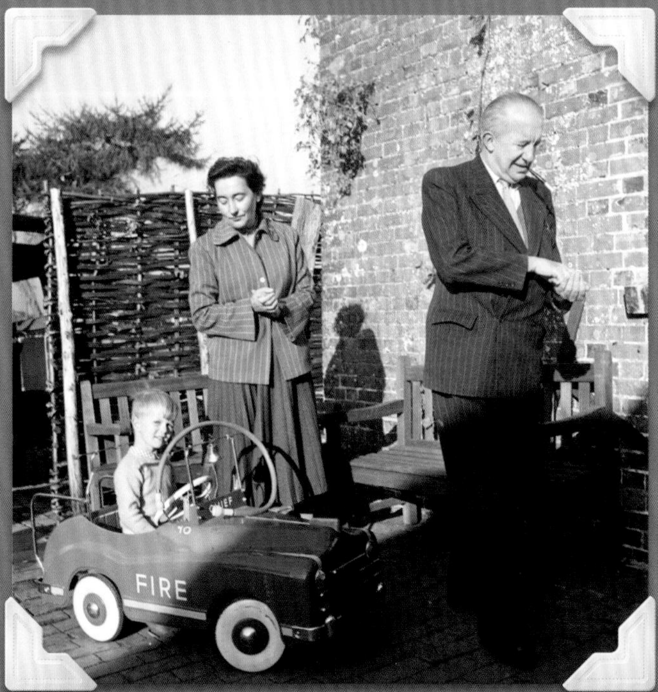

Antony Penrose, Dominique and Paul Eluard,
Farleys garden 1951

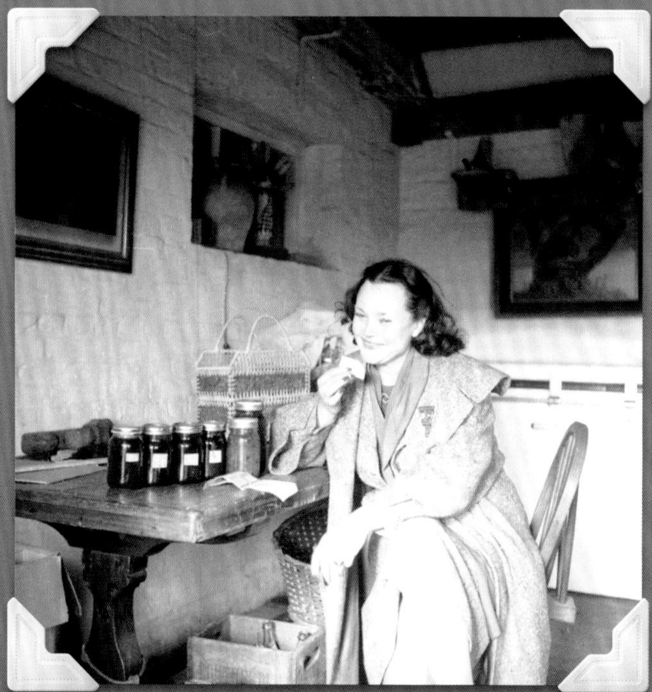

Margaret King-Farlow (Actor) labelling preserves
in the old kitchen, Farleys 1954

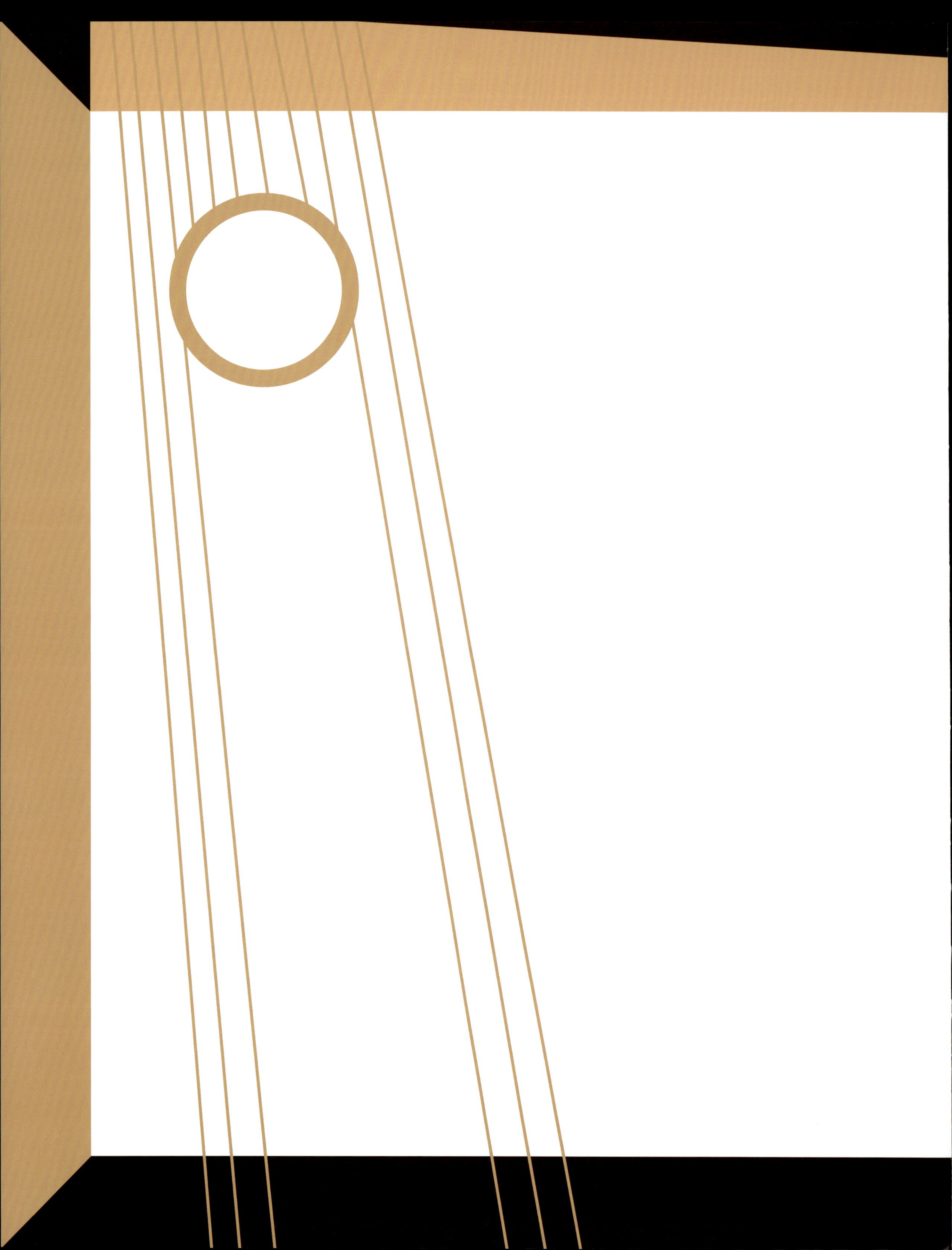

CHAPTER 08

‘I AM SMILING INSIDE’

TIMMIE O’BRIEN

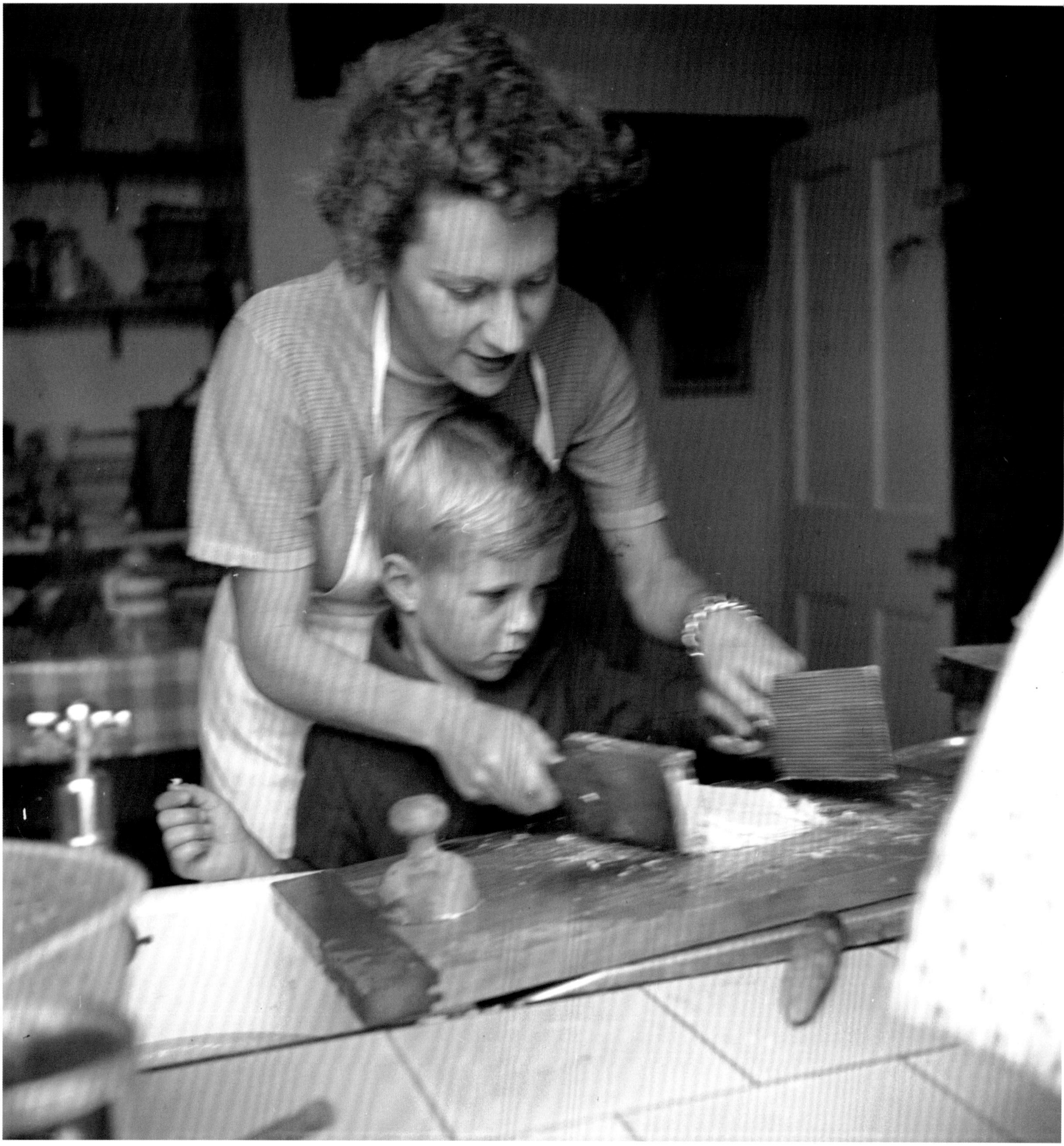

One of the most frequent entries in the visitor's book until the late 1950's is that of Timmie and Terry O'Brien. They were a couple so loved and so intimately part of our lives they seemed an extension of our family.

Timmie, a slim graceful woman with a mass of curls surmounting a kind and lovely face, came from South Africa just before the war. *Vogue* Editor Audrey Wither's appointed her as managing editor and in the post war years in a manner unlikely to be found in today's corporate world one of Timmie's main duties was to look after Lee. Audrey was one of the few people to recognise the full impact of the emotional, mental and physical damage Lee had incurred with her war reporting for the magazine. That the term Post Traumatic Stress Disorder was not invented until 1980 shows us how prescient Audrey was with her unique and profound sense of understanding and also loyalty. Most editors would have fired Lee as her behaviour became egregious and her ability to meet deadlines changed from utterly dependable to hopelessly erratic.

The challenge of pulling a contributor with Lee's forcefulness and reputation into line would have made the stoutest heart quail. Timmie solved the problem by not even trying. In a way that was part filial devotion, part maternal affection, part authority and always with a high voltage intelligence, Timmie became one of Lee's closest friends. She realised from the outset that no-one could force Lee to do anything. Her strategy was to sit up far into the night keeping Lee company while she wrote. She knew enough to not try and suggest phrases but by talking around the subject she helped Lee get the words moving or the fashion shoot motivated. Timmie knew how much Scotch Whiskey to pour. She knew how to limit the distractions and gently keep Lee's focus on the job. It worked and the two women began a collaboration that had a touch of rebellious naughtiness.

Lee was supposed to work exclusively for *Vogue*, but on one occasion she and Timmie went 'moonlighting' for *Picture Post*. It was probably a little to do with resenting the reassertion of control by American *Vogue* and may well have had Audrey's tacit approval as neither would have betrayed her. The chosen location for one fashion shoot was our local railway station of Horam and Farleys, and Lee simply re-purposed all she knew from the improvised shoots she did on the streets of London during the war when *Vogue* studios were bombed or there was no electricity. Today we look back with the nostalgia of steam and the rural station. Then it was an entirely normal part of life and a good natural setting for the women and their stylish coats. The feature ran to 4 pages and 8 photographs in the Vol 47 No 9 issue of *Picture Post*, 27th May 1950. A success in its own right and a joint venture repeated a couple more times that same year.

Timmie O'Brien and Antony Penrose with butter pats, Farleys House c1952

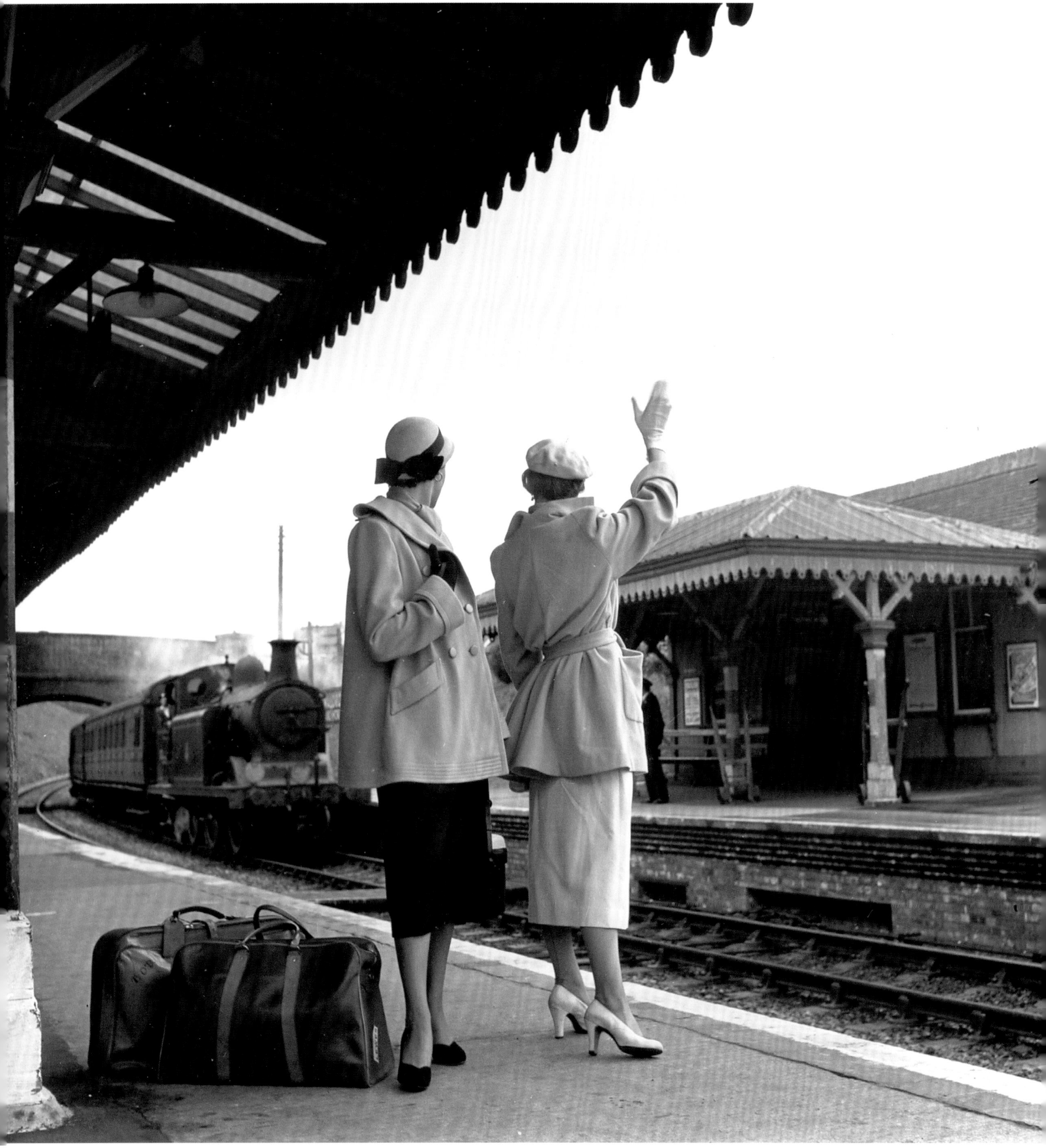

Travel light for Whitsun, Horam Railway Station, East Sussex 1950

Timmie was a devoted friend to Lee, and when I was born, to me. She took me on my first visit to London Zoo and when we moved to Farleys she was a frequent visitor. She was married to Terry, an Australian who had come to England to join the RAF in 1940. Soon after he met Timmie he was posted to India and had a remarkably distinguished wartime career flying in South East Asia. He returned to England in 1945 and was now struggling to establish his career as a novelist and journalist, but that did not matter to me. What I found impressive was he was intensely practical with that gift of improvisation common among Australians of a rural background. It was he to whom I turned when my toys broke or my chums and I had a structural problem when building our tree house in the garden.

At Farleys during the week, it was normally just Patsy, our housekeeper, me and Heather the Labrador dog on our own. We were never lonely as there was always so much activity on the farm or in the garden. At weekends Patsy's attention was diverted by the return of my parents and their guests, not all of whom were child friendly, so when Timmie

Lunch outdoors, Farleys garden 1951

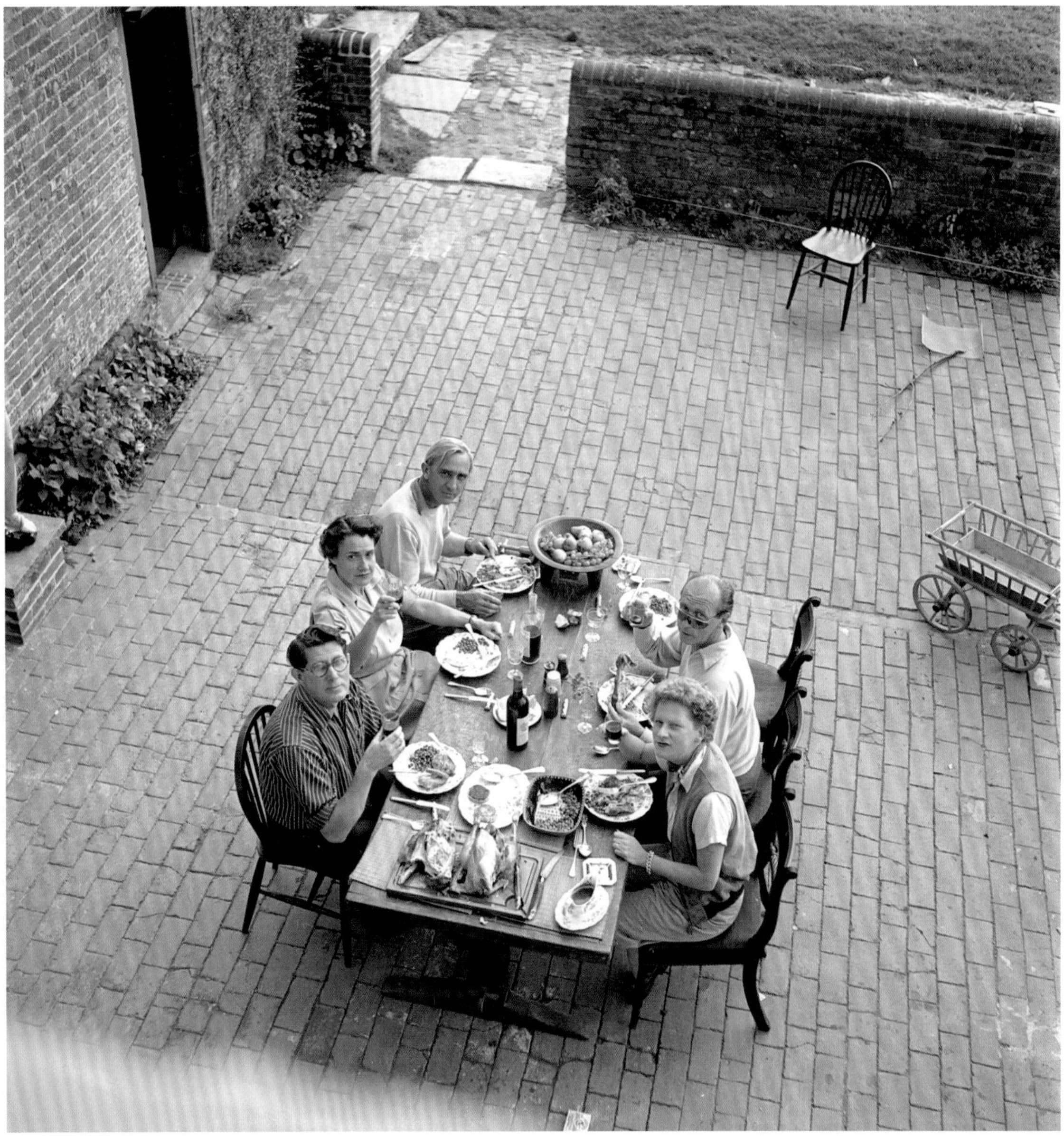

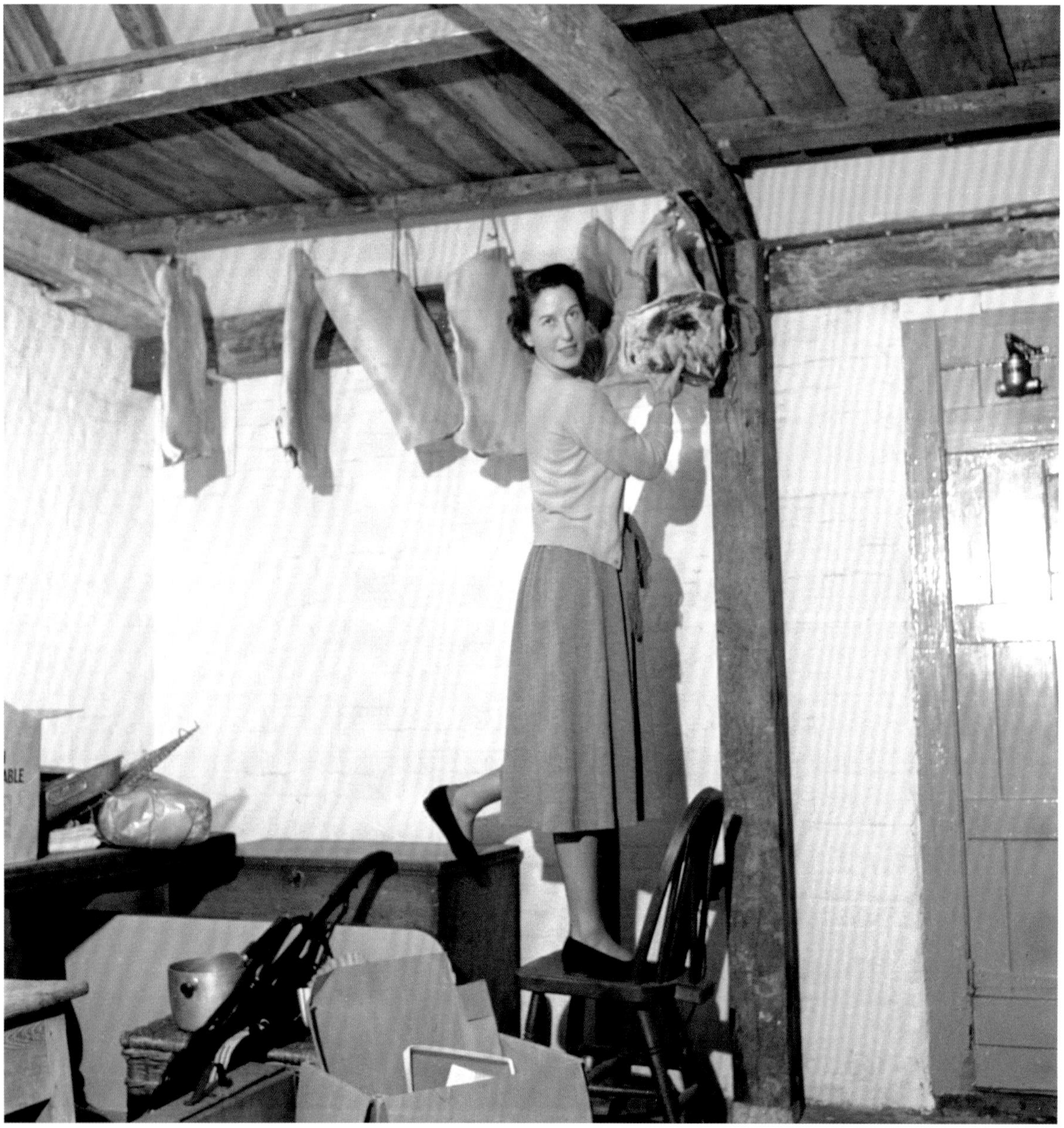

Peggy Bernier (Actor) curing ham, old kitchen, Farleys House 1952

and Terry arrived it was always a joyful moment for me. Timmie had her two boys later so when I first knew her, I was the sole recipient of her warmth and her generosity. We spent endless time together, taking long walks on the farm and building stick houses in the woods. Or, if it was wet, she would get down on the floor for games with my toys, building wonderful palaces for my teddy with wooden blocks or putting my cuddly animals in my toy truck and taking them on a kind of reverse polarity safari through all the rooms in the house so the animals could see the people. For Timmie, the bigger the stretch of the imagination the better. Nothing seemed too trivial or too much trouble.

About this time Lee's interest in cooking was rising and this coupled with her desire to make the best of the food opportunities the farm offered powered a craze for self-sufficiency. She attempted making bacon and ham and tried every known form of preserving fruit and vegetables. It was her cheese and butter making that was the most

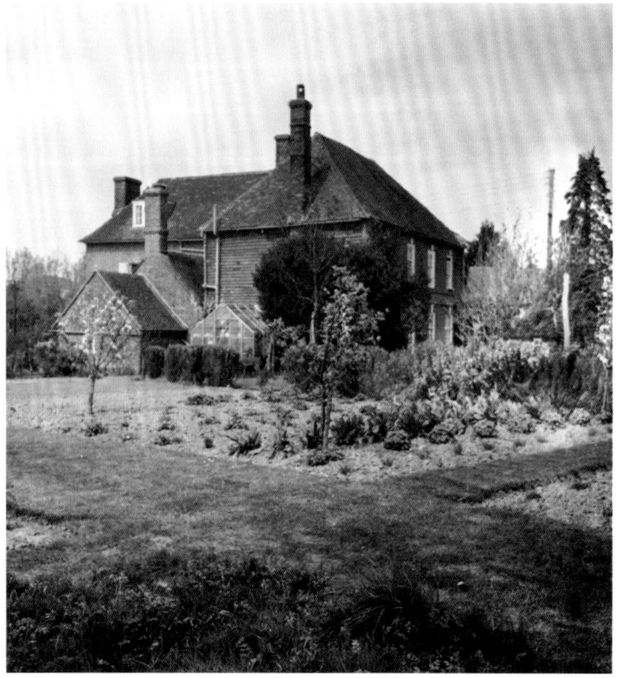

Farleys House

entertaining. For this she had a wonderful supply of rich creamy unpasteurised milk from our herd of Ayrshire dairy cows. Huge muslin covered teardrop shapes of soft cheese hung in the back kitchen, emanating an enticing sharp aroma. When matured and ready to be eaten it was scooped into bowls and decorated with snippings of chives from the garden. But it was butter making where Timmie excelled herself. No one other than Timmie (watched by me) had the patience to crank the churn for the hours required. I loved the process, with the little bevel gears whirring as they transferred the rotation of the crank to the two wooden paddles in the glass churn. Hours passed with no change to the contents and then suddenly the contents solidified into butter as if by magic.

And then the best bit followed. Making the butter pats was endless fun. Timmie scooped the butter out of the churn and chilled it a little in the fridge. When it was the right consistency, she would put a huge dollop on a wooden board. It was my job to shape the round butter pats using two paddles. They were ribbed and left a pattern of parallel marks on the surface of the butter. Then the greatest joy was decorating the pat with the wooden stamp that left embossed wheat ears on the surface.

In the late 1950's Timmie and Terry pursued their life-long dream and went to settle in the Canary Islands where they bought a small hotel. They had two sons of their own and became part of the artistic scene of Tenerife. It was many years before they returned to England and bought a house in Selsey where they welcomed me, my late wife Suzanna, our two little girls and later our son. Watching Timmie play with the girls gave me a sense of *déjà vu*; unsurprisingly there seemed to be a direct familial link we all enjoyed. We felt as Timmie described when she was happy, "I am smiling inside".

Timmie died in 1996 and Terry followed her three years later.

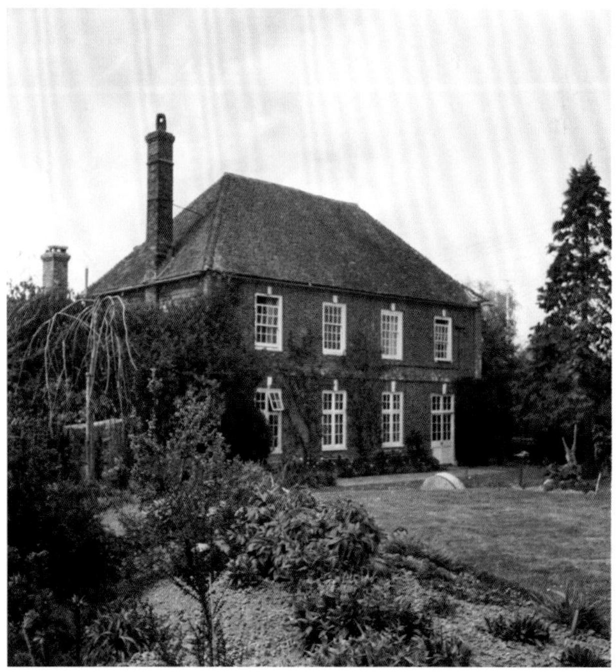

Farleys House

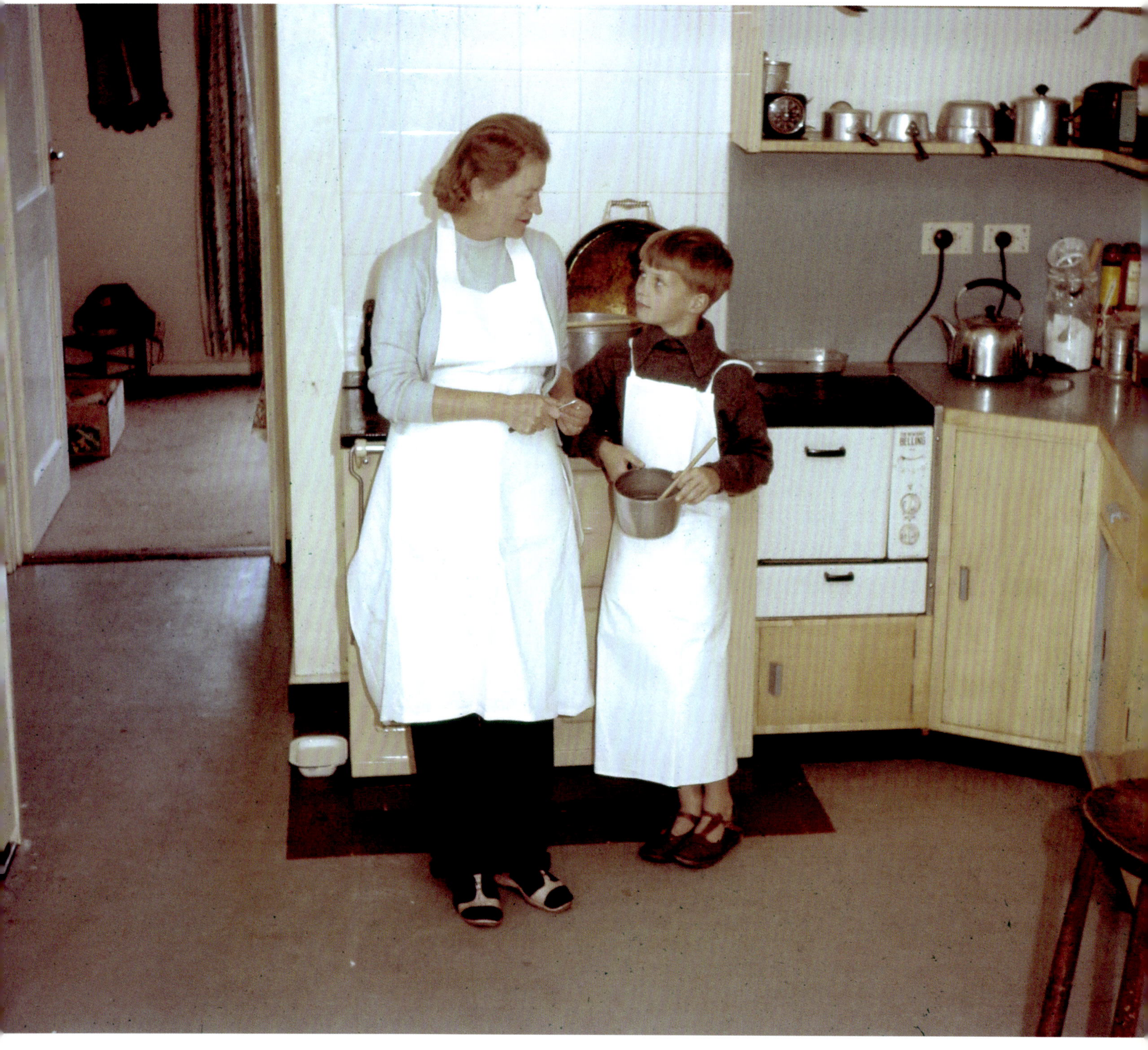

Lee Miller and Antony Penrose, Farleys kitchen 1955 by Roland Penrose

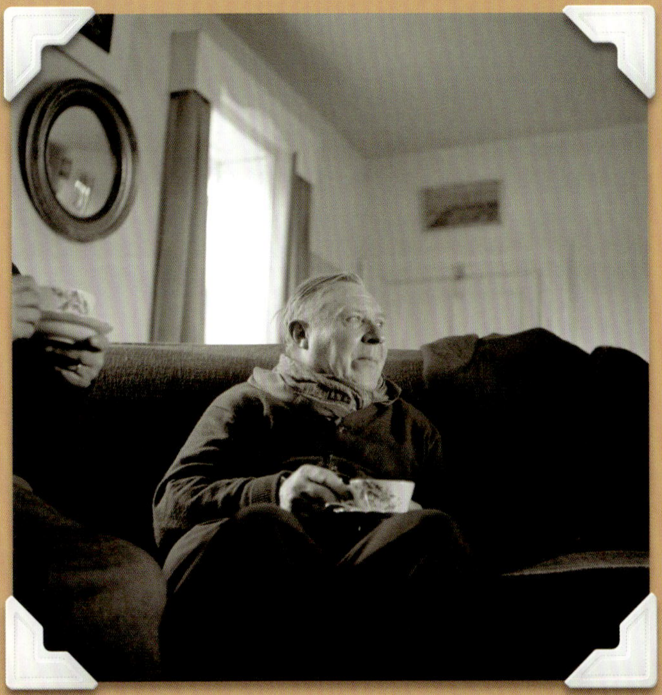

André Masson (Artist), Farleys sitting room 1955

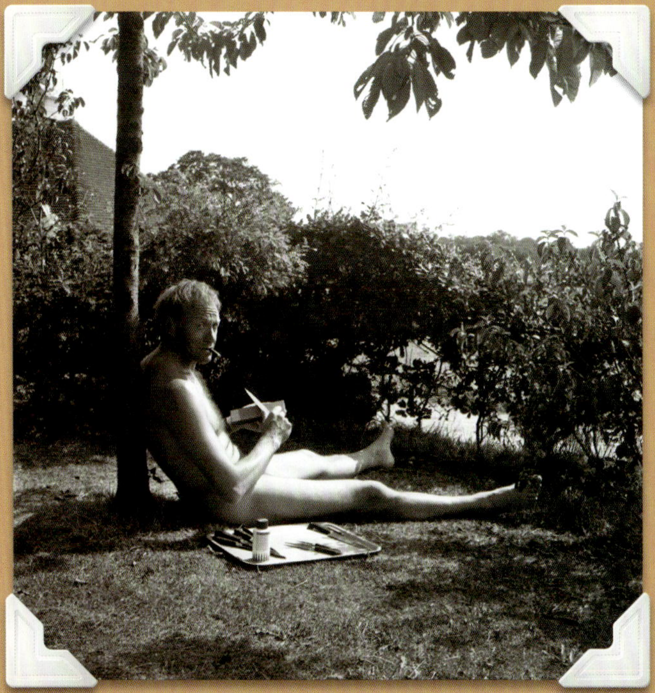

Lynn Chadwick naked sharpening Lee's kitchen knives, Farleys garden 1957

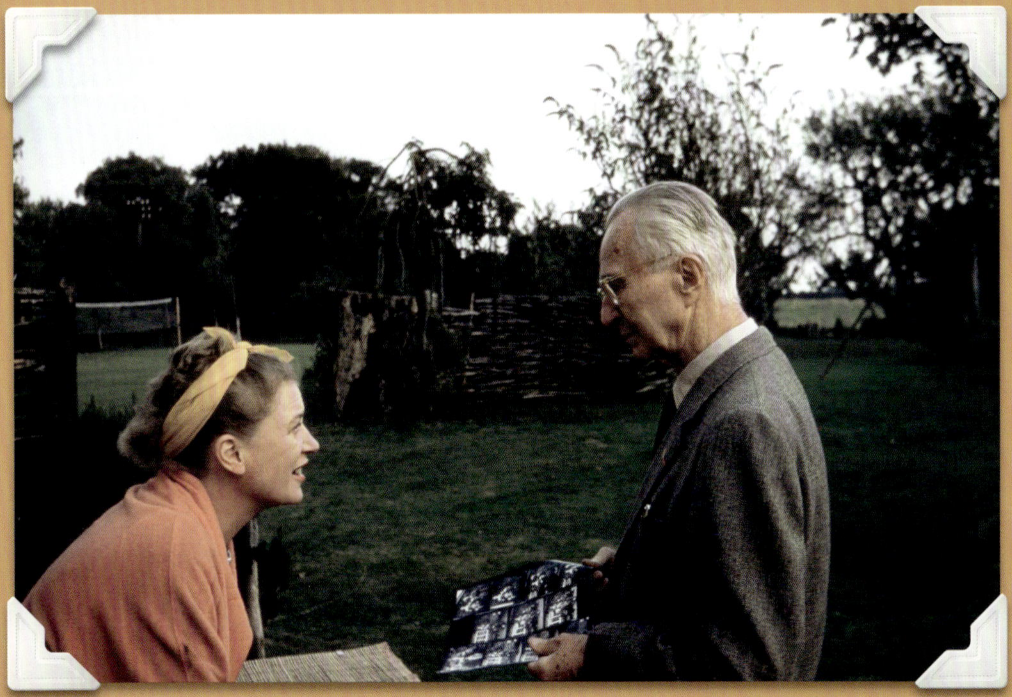

Lee Miller and Edward Steichen (Photographer), Farleys garden 1955 by Theodore Miller

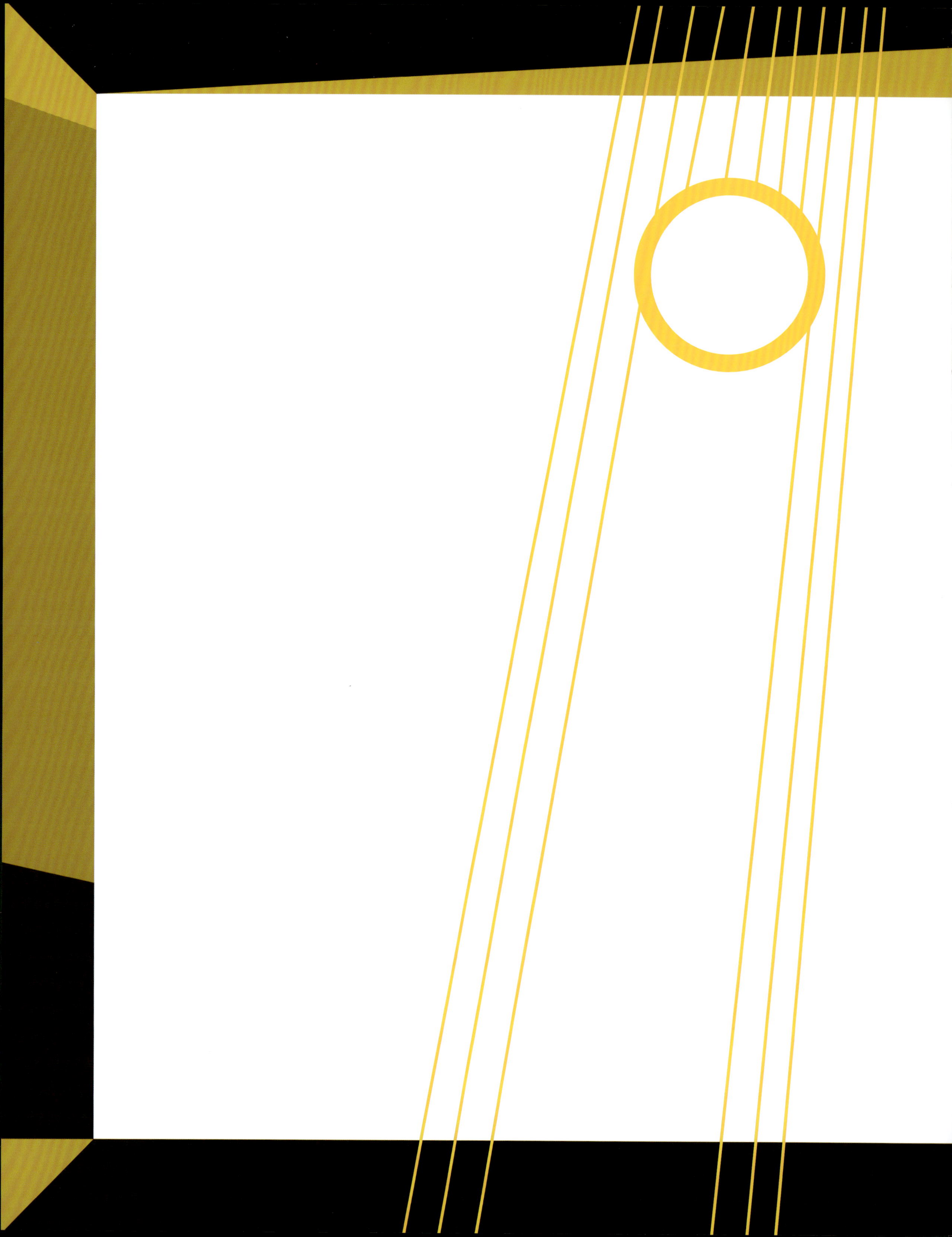

CHAPTER 09

SNAKE CHARMING AT FARLEYS

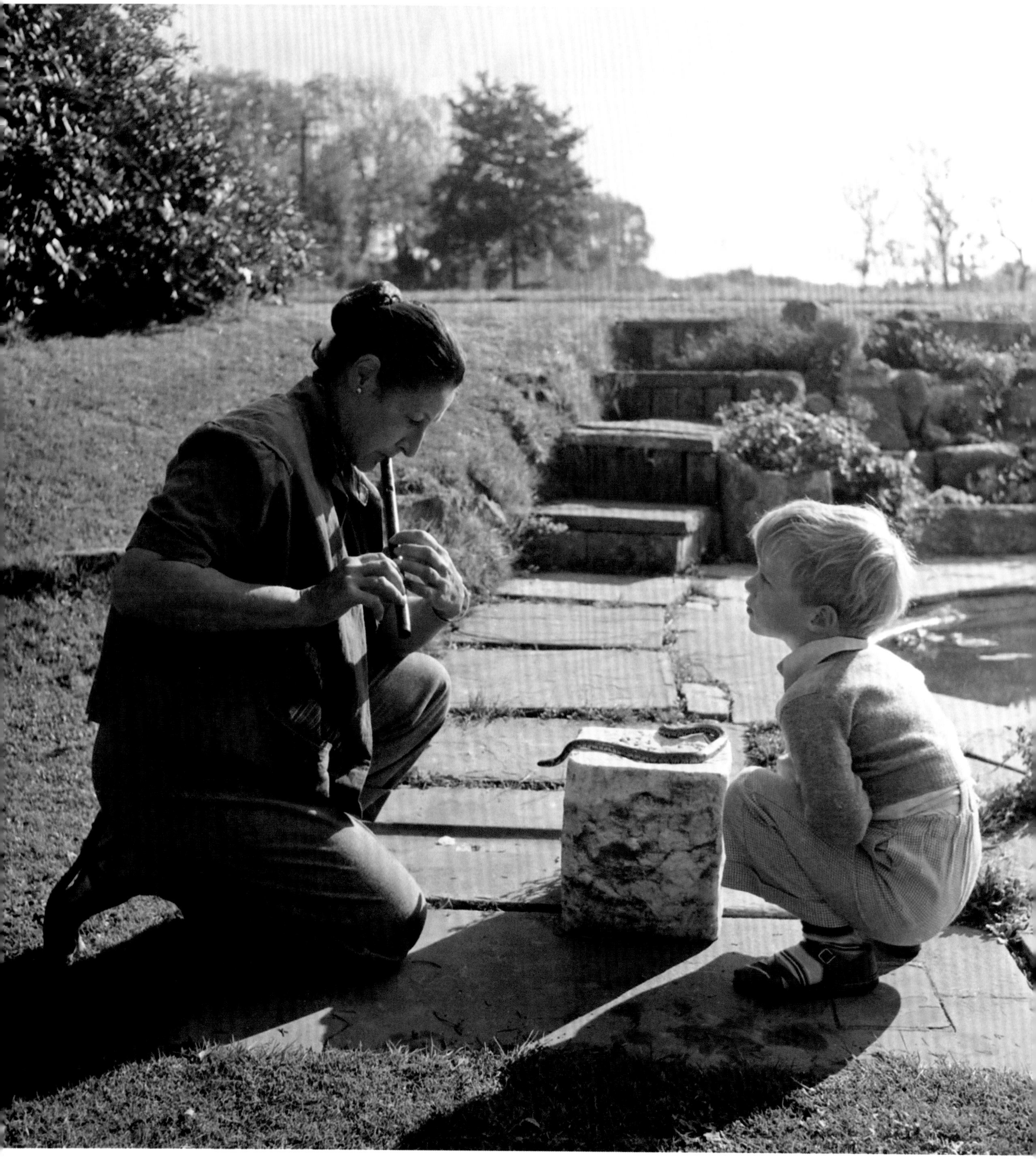

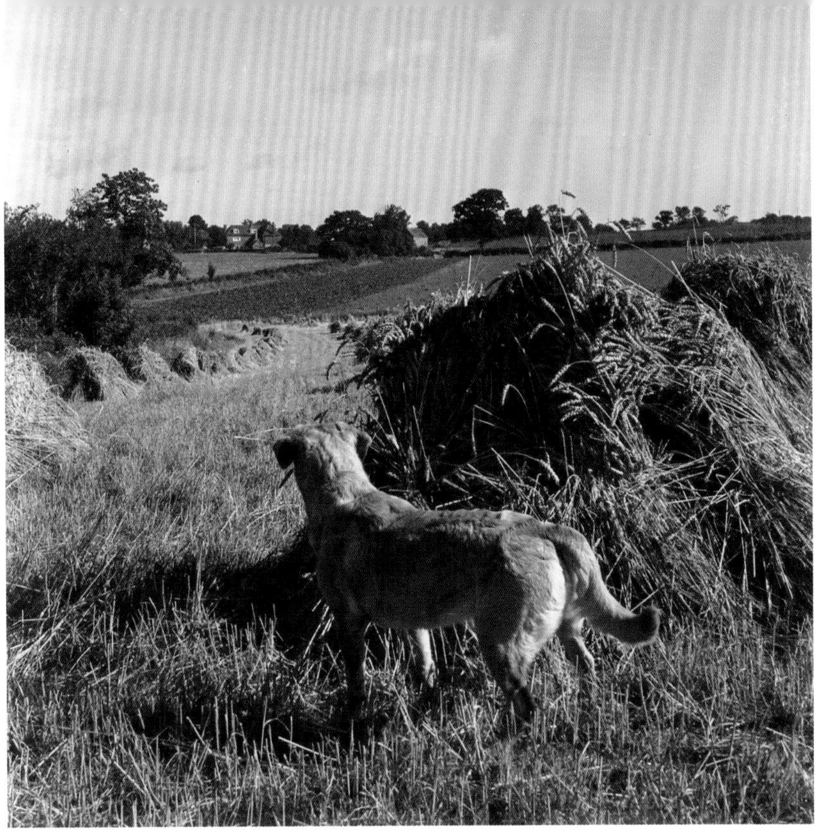

Wheat field, Farley Farm c1951

Some people believed that Valentine Penrose née Boué was a witch. This opinion was held not with malice but with admiration for there was no other explanation for her intense rapport with all living creatures and her unworldly manner of being. She would go on long walks by herself and when she returned the large deep pocket of her coat sometimes contained a bulge that wriggled. Once it was a hedgehog she brought back to show me, a mass of prickles on a tightly curled little body. We watched for ages without making a sound as the prickles parted to reveal a pair of beautiful little bright eyes set in a furry face ending in a sensitive oddly shaped button nose.

The most impressive creature she brought home was a grass snake. She held it gently with her fingers behind its head and its body looped over her wrist. One-handed she got her flute from inside the house and then she settled the snake on a block of stone in the garden by the pond. I did not know it at the time but the tune she played was similar to that of an Indian snake charmer. It was deep-seated in her as she had travelled India extensively with my father in 1932 and later when they parted, she had gone to live in an ashram at Mirtola.

The snake flickered its tongue, clearly appreciating the authenticity of the flute music and the connection Valentine established with it. As a small child, to me it seemed entirely natural, but looking back it was extraordinary that the snake was so calm. It lay on the stone motionless and allowed me to gently touch it. When Valentine stopped playing, she picked it up, caressed it briefly and put it down in some long grass where it promptly disappeared.

Other witch like gifts Valentine possessed were astrology and clairvoyance which was of importance to us all. I don't mean to imply she could predict the football results, but she frequently foretold our personal futures with surprising accuracy using a beautiful set of Tarot cards. If she agreed to do a reading there was the ritual shuffling of the cards, the dealing, the selection of them and placing them face down in a precise pattern. Then the moment came for revealing the images. Great concentration was evident as she interpreted the line-up. Both good and bad news were delivered gently. When thieves raided Roland's flat in London and stole the key works from his collection Valentine assured him they would be returned. Against all odds they were. On my travels in 1971 I was briefly in Islamabad during the India – Pakistan war. As Indian Airforce jets bombed close by, I remember thinking 'This can't be the end, Valentine assured me I would have a long and happy life'. She was right, and she told me how I would discover who I would marry and how many children we would have. Our first-born daughter has Valentine as her middle name.

Valentine Penrose and Antony Penrose, Farleys garden 1952

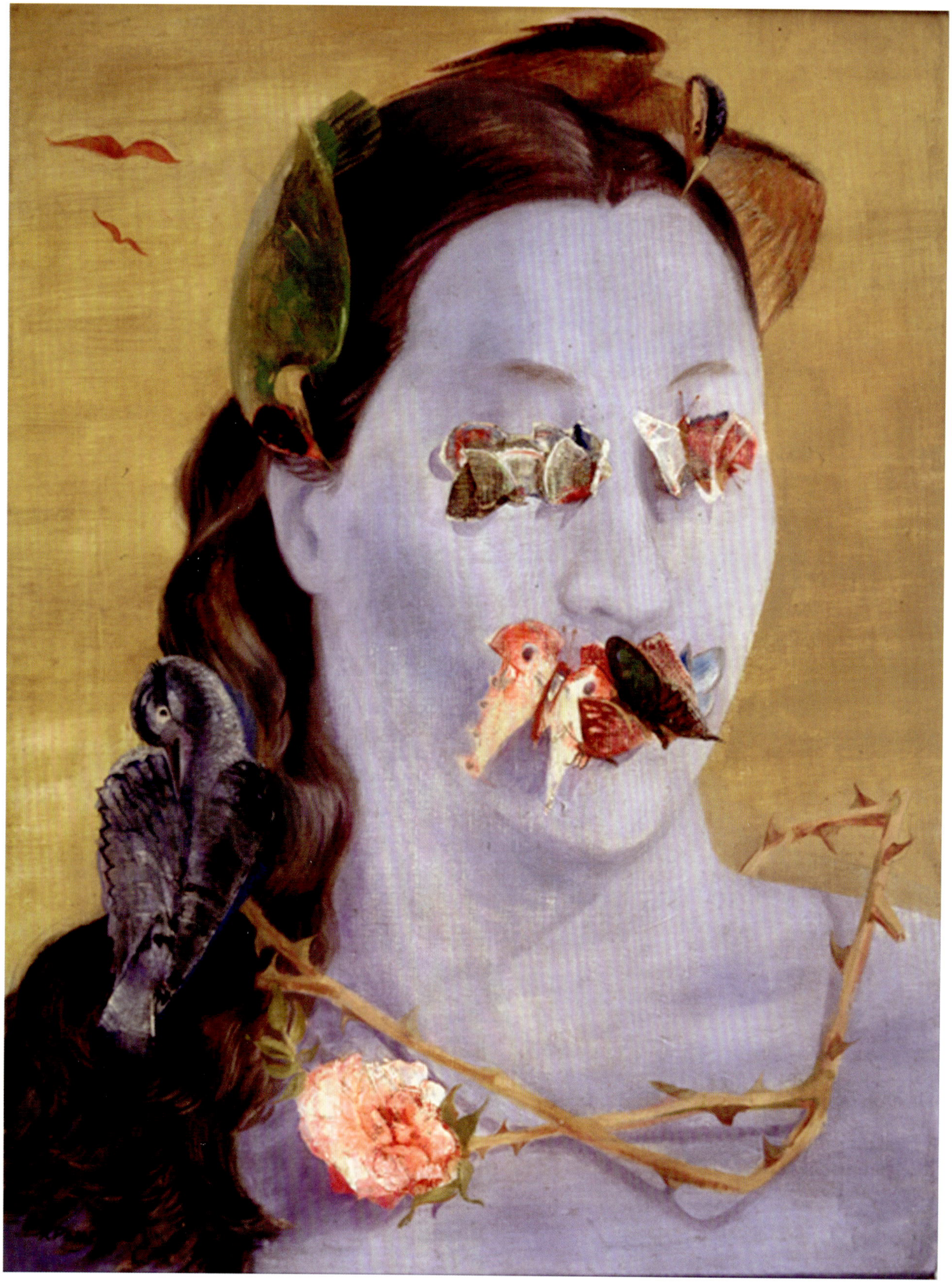

Valentine was my father's first wife. They met when he was living in Cassis sur Mer on the Mediterranean coast and later moved to her native Gers and her wonderfully named home town of Condom sur Baise, buying the dilapidated Chateau le Pouy. She was a surrealist poet already known to Andre Breton and Paul Eluard. They married in 1925. After eleven years and many wonderful adventures the divergence of their paths split them apart. Roland, moderately successful as a painter became passionate about curating and presenting the work of surrealist and other modern artists. Valentine became dedicated to her own spiritual life. She learned Sanskrit and immersing herself in the Hindu religion, went to live in India. The divorce came through in 1937 and to expiate the grief of losing her Roland painted her as '*Winged Domino*'.

Valentine's face is blue for the distance of their separation. She is already on her route to Nirvana. Her eyes and lips and hair are clustered with birds and butterflies, an attestation of her closeness to nature. Around her neck is a rose, the symbol of love and the motif for the Penrose family motto *Nulla Rosa Sine Spina (No Rose Without Thorns)* to which Roland's rejoin in that moment was probably 'No Love Without Pain'. We see the thorns piercing Valentine's tender skin. There is no blood. She is not there to bleed, but the pain is there and will remain for some time to come.

When war was declared, Valentine, whose father was Colonel Boué, a hero of the siege of Verdun, decided to return to France and join the army to fight the Nazis. While she was at sea, France fell and her ship diverted to London. The hotel she was in got bombed and as a last resort she contacted Roland who asked her to meet him in a Hampstead pub. When she arrived, still shocked and with a cut face, she was greeted in French by a woman who calmed her, dressed her wound, and gave her wine. By the time Roland arrived Valentine and the woman had become friends. "Oh Roland", Valentine cried, "I am so sorry to bother you, I don't want to make trouble for you and Lee Miller, but I have nothing, everything was lost in the bombing". "Well", said Roland, "the woman you were talking to is Lee Miller". Lee invited Valentine to move in to Roland's house in Downshire Hill with her and Roland and from that moment on they had a strong and unique friendship.

During the war Valentine served with the Free French in Algeria and then went to live in Paris. She was one of the first and thereafter the most frequent visitors to Farleys, staying for long periods and greatly loved by everyone who knew her. Her poetry continued to be published and was highly acclaimed. Pablo Picasso, Joan Miró and Eileen Agar contributed work to illustrate her published work. To my everlasting pleasure she wrote me a poem for my 21st birthday which we all celebrated at Farleys. She had been watching as I carried in armfuls of fresh hornbeam branches, a sheaf of our own wheat and bundles of reeds I had cut from the farm I was working on in Norfolk.

This is her own translation and spelling;

'To Tony along this year
As he knew that the witches
After fairies are the mad people of the reeds
When the fairie she flies, she flies
Holding fast the trusted child of life
Telling him of lightness and the watery syllables
Three times she spoke, three times he bought
A sheaf of grey wheat. Some hornbeam branches
Then a sheaf of reeds
Reeds rough and pink having slept
Under the planets of the year
Then all dazzling he said the wood was going to Dunsinane
It is true that the wood was going to Dunsinane
Believe, you, in this wood, in its hair and branches
I of the fens, the sad contented witch,
I say it
In the vaults of the night which go to Dunsinane:
It is true: You carried as no one else the sheaves and leaves
You will be happy.'

Valentine Penrose 9th September 1968

In her final years Valentine stayed at Farleys for ever increasing periods until she died in 1978, a year after Lee. Roland and I scattered her ashes beneath an oak tree she loved. She had planted cyclamen she took from their old home in the Gers around its base.

Winged Domino 1937,
Oil on Canvas by Roland Penrose

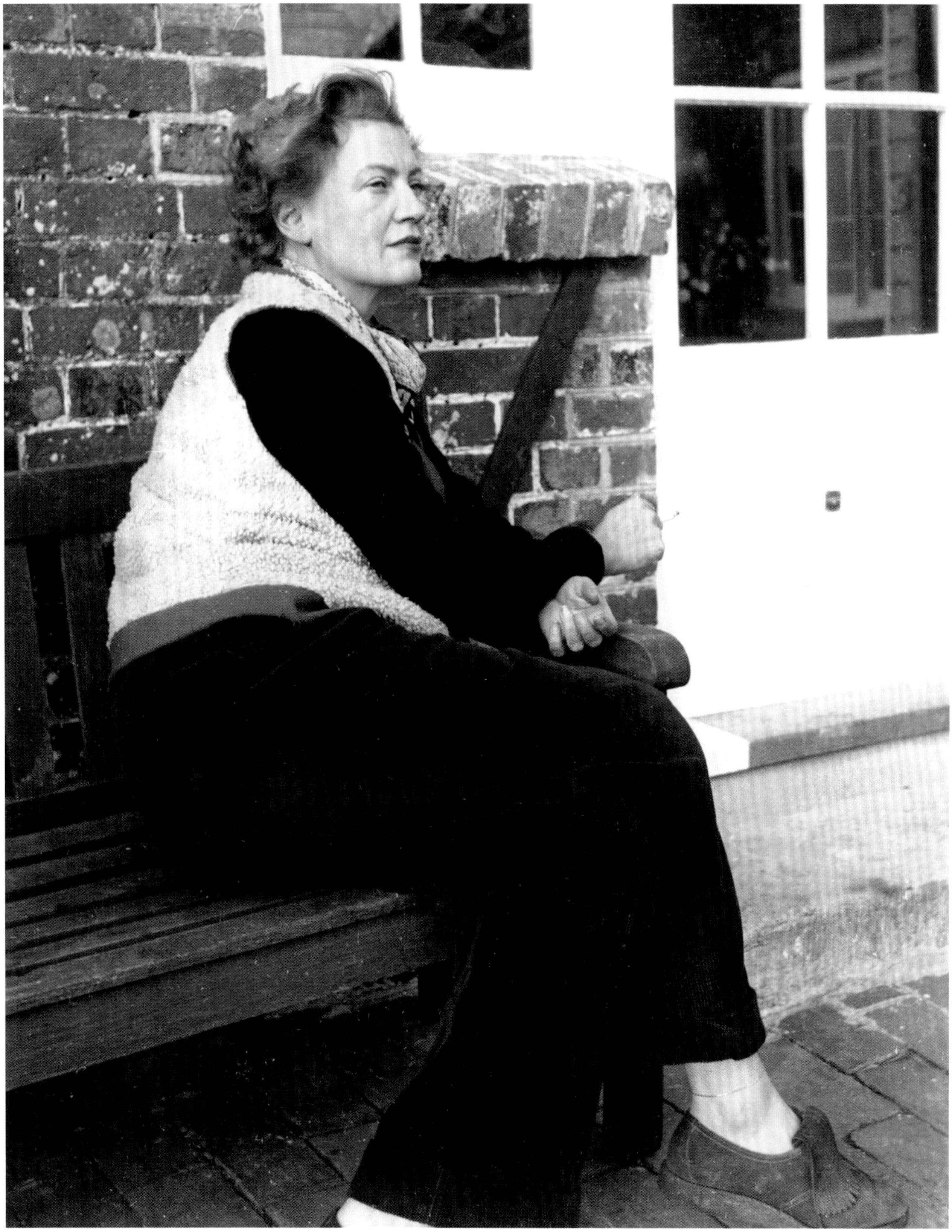

Lee Miller, Farleys garden 1953 by Roland Penrose

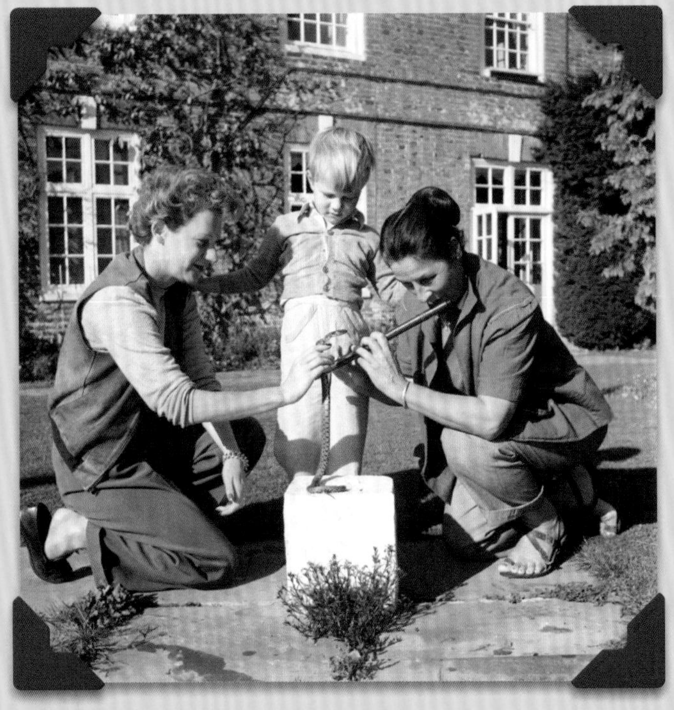

Timmie O'Brien, Antony Penrose and Valentine Penrose, Farleys garden 1952

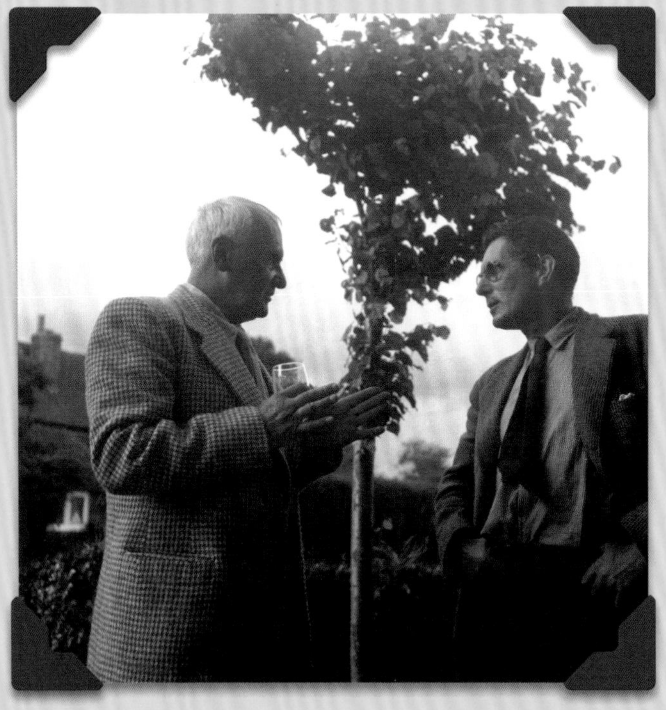

John Gunther (Journalist) and Roland Penrose, Farleys garden c1955

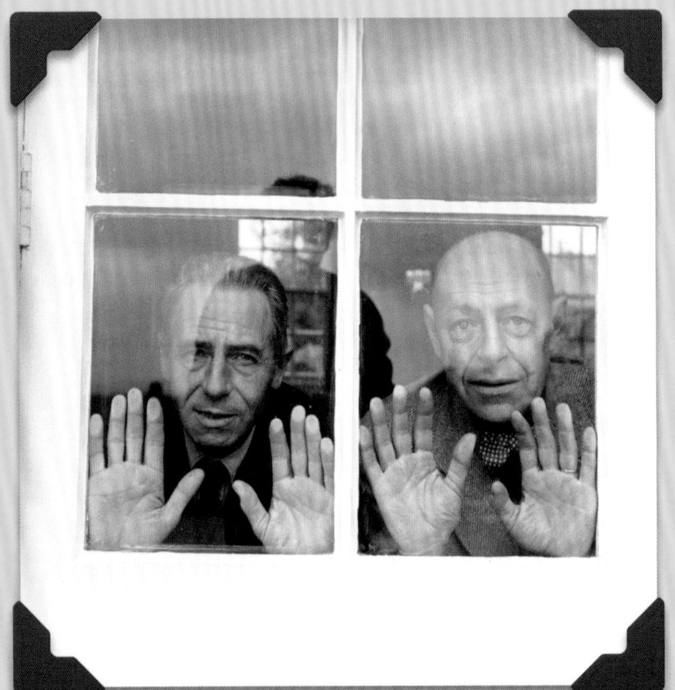

Georges Limbour (Writer) and Jean Dubuffet (Artist), Farleys House 1955

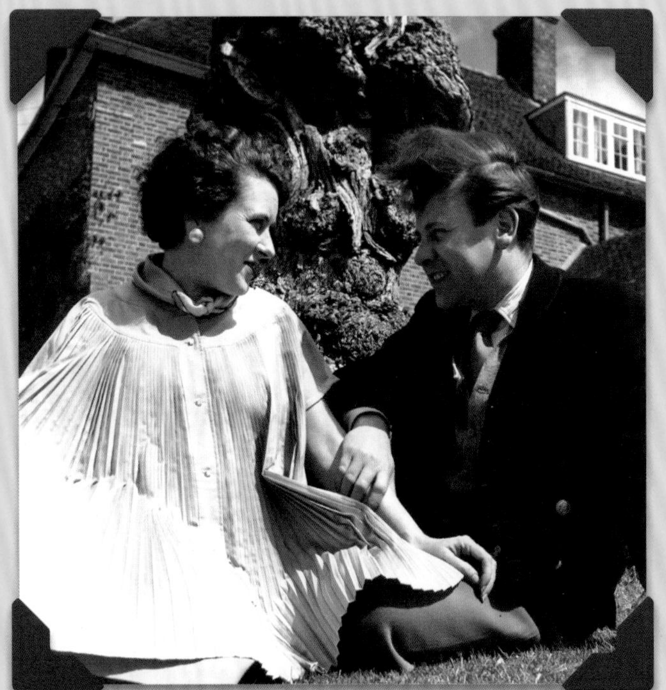

Siriol and Derek Hart (Actor), Farleys garden 1955

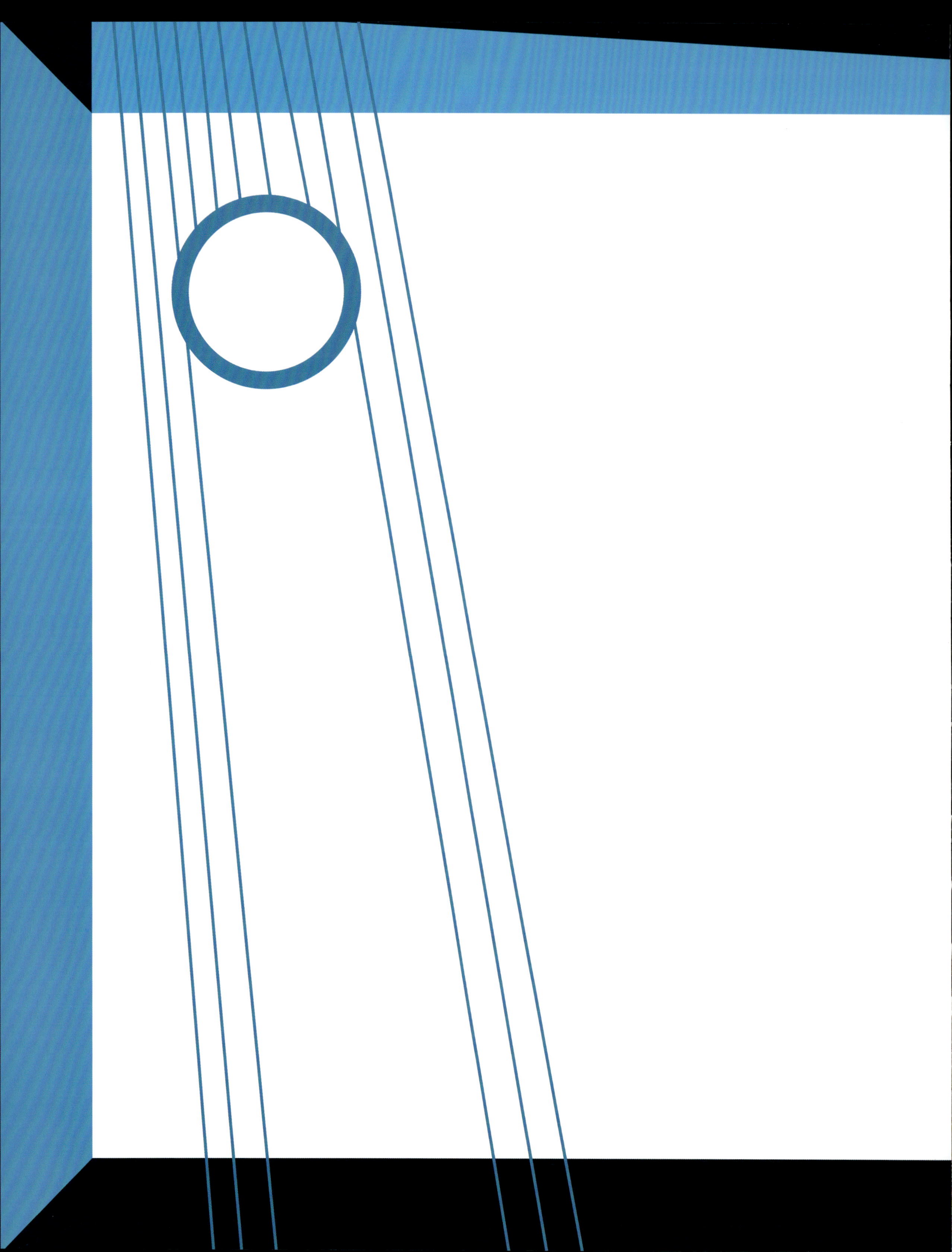

CHAPTER 10

INDIVIDUALITY AND FREEDOM

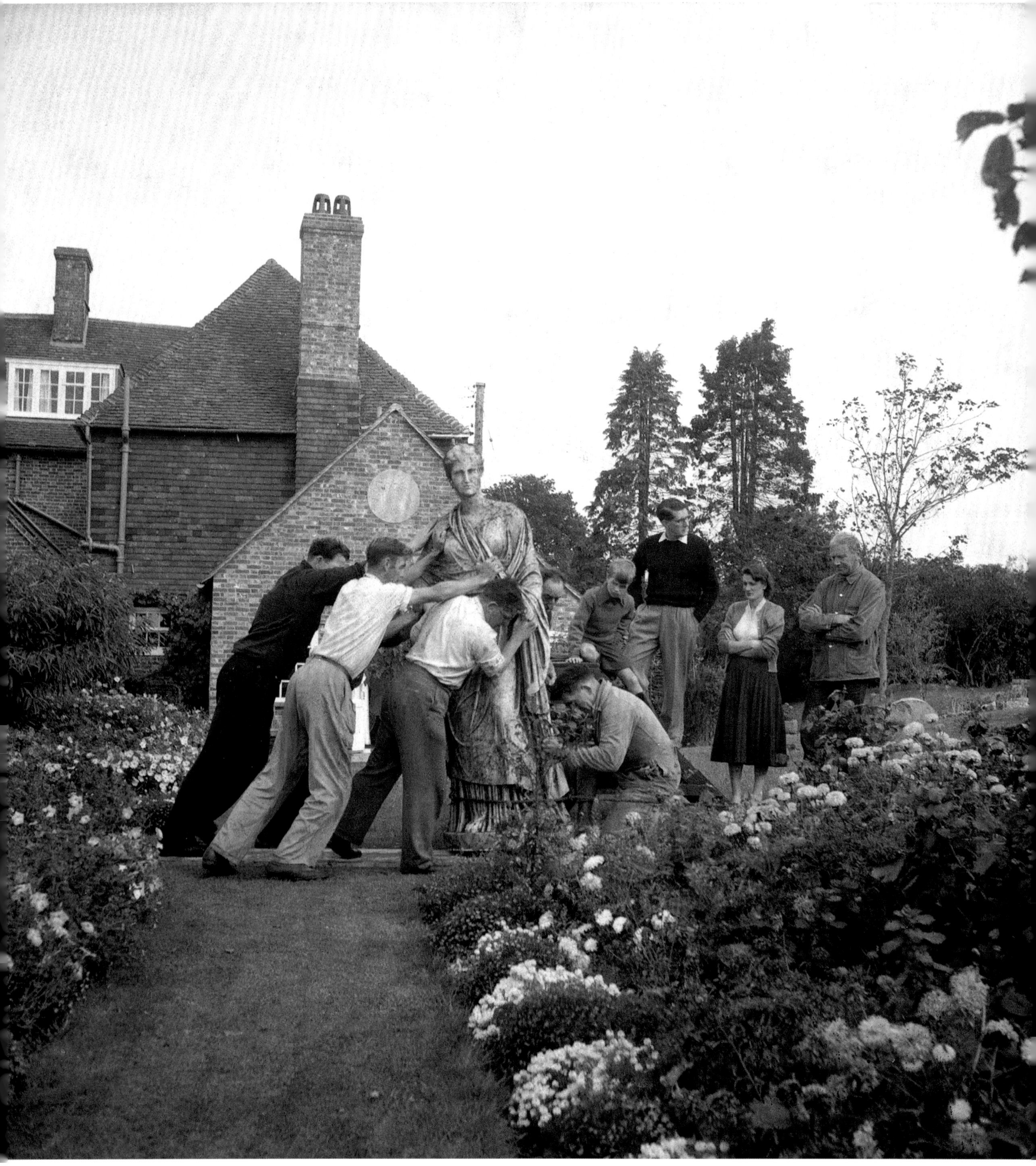

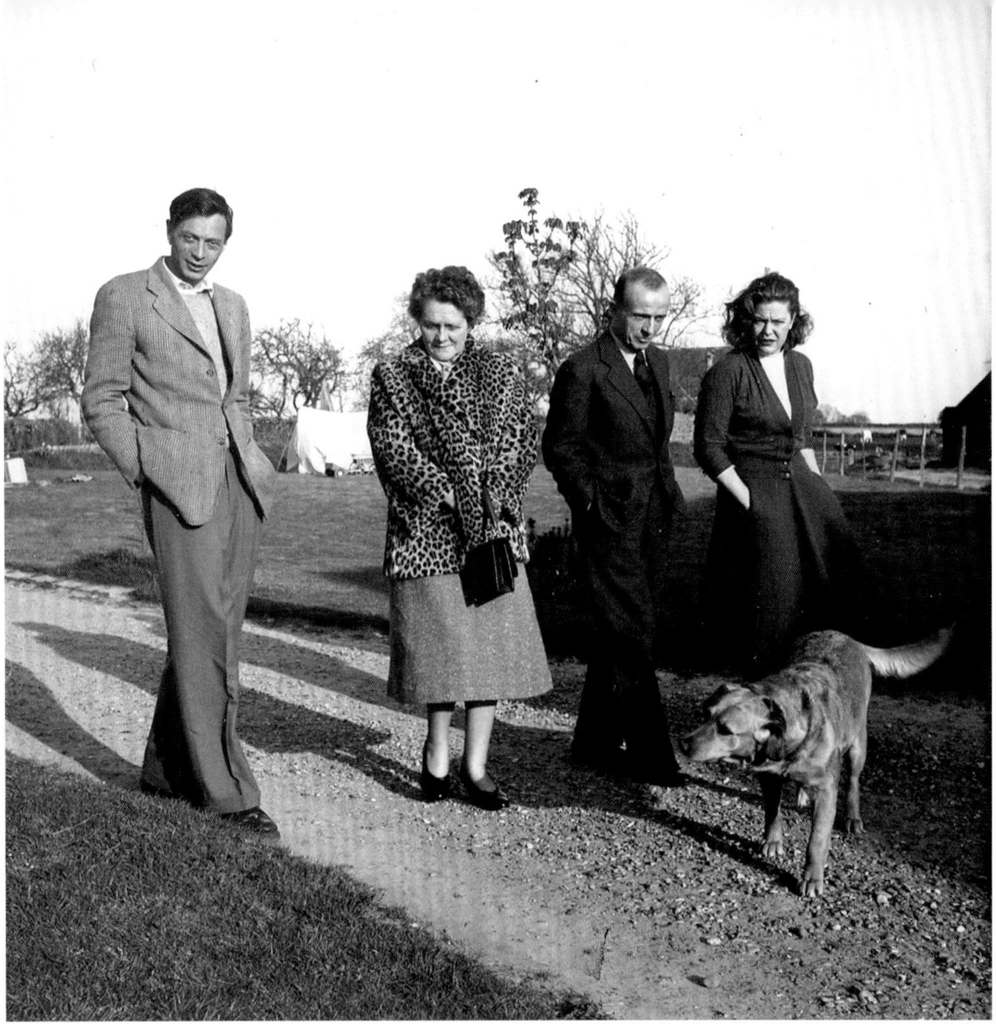

Peter Watson, Zette and Michel Leiris (Writer) & Sonia Orwell, Farleys garden 1955

As a child, how was I to know Sonia Orwell was such a distinguished literary figure and had an involvement with government propaganda during the Cold War? Among the visitors to Farleys, Sonia was a great favourite of mine. Warm, funny and with a low-pitched slightly gravelly voice, she had this huge laugh that could be heard rooms away. She was not an affectionate maternal figure, but I had a great sense of connection to her as a child and later as a young adult. She had a vitality and sense of fun that was infectious and made her the best ever target for practical jokes. A kind but misguided visitor gave me a box filled with fiendish devices. There were the usual fake cat turds, puddles of vomit, a severed finger, huge spiders and a glass of brandy that could not be drunk but my favourite was a clockwork gadget with legs like a giant insect. Hidden under a pillow or bedspread, when disturbed it would whir into life, beetling across the bed, drop onto the floor and keep on going. All these tricks and more were visited upon Sonia and I would lie in wait, listening for the highly gratifyingly dramatic shrieks of anguish she always made to oblige me.

Sonia's visits to Farleys began on New Year's Eve, December 1950 and the last of the thirty-eight times she came was in July 1975. Her strong and beautiful face had been the subject of portraits by several artists who were at that time my parent's friends including Victor Passmore, Lucien Freud, Rodrigo Moynihan and Pablo Picasso. Fluent in French and with a background in editing medieval literature, her career in modern literature would have been impossible for anyone who did not share Sonia's all-embracing mind. It was her work as editor of the *Horizon Magazine* in the 1940's with Cyril Connolly, Stephen Spender and Peter Watson that formed the connective tissue with my family. Devoted to modern literature and with some reference to the visual arts, Horizon was heroically kept going during the war as a unique avant-garde production, widely read and forming many important connections within the art world then and later in the post war years. This led to the huge number of mutual friends Sonia shared with my parents including the French surrealist writer Michel Leiris who would become a leading figure in 20th century French literature, sociology, and cultural criticism.

Installation of the Classical Greek sculpture, Farleys garden 1957

Among them all was a common thread of opposition to the totalitarian state, to the unthinking constraints of bourgeois life and a passionate conviction of the importance of peace, freedom and justice. These strongly held beliefs gave Sonia a perfect understanding of George Orwell. They met in about 1941 when she was at Horizon, and then again later after Orwell was widowed in 1945. The impression she made on him can be judged from his portrayal of the character of the heroine *'Julia'* in his dystopian novel *'Nineteen Eighty-Four'*. To quote from the biography of Sonia by Hilary Spurling titled *'The Girl from the Fiction Department'*;

> *The novel's hero Winston, loves Julia for her boldness, her bossiness, and the uncompromising rejection of the Party that fuels everything she does. Julia's fearlessness electrifies him. Even the coarseness of her language strikes him as symptom of revolt, 'natural and healthy like the sneeze of a horse that smells bad hay'.*

The description continues:

> *Winston's agonized intellectual reservations are overwhelmed by Julia's fierce, blind, animal abhorrence of the totalitarian system that seeks to abolish individuality and freedom.*[1]

Sonia married Orwell in 1949 as he was dying of TB. No doubt recognising her supreme integrity and her ability as an editor he entrusted her with his literary estate. His book *Animal Farm* had been a huge success and *Nineteen Eighty-Four* was about to achieve the same. For the next thirty years Sonia put her heart, soul and eventually all her wealth into following Orwell's insistence that his work should not be 'monkeyed about with' by publishers and editors. Part of her work was to create the George Orwell Archive in 1960 and to publish three volumes of his previously unpublished letters and manuscripts. Her work earned her cruel condemnation by figures of the literary world who unjustly accused her of obstinacy and greed. Her hatred of Stalin's regime helped lead her into unexpected associations with the Information Research Department, a secret propaganda wing of the British Foreign Office and the CIA – organisations that seem in themselves parallels of all Orwell hated, but which saw both his books as a counter to Soviet propaganda.

As a young person this mostly went way over my head. At Farleys Sonia held a much-loved place in all our hearts, and I could not understand why she was viciously attacked in the press in a manner that appalled my parents and baffled me. How could anyone not see Sonia as the champion of all things that were right?

In 1958 she married Michael Pitt-Rivers, the grandson of General Augustus Pitt-Rivers, who amassed the legendary collection of ethnographic material, now the Pitt-Rivers Museum in Oxford. Part of the collection was then housed near Blandford and was my favourite destination on days out from my boarding school. They lived in King John's House at Tollard Royal, where my father and I visited them in about 1961. Michael, way ahead of his time, was dedicated to nature conservation and had planted massive areas of woodland on the estate. Sonia missed her literary life acutely but flung herself into being the landowner's wife with style and enthusiasm. She organised the Larmar Tree Pageant in the grounds to raise money for the local church. With her formidable talent for organisation, she created a sort of promenade theatre relating the history of that area back to Neolithic times. It was stunning, way ahead of its time, completely outclassing every other Village Fete in the land. The final act was a stunt Tiger Moth biplane that thrillingly made a forced landing, fortunately without hurting anyone.

Roland Penrose, Sonia Orwell and John Hayward,
Palace Pier, Brighton, England 1955

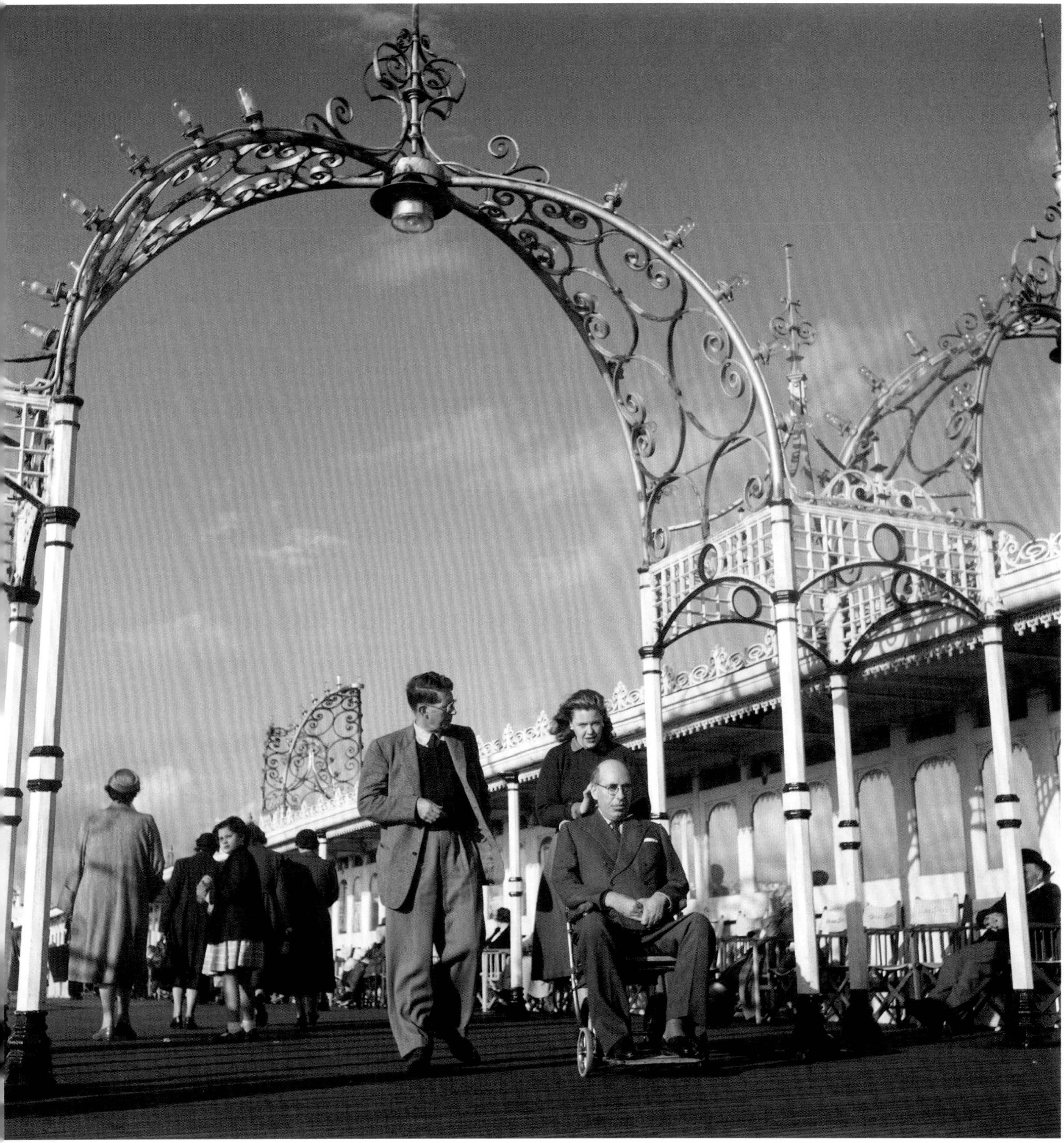

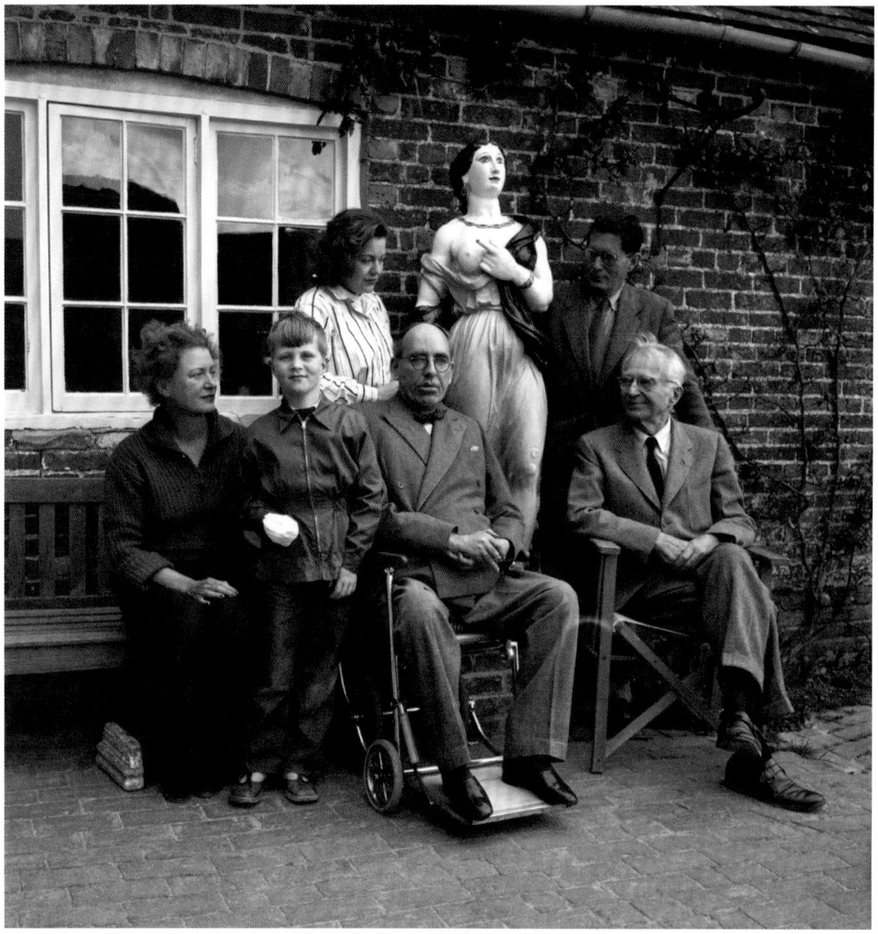

Lee Miller, Antony Penrose, Sonia [Orwell] Brownell, John Hayward (Historian), Roland Penrose and Edward Steichen, Farleys House 1955

At Farleys Sonia had a particular friendship with my mother. Looking back, I recognise they shared the torment of innumerable internal demons from unexpressed traumas in their lives. Over the years my studies have given me an understanding of the roots of my mother's traumas but those in Sonia's life are harder to understand. Probably the best hint is to be found in her hatred of the Catholic church, resulting from her early convent schooling. Clearly both women shared a deep distrust for authority in general and particularly in totalitarian regimes. It was not something that openly bonded them, neither being inclined to discuss such things, but I think it gave them a firm mutual recognition of each other's drives and perhaps a notion of their hidden suffering.

Sonia's friendship with my father was more straight forward. With so many friends in common, there was an easy flow of stimulating ideas. Cyril Connolly was a near neighbour in the 60's and often came for lunch when Sonia was with us. Another favourite friend was John Hayward, a formidable scholar, critic and friend of T.S. Elliot[2]. His severe disablement due to muscular dystrophy did little to damp his humour or his zest for life and a visit to Farleys often meant an outing to Brighton or Hastings to enjoy the British seaside at its best.

The last of Sonia's many visits was on 11th July 1975. Age had been kind to her looks and all the old flashes of wit and often outrageous humour were there. I had returned home from my travels with my late wife Suzanna. Sonia greeted her with warmth and affection, and for me the intervening five years since I last saw her counted for nothing. I was not to know it was her last visit. Although she saw my parents in London, we never welcomed her at Farleys again. She died of a brain tumour in London in 1980. She was only 62 years old.

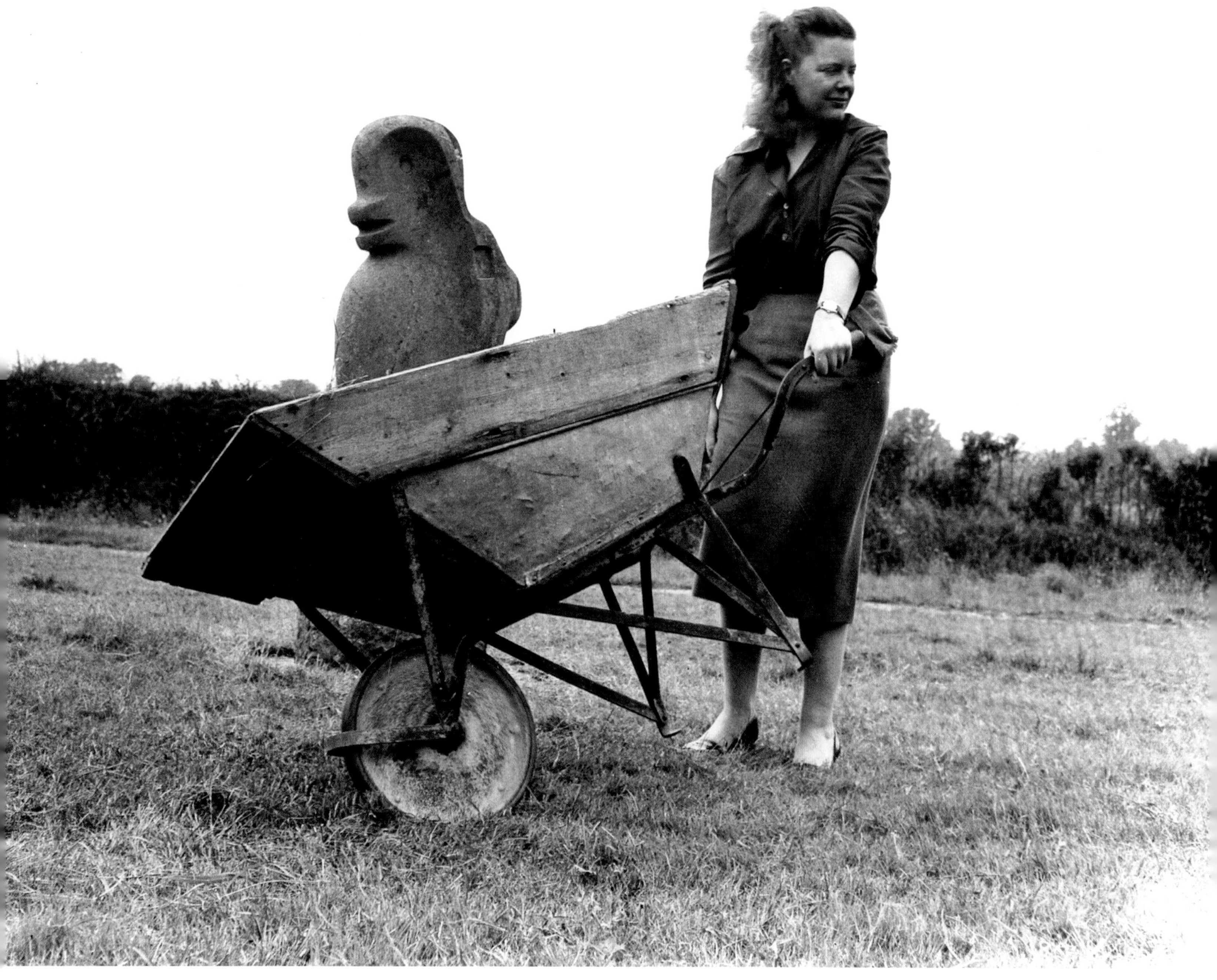

Sonia Orwell, Farleys garden 1953

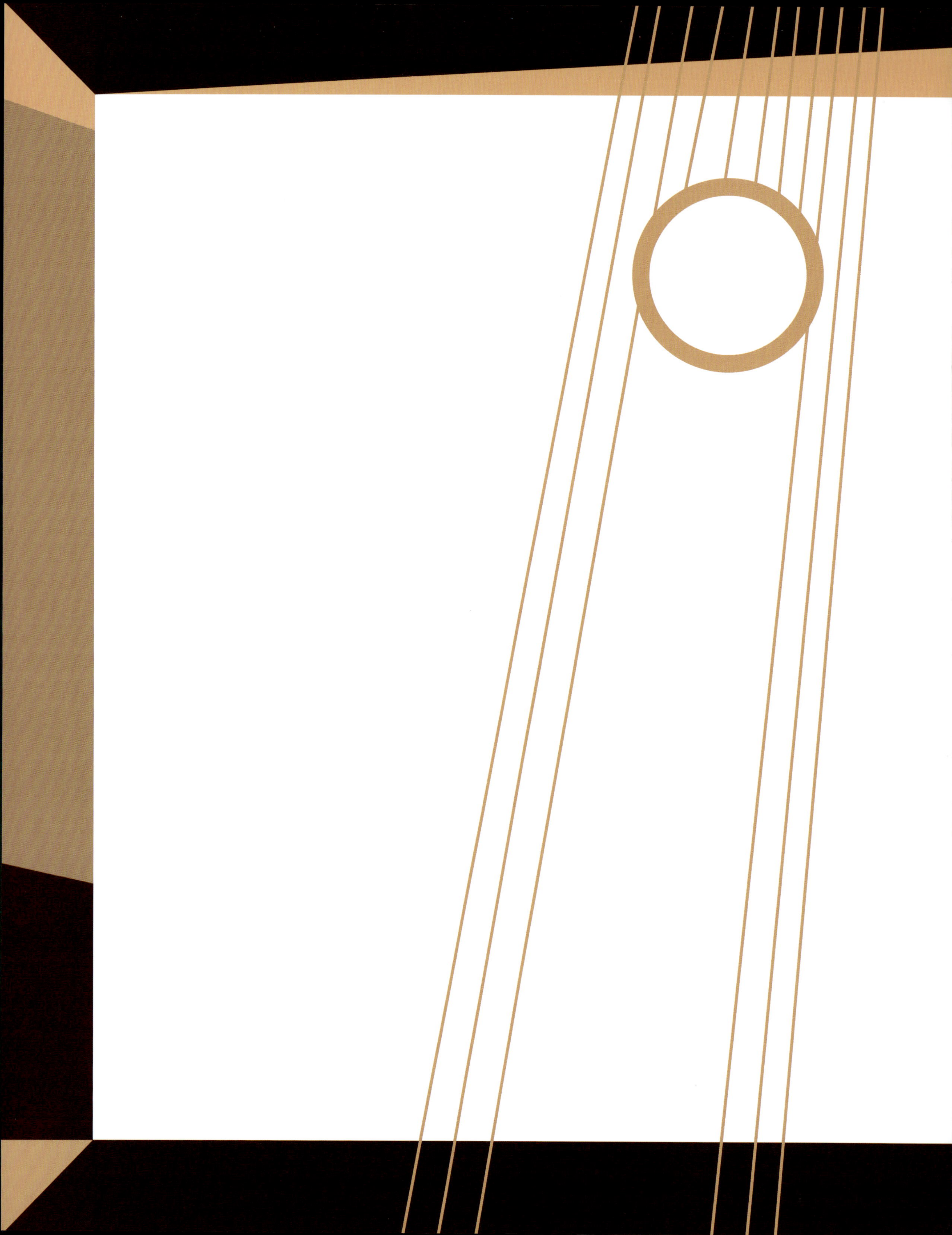

CHAPTER 11

BIG SPECTACLES AND BUSHY EYEBROWS

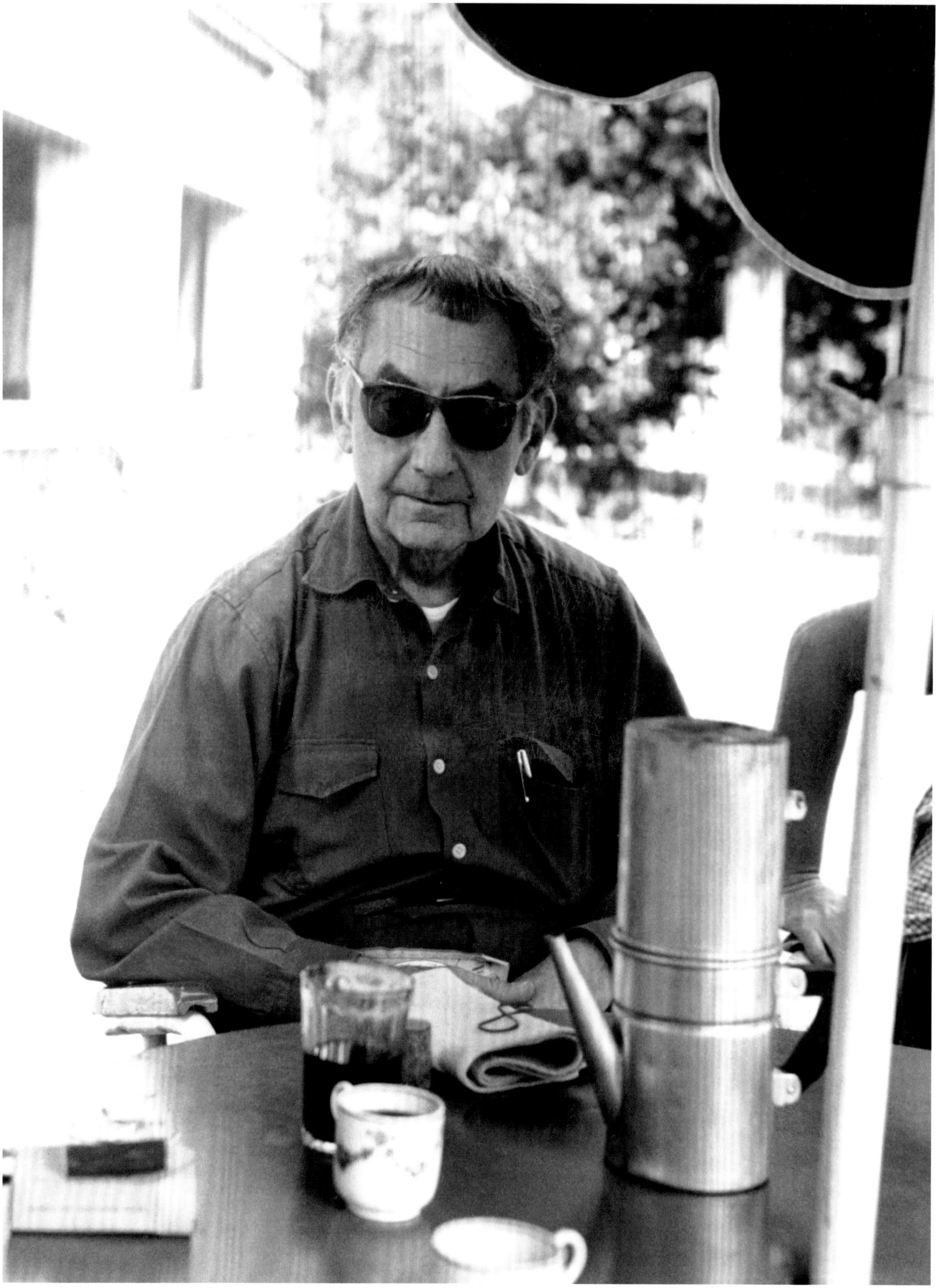

Man Ray was not very tall. He had big spectacles and his bushy eyebrows made him look a bit like an owl. He always wore a French beret when he went out and he seemed much more French than American. When he spoke English he had a strong accent like the New York gangsters in the movies, but that is where the similarity ended because he was funny and gentle and I liked him very much. When I was little, he was not 'child friendly'. I don't think he could see the point of small children but as I grew older, I found a different side to him. Together we built a model of a medieval siege catapult on the kitchen table capable of flicking dried beans across the room. We were having a great time until my mum got cross and made us stop.

His intense creativity was evident in his prodigious output of works of art. In the post war years his photography slowed down but not so his painting or the flow of his objects. Once carelessly scattered around his studio, they are now enshrined in private collections and top museums but I do remember one piece that did not make it into a museum. It was his device for swatting flies. I was surprised he knew so much about flies; their habits, the field of vision from their compound eyes, their flight technique. I guess when he was young and poor, he had had plenty of time to study them. His fly swat invention was a length of elastic rubber from a broken chair. He stretched it back, took careful aim, let go and splat! Even in my hands it worked every time and our success was marked by us getting a frightful telling off from the grown-ups for the splat marks all over the walls.

Man Ray's first visit to Farleys was in October 1954. Roland, my dad, had invited him to give a lecture at the ICA[1], titled *Painting of the Future and The Future of Painting.* I was too young to go but knowing Man Ray it would have been full of enigma and outrageous puns.

We can see from Lee's photos that Man Ray is not a country boy. He does not even look comfortable in the garden, and Roland confirmed Man Ray's dislike of rural life on his first visit with a walk round the farm. Roland loved all aspects of nature and his walks were more like a forced march of at least an hour and a half, with complete disregard to the weather. Man Ray was kitted out with wellies and a big oilskin coat and off they went. The rain lashed down and darkness came early. Roland, realising Man Ray was suffering took a shortcut home across a field where our cows had recently grazed kale in heavy rain. It was a bad move. Our clay makes the stickiest, deepest mud, favoured by the brick and tile makers of the 19th Century and Man Ray really struggled. He arrived back at the house exhausted, plastered in mud and determined to never venture out doors until the next drought.

Man Ray had been the lover and photographic partner of my mother in the 1930's. In 1946 whilst in California he met and married Juliette, a woman of great grace and beauty, a dancer with Martha Graham's company. Juliette and Lee became very fond of each other, a mirror image of the deep friendship between Roland and Man Ray. A French friend, marvelling at the closeness between Roland and Man Ray opined "The shortest distance between two men is the love of the same woman"[2]. The opposite polarity of that wisdom applied equally to these two women.

Man Ray, La Brosse, France by Antony Penrose

A version of Man Ray's famous smoothing iron with a menacing row of tin tack glued to its face titled *Cadeau* and *Indestructible Object*, the metronome with my mum's eye on the pendulum, had been at Farleys from the earliest days. The familiarity with the way Man Ray could take everyday objects and change their meaning always whispered to me, encouraging me to make my own. One summer I was dismantling a redundant reaper and binder that had lain hidden in the brambles for decades. I wanted some steel rods but more interesting were the beautifully shaped tines from the reciprocating knife bar that cut the corn. To me the shape suggested the figure of a girl. I used two nuts to form her breasts barely contained by her evening dress. A scrap of wood became the base into which I tapped the sharp point of the tine. I gave it to my dad – he liked it and so did Man Ray who was with us at the time. Man Ray often made editions of his objects so why should not I do the same? I went back to the old binder and unscrewed another tine, made another figure and gave it to him.

I thought nothing of this for decades and then recently a friend found a photo Man Ray had taken of the back area of his studio and there on the top shelf, among his own objects, was my *Girl in an Evening Gown*. He had liked her enough to give her a place amongst his own work.

Man Ray's generosity extended to my school friends Ian Barker and Andrew Lanyon when we visited his studio in Paris. Andrew was a keen photographer using a battered old Leica with a home-made lens cap and the back held shut with rubber bands.

Man Ray thought it showed excellent promise. He said "The camera you use is not important. It is what you choose to photograph that matters. People ask me what camera I use – I say to them why don't you ask me what kind of paint brushes I use? It's the same irrelevance". Andrew's immediate reaction was to ask Man Ray if he would pose for a portrait. It took a lot of nerve to ask that of someone who by now was one of the most famous photographers in the world, but Man Ray was so friendly and kind that he made it easy for Andrew. Ian tilted up the lamp shade to allow more light to fall on Man Ray's face and I held a chess board behind his head. Back at school Andrew developed the film and made his prints, sending one to Man Ray. He received a note back that said "This is the portrait of me I like the best". That has to be the nicest compliment a young photographer has ever received. Andrew went on to become a very significant artist, photographer and maker of artist's books.

The last time I saw Man Ray was in London the year before he died. It was 1975 and my dad had organised an exhibition of his work at The Institute of Contemporary Arts. It was a superb show, with all my favourite works in it including a huge mobile made of coat hangers he titled *Obstruction*. It floated just above the floor turning gently in the changing air currents. Man Ray was in a wheel chair but that did not slow him up. He was delighted to meet his old friends and to see his work honoured and appreciated by all who came. I like looking back on the photos of my parents with him that evening. They look so happy together and their smiles tell me of their friendship that stretched back more than fifty years from that moment.

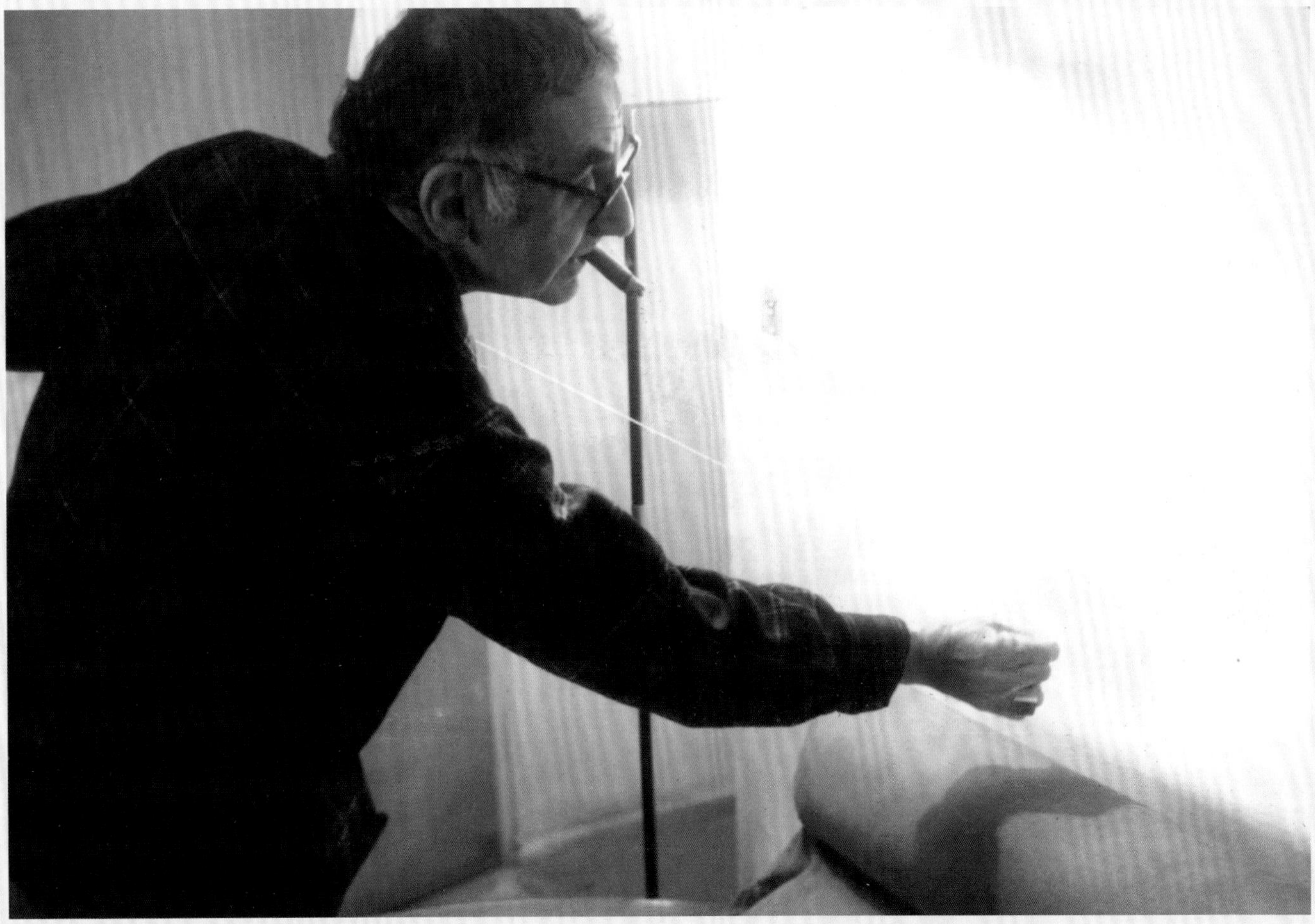

Man Ray, La Brosse, France by Antony Penrose

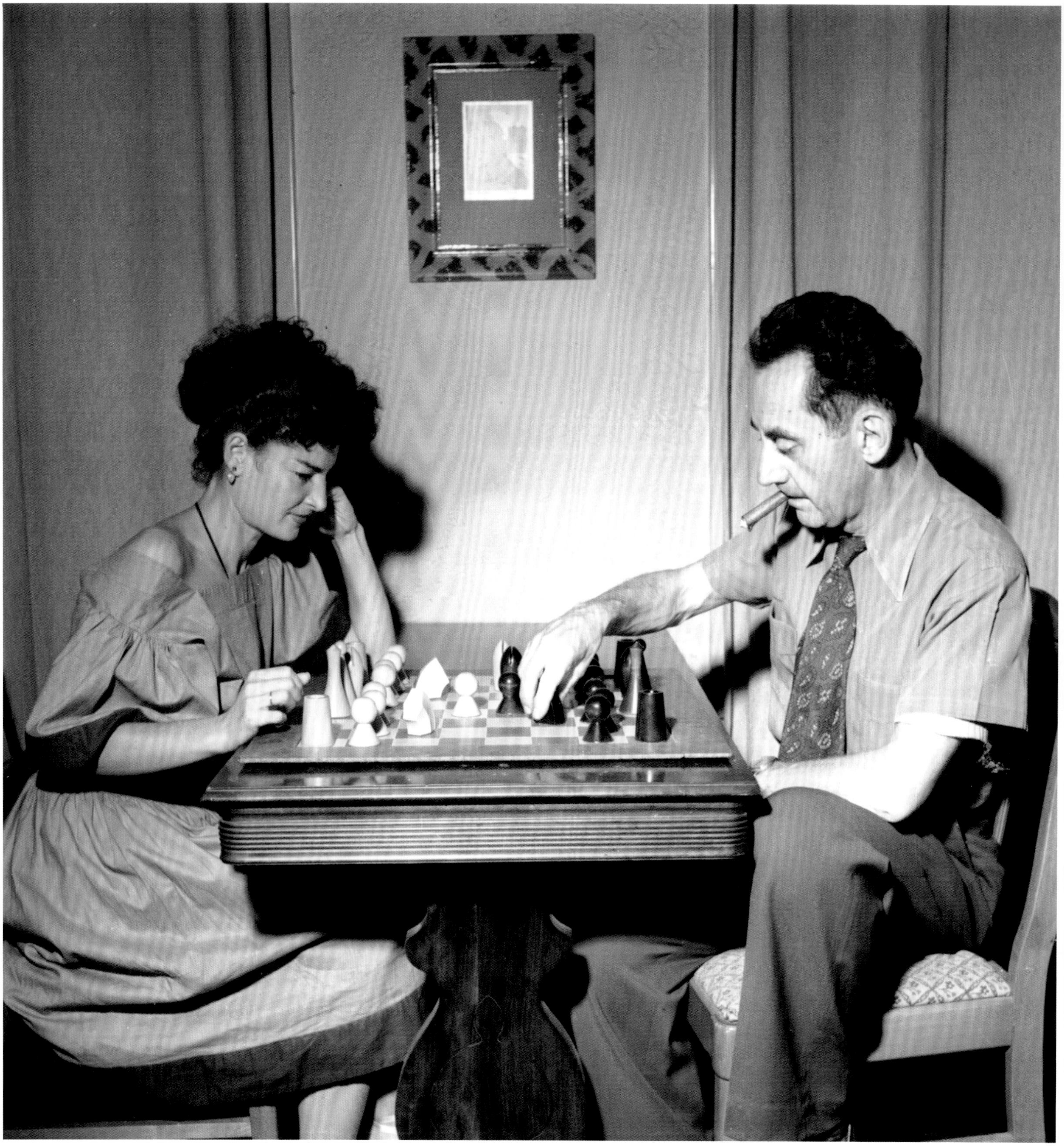

Juliet (Browner) Man Ray and Man Ray, Los Angeles, USA 1946

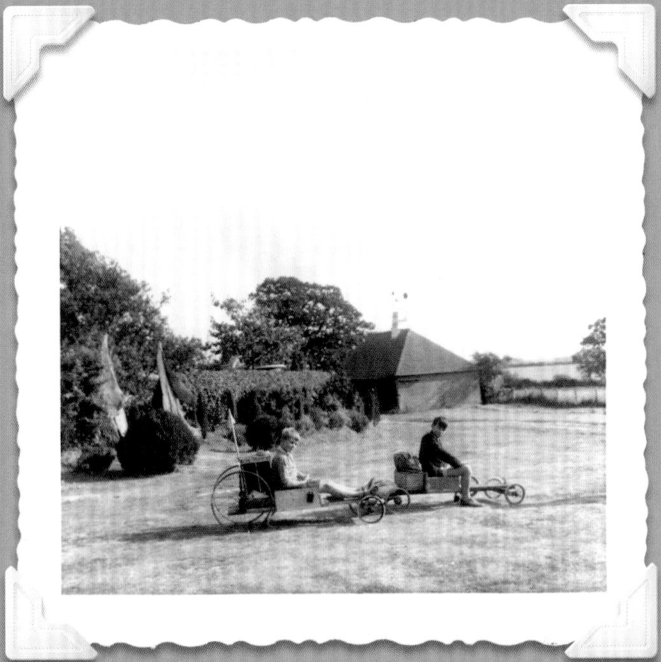

Antony Penrose and John Funnell on the Bone Shaker and Clarabell, Farleys garden 1959

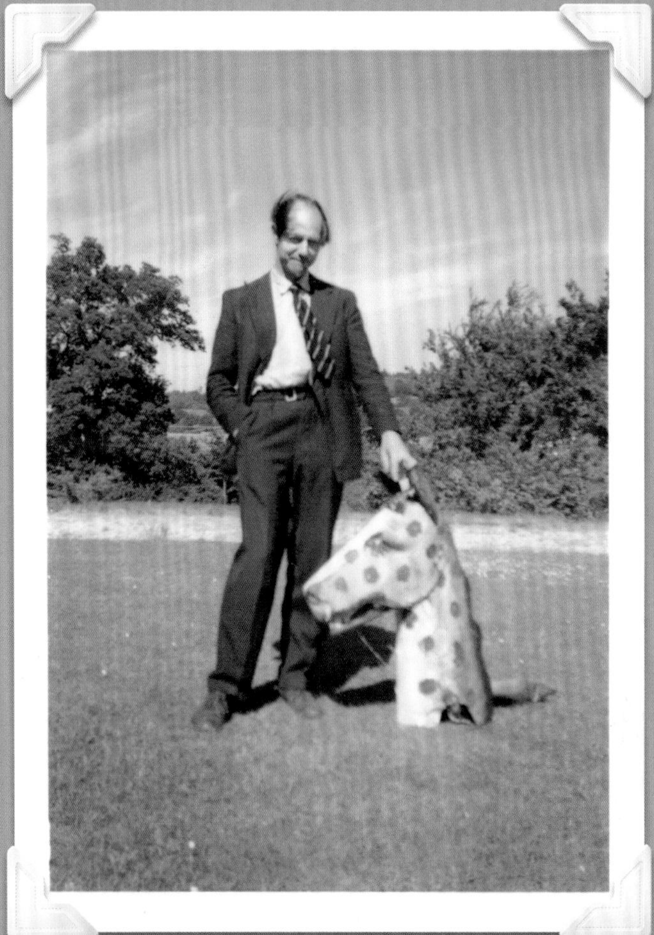

Mr Mellor and Brigett, 1959

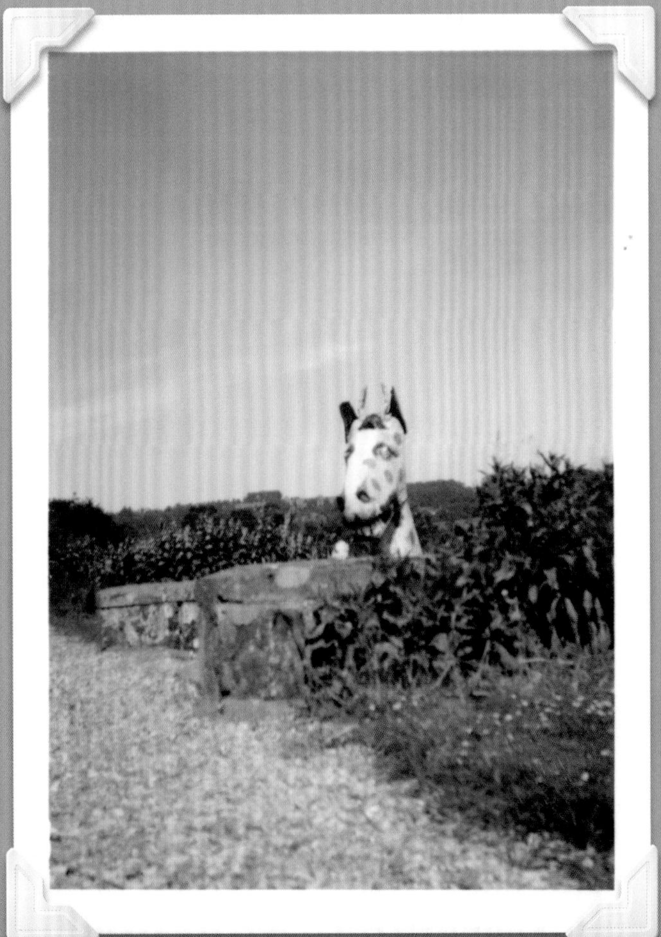

Brigett, 1959

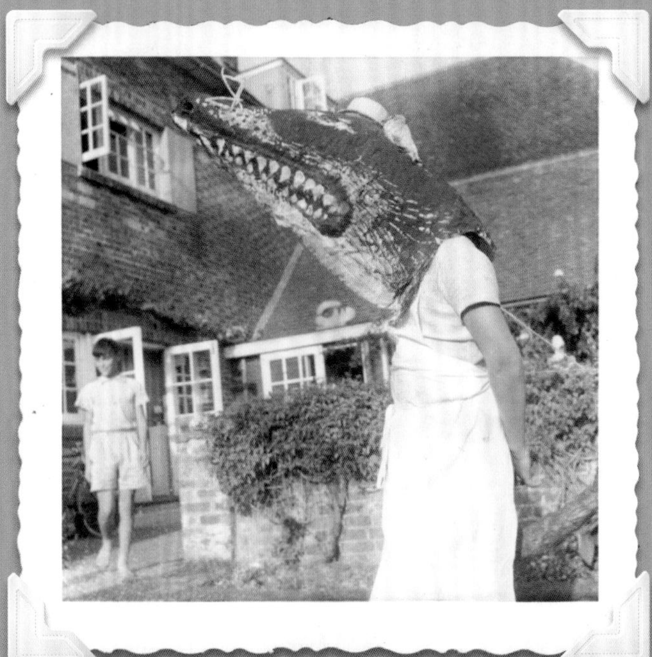

John Funnell and Antony Penrose wearing rat's head, Farleys garden 1959

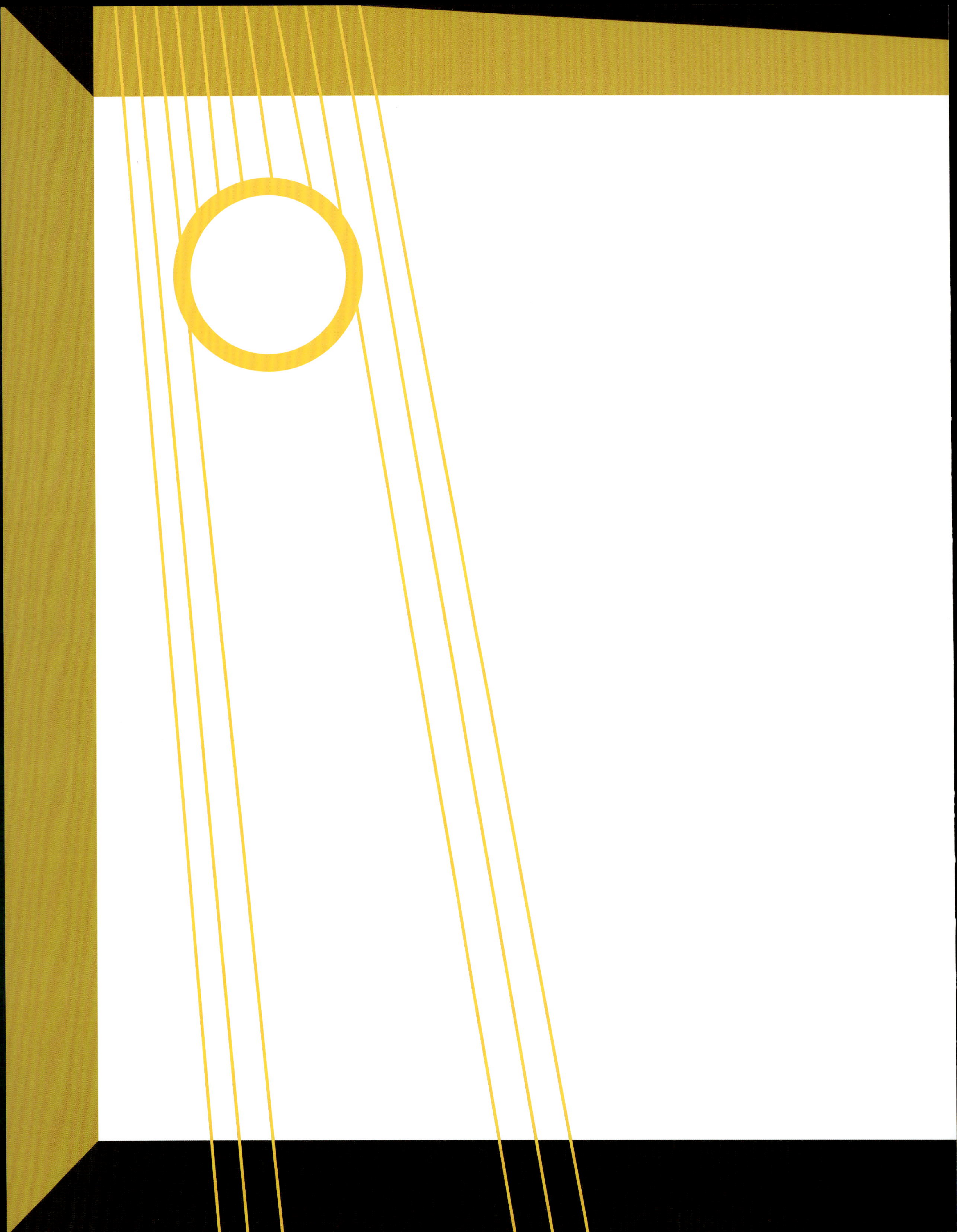

CHAPTER 12

RADIATING WARMTH, INNER STRENGTH AND EXCEPTIONAL INTELLIGENCE

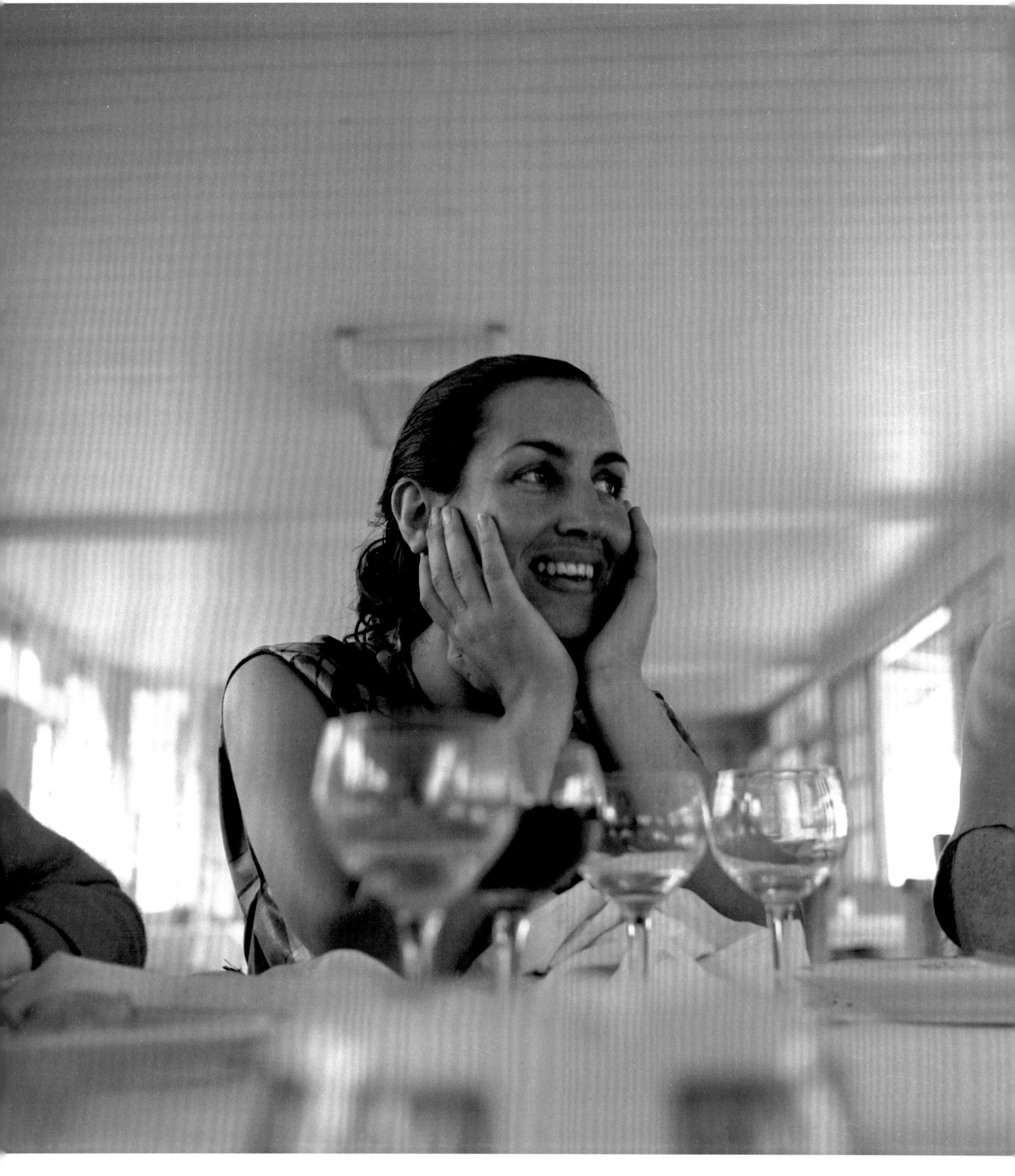

Françoise Gilot had a beauty that went way beyond her appearance. She radiated warmth, inner strength and exceptional intelligence. For me as a five-year old she was unbelievably exciting. She had an embracing maternal kindness and she and the world she inhabited were packed with exotic wonders. Coming from post war England with its food rationing still in place I felt I had landed on a different planet. She plied me with wonderful patisseries. In complete contrast to home, fruit – grapes, melons, peaches and pomegranates were plentiful and delicious. It was warm, the sea was clear and the beaches offered endless sand. I had never seen or tasted anything like it.

In 1938 Françoise had graduated from the Sorbonne in Philosophy and later got a Cambridge degree in English. Her family had hoped she would make her career in law and indeed she would no doubt have been very successful but it was painting that was her passion. Her desire to be an artist drove her from an early age. Her mother was a demanding teacher who from the age of six insisted Françoise drew in ink or crayon so every line was permanent. The sureness of Françoise's line can be unmistakably seen in all her drawings. Two large works in blue crayon and some smaller pencil drawings are in The Penrose Collection, dedicated to my parents in a way that shows the strong bond of affection between them at the time.

That bond endured after Françoise parted from Picasso in 1953 and moved to London with Claude and Paloma. Her first visit to Farleys was in August 1959 and was probably the moment when Roland took her to see the spectacular local wonder of Beachy Head, the massive 160 metre high chalk cliff with a sheer drop to the toy-like, red and white striped light house at its foot. The sea has cut into the solid permanence of the land with the precision of a knife. At the foot of the mighty cliff the defiance of the tiny lighthouse may have offered Françoise a metaphor. She painted it standing bravely against all adversity. By now her work was emerging from the shadow of Picasso and her paintings were well received in their own right. She had exhibitions in Galerie Coard in Paris and The Mayor Gallery in London in 1960 and '62. Sadly her Beachy Head painting was not one that Roland bought from her shows, although there are others in our collection, still with the gallery stickers on their frames. Roland hung them throughout Farleys in prominent positions and for me they were always particular favourites, reminding me of Françoise and attesting that my parents' friendship endured beyond her separation from Picasso. It was not long to be so.

In 1961 she began writing her memoir *Life with Picasso* assisted by the art historian Carlton Lake. She wrote in English and eloquently gave an intimate account of life with Picasso. Her observations of his work process were fascinatingly insightful and revealing, as are her accounts of the

Françoise Gilot, Cote d'Azur, France 1949

bizarre machinations of the Communist Party of France of which Picasso was their highest profile member. We learn a lot about Picasso's attitude to his friends and to the other women who had constantly vied with her for Picasso's attention.

When it was published in 1964 it had a cataclysmic effect on Picasso's friends. Reading the book today we can gain an understanding of how it was to live and work with the powerhouse of mercurial and creative energy that was Picasso. We can see his self-doubt, his flaws and his ability to create and destroy with equal passion. We are also given an intimate understanding of how he and Françoise related to each other and that for many, including my parents, was a step too far. The surrealist ideal of free love made them open to sexual freedom within their group, but the golden rule was to never, ever, go public about it and now Françoise had, in their view, unforgivably violated Picasso's personal privacy and broken the trust placed in her.

Picasso was furious. He tried to get a legal injunction to stop the publication, but that failed. He grudgingly acknowledged she had won, but cut her and the children out of his life. The media immediately fanned the flames. Roland, following the publication of his biography *Picasso His Life and Work* and the huge success of his 1960 Picasso retrospective at the Tate became known as the 'The Picasso man'. He found himself front and centre of this bitter schism with interviews in the press and on the radio. Positions among Picasso and Françoise's friends became totalitarian and all had to declare which side they were on. My parents firmly supported Picasso. Their friendship and loyalty to him went back to the thirties and they felt Françoise had betrayed him by disclosing so many intimacies. Overnight, to my great sadness, all of Françoise's works disappeared from the walls of our home at Farleys.

Françoise went to live in the USA and married another childhood hero of mine, Jonas Salk, the developer of one of the first successful polio vaccines. My affectionate memory of her never faded and after Roland died in 1984, I found where he had hidden all her works and replaced them on the walls. It was like welcoming the return of old friends but I could not rid myself of the disquieting thoughts of that quarrel. Later I began to write my memoir, *Roland Penrose the Friendly Surrealist*, and I felt I had to understand Françoise's position so I called her. It began as a wary, stilted conversation but very soon the warmth I remembered so well broke through. She bore no malice for the way Roland had been so outspoken against her in his defence of Picasso and after a long and for me a healing conversation we parted friends. Today her paintings are even more loved and fascinating than before.

On the 26th November 2021 Françoise Gilot was 100 years old. She lives in New York and she still paints.

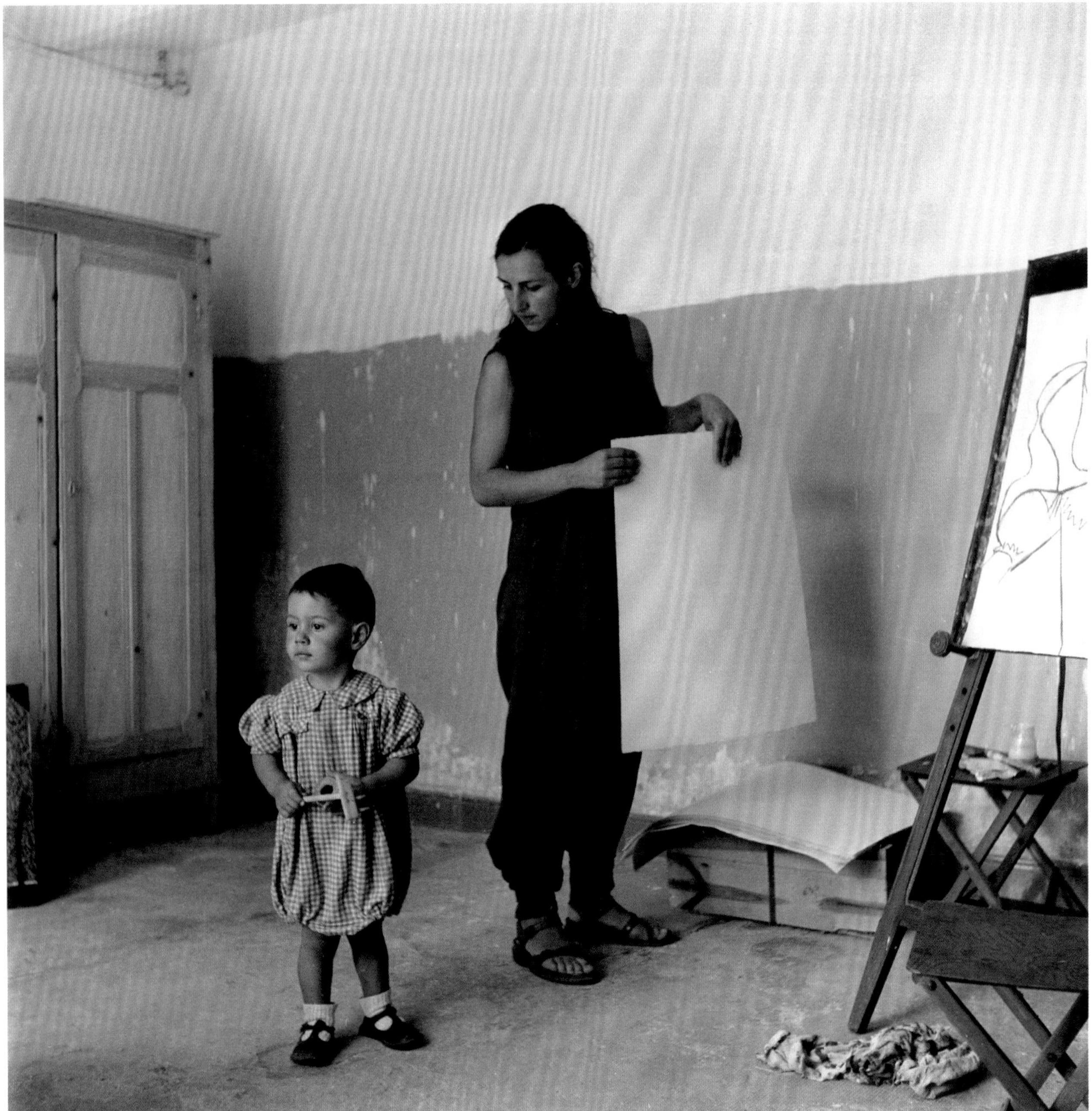

Claude Picasso and Françoise Gilot, La Galloise, Vallauris, France 1949

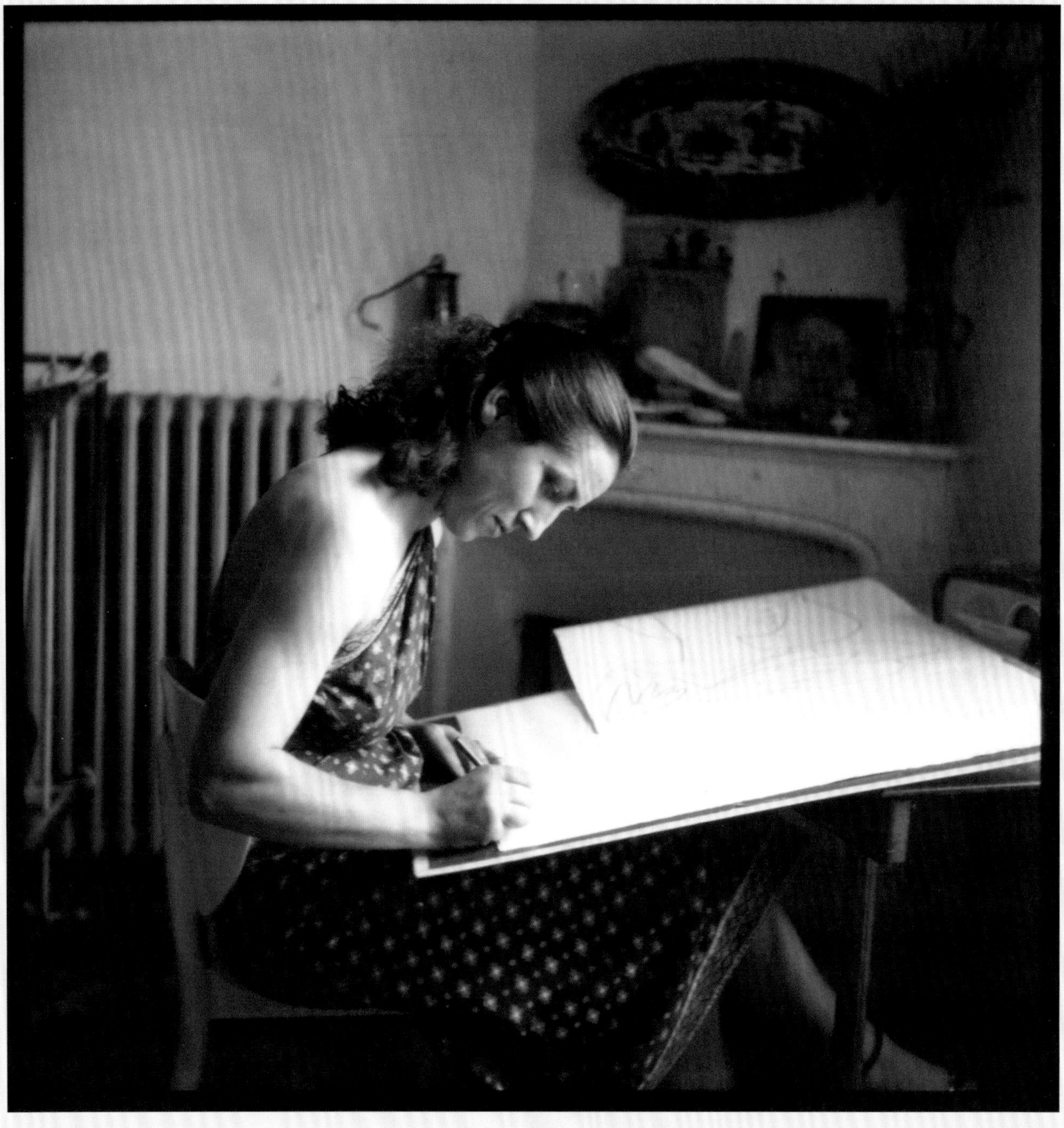

Françoise Gilot working, La Galloise, Vallauris, France 1953

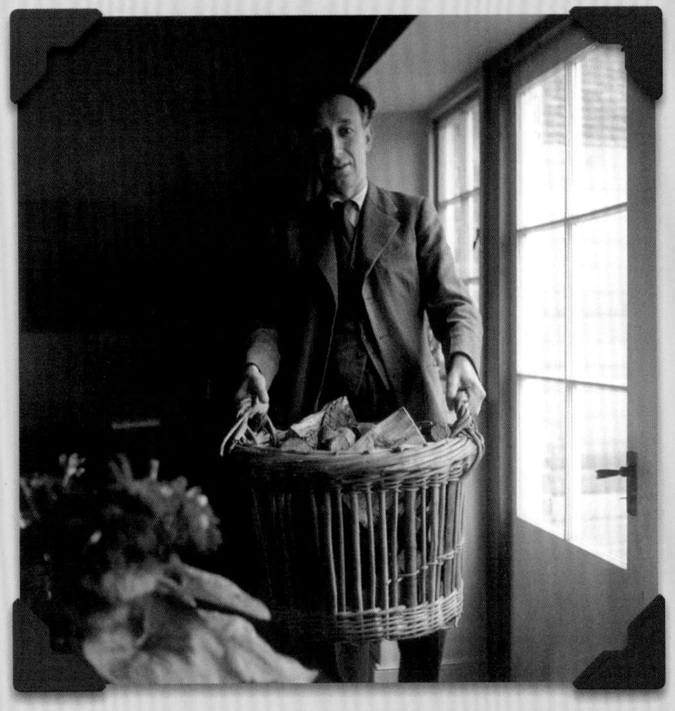

Alfred Jules (Freddie) Ayer (Philosopher), Farleys sitting room 1951

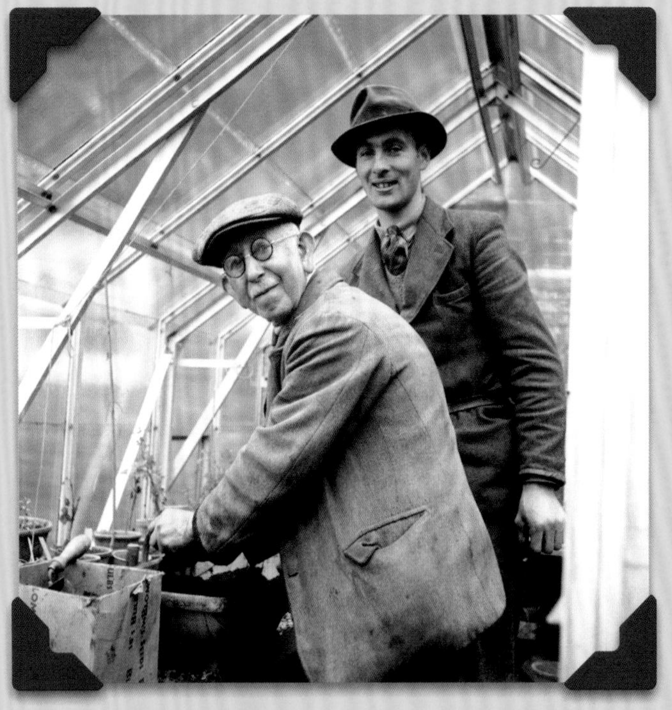

Grandpa White and Fred Baker, Farleys garden 1953

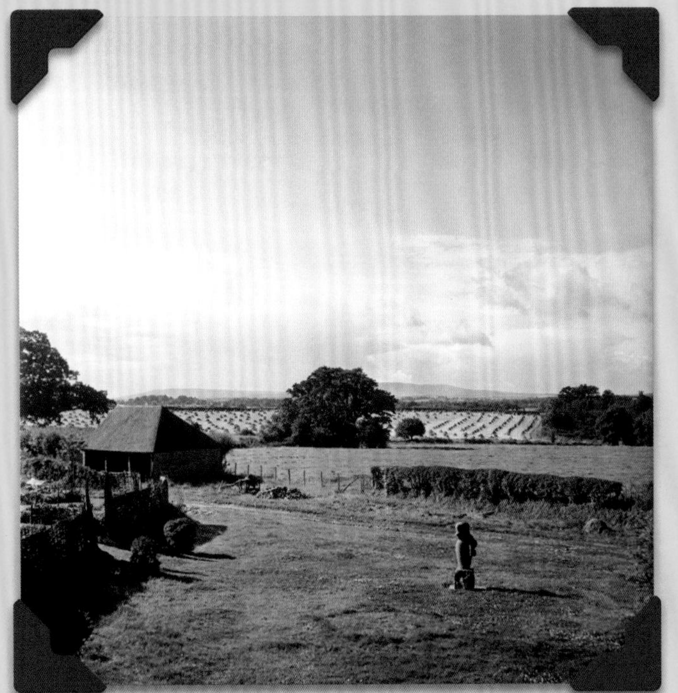

View from upstairs at Farleys House 1951

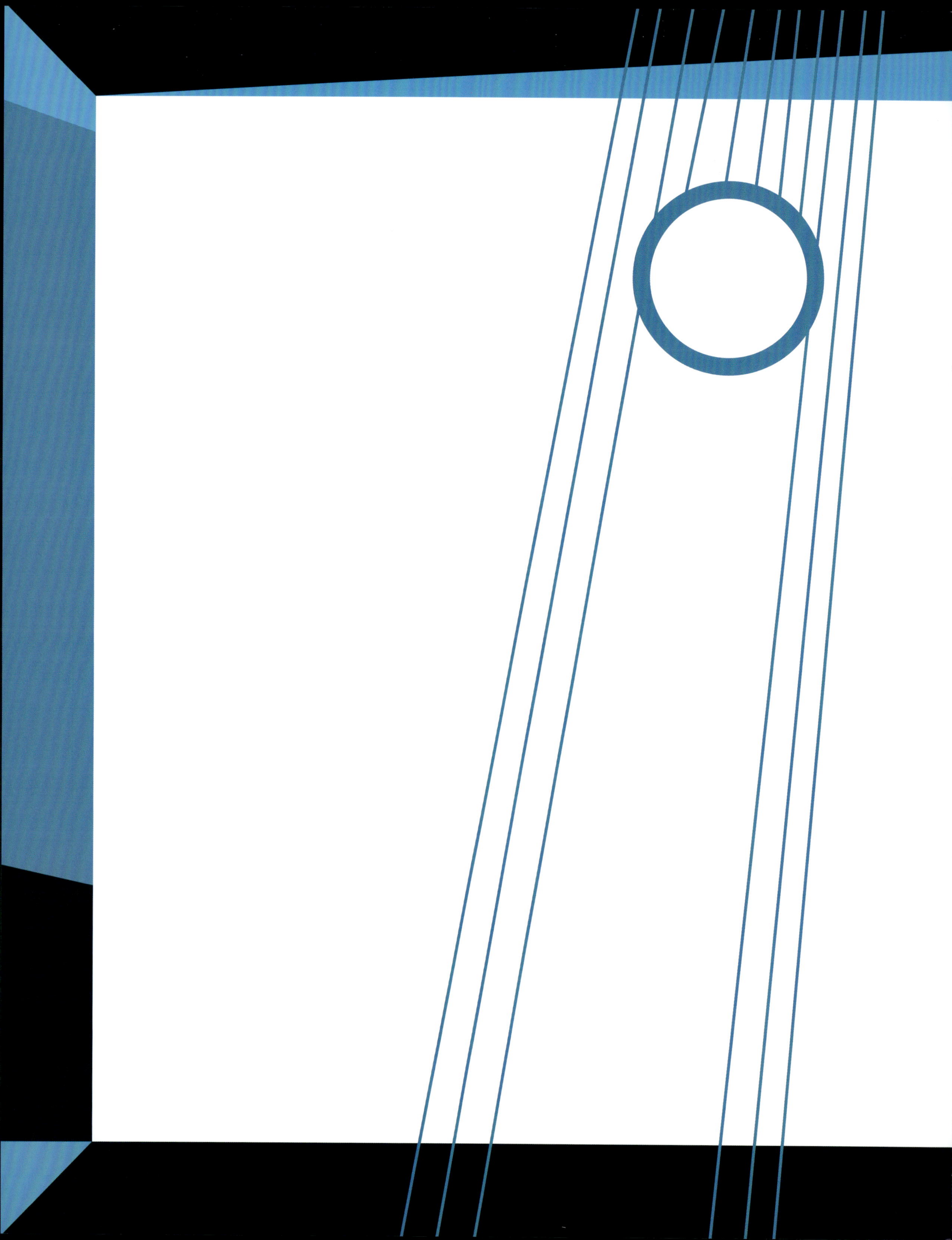

CHAPTER 13

‘TO BE AN ARTIST IS TO BELIEVE IN LIFE‘

HENRY MOORE

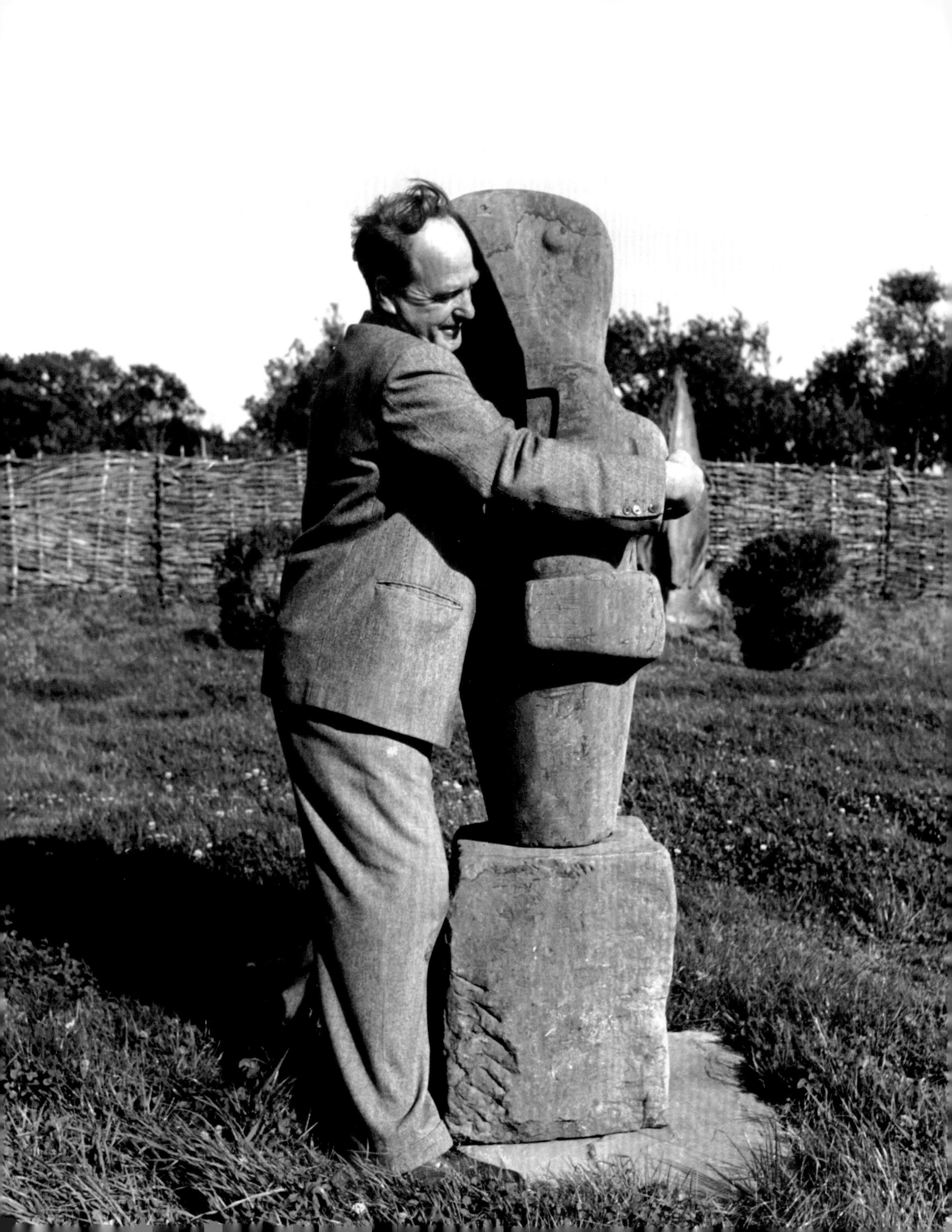

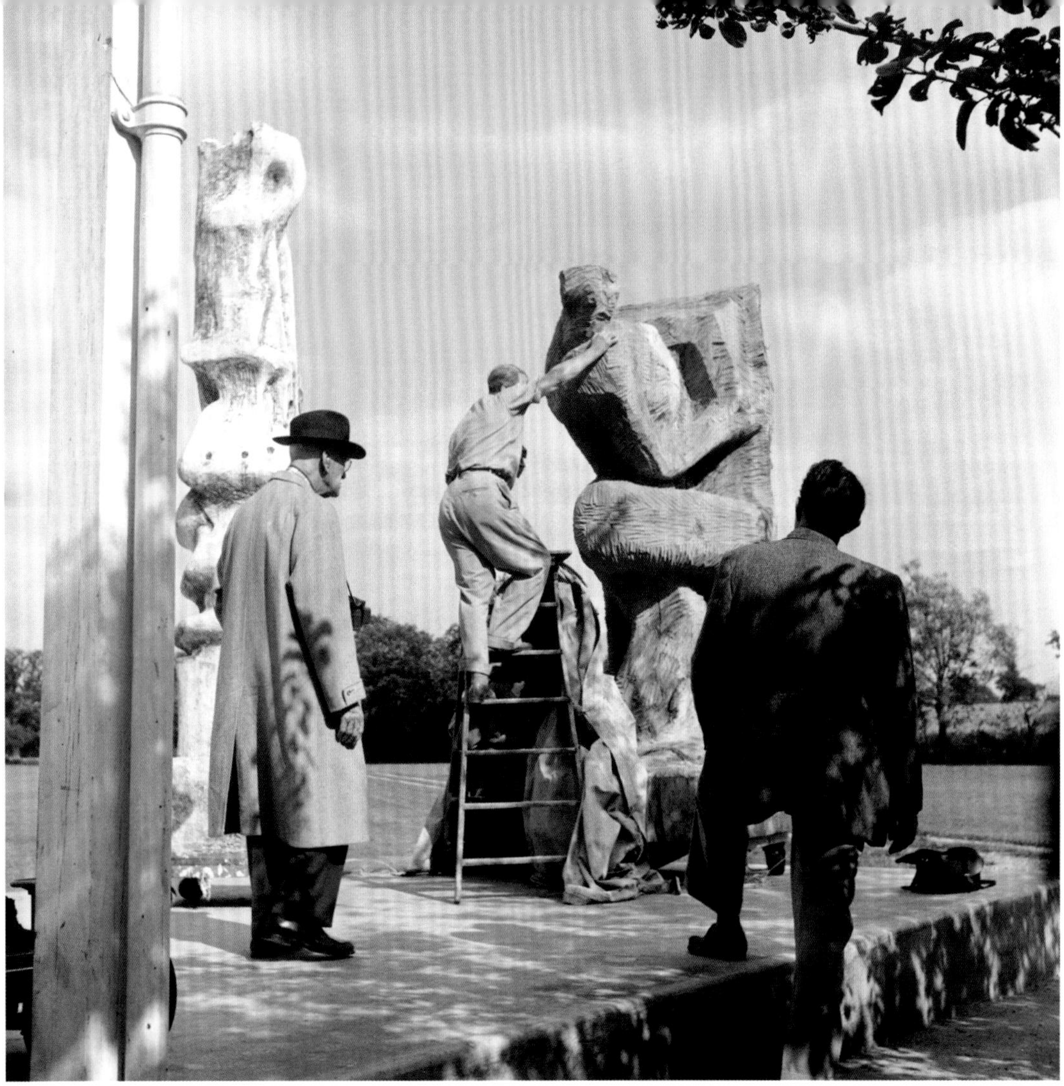

Theodore Miller, Henry Moore and Roland Penrose, Perry Green, Hertfordshire, England 1943

Henry Moore never lost his Yorkshire accent. His voice instantly projected his warmth, his gravity and an unshakably grounded nature. These qualities might be expected in the son of a Yorkshire miner, but not readily associated with the kind of personality who took British sculpture to an entirely new plane of the imagination and level of importance.

Henry had become friends with Roland through the painter Wolfgang Paalen at the time of the International Surrealist Exhibition Roland initiated in 1936. Henry had loaned two works to the show and installation photographs show them boldly placed in the gallery. Although firmly welcomed by the surrealists in this moment, some were to turn on him later when he carved an image of the Madonna, contrary to the anti-religion principles of the group.

The following year in Paris he and Roland visited Picasso's studio in 7, Rue des Grands Augustins, to see his master work *Guernica* in progress. Later Henry and his wife Irena joined Roland and Lee for part of their holiday at Lambe Creek in Cornwall. It was about this time Henry drew his feet seen from his own point of view, set against the Cornish coastal landscape and titled '*Feet on Holiday*'.

Later in the year, on his way back from France by road, Roland visited Henry's studio near Canterbury where he encountered Henry's powerfully enigmatic sculpture *Mother and Child*. He bought it on the spot. Henry later told me it was the first big work he had ever sold and it gave him money and encouragement when he needed it most. He delivered the sculpture to Roland's house, 21 Downshire Hill in Hampstead, telling him with characteristic modesty that if he ever tired of it, he would replace it with another. The work drew caustic criticism from the neighbours and local press; '*Grievance over Modernist Statue in Front Garden*' was one of many rants. Ironically in post war years this much reviled work starred in the British pavilion of the 1948 Venice Biennale and was shipped by the British Council to Australia and the USA representing the finest of British sculpture.

Henry Moore with his sculpture 'Mother and Child', Farleys garden 1953

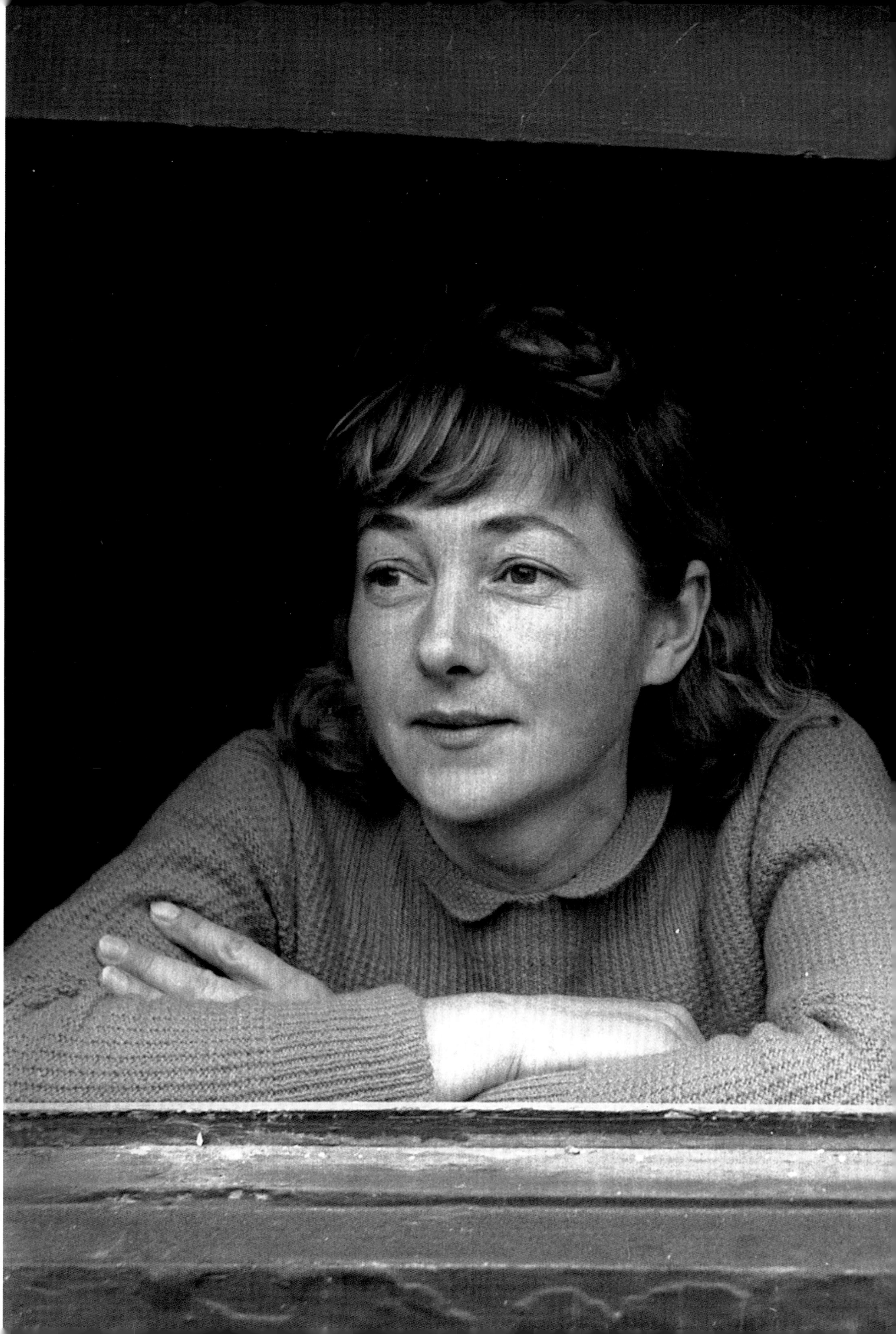

Irina and Henry Moore, Hertfordshire, England 1942

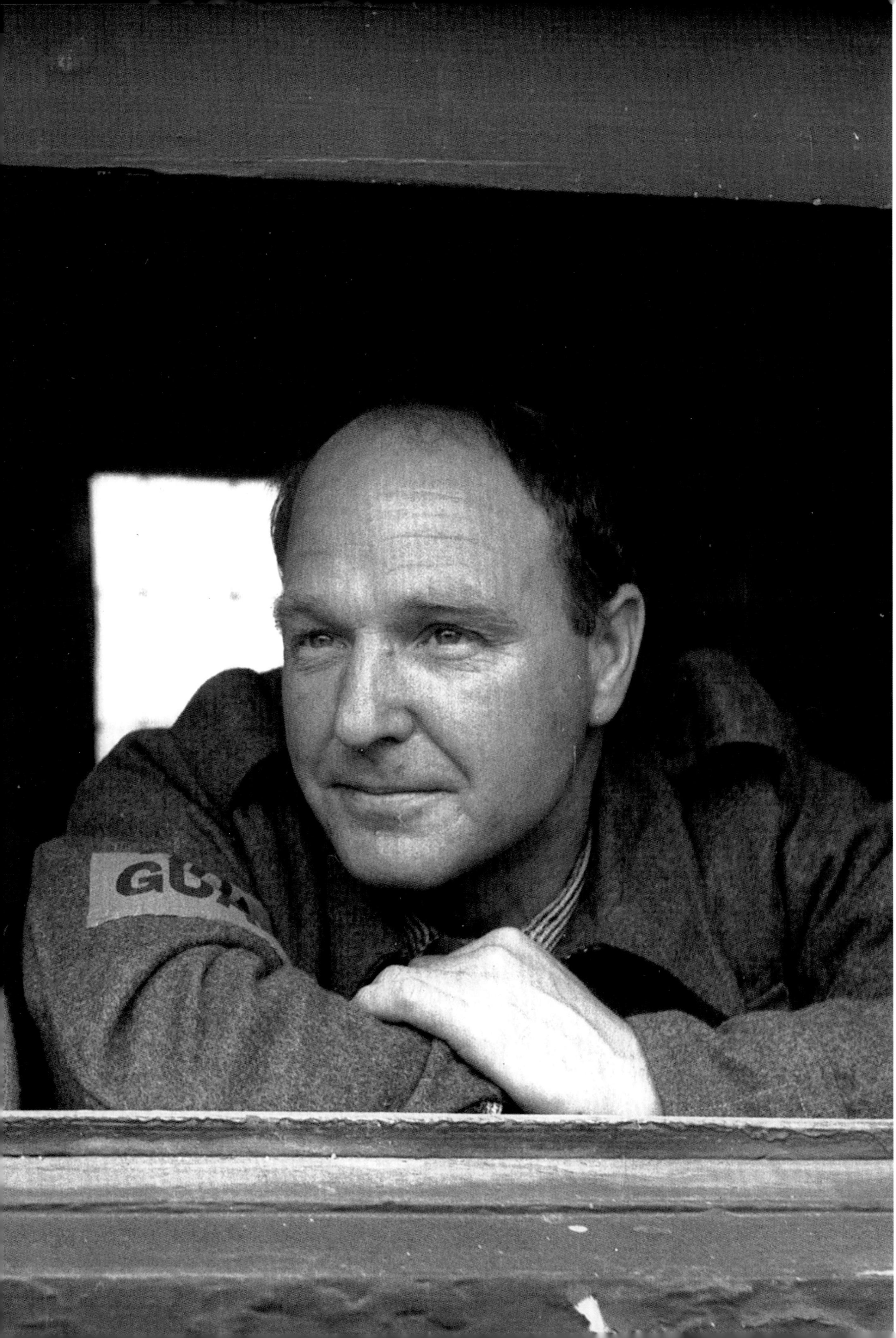

During the war Henry served as a war artist, with drawing as his main output. Lee photographed him on the platform of Holborn Underground station making some of his famous '*Shelter*' drawings of people seeking refuge from the air raids. Rows of vulnerable bodies lie huddled in rows giving us an impression so strong we cannot fail to empathise with the fear, suffering and utter exhaustion of those people. The photo session occurred during the filming of a documentary titled *Out of Chaos*. Henry's inclusion in the film further countered the complaints of Roland's Hampstead neighbours. He was well on the way to becoming established as Britain's best-known sculptor.

Mother and Child came with us to Farleys and Roland positioned her on the lawn. It was an inspired choice of location. She would stand alone, watching over all arrivals and departures from the back door of the house, the preferred route for everyone. She could be seen clearly from the sitting room window, a fringe of daffodils decorating her base in the spring. It was the perfect location and in a mysterious way her maternal strength seemed to make her the axis around which everything on the farm revolved. Although her placing was theatrically perfect, there was a more important but invisible feature about her location. Roland had intuitively positioned her on a ley line connecting Farleys House to *The Long Man of Wilmington*, a Neolithic figure drawn in the chalk of the slope of South Downs.

Since reading *The Old Straight Track* by Alfred Watkins, Roland had been fascinated by the concept of ley lines. It was many years later that a dowser confirmed Roland's earlier hunch that he had sited her on a ley line that passes from the *Long Man*, close by the house and on through Chiddingly Church to traverse northwards leaving England from the coast just east of Hull. Roland's close observation of the *Long Man* revealed he is a solstice marker, catching the sun in the early spring when it rises high enough to light his north facing slope. At mid-day on midsummer's day the sun is directly over the *Long Man* and then in the autumn the sun sinks to a point where it leaves him to sleep until the next spring but for one more instance in his role a keeper of seasonal time. At midnight on midwinter's night the constellation of Orion, the biggest giant in the universe, hangs above him when seen from Farleys. Towards the end of Lee's life Roland put all these observations into the book plate he made for Lee's library of cook books. The sun and Orion can clearly be seen and the dark shape in the foreground could be read as the top of *Mother and Child*.

When Henry came to Farleys with Irena and their daughter Mary in 1953 he evidently approved of the new location for *Mother and Child*. Her sense of quiet authority fitted perfectly with her alignment with the *Long Man* and her placement in her surroundings. She was clearly in a key position in our home and our lives. In Lee's photograph Henry appears to be giving her a big hug, an affectionate embrace to a fellow survivor of the war and the London Blitz. It is more likely he was trimming her installation by rotating her a few degrees on her base to give her a better profile when seen from the house, or perhaps it was both, delivered in his usual sensitive but no-nonsense style.

Mary loved the cats and our big soppy old Labrador dog, Heather. Her teddy made great friends with mine. Many years later as teenagers we jokingly tried to recreate the shot but it just didn't work without the long since discarded teddies.

Visits to Henry's studio in Much Haddam followed, where Henry now had the space to work on the monumental pieces he had been commissioned to make. Roland had been working in Paris for the British Council at the time of the unveiling of the great sculpture Henry made for the 1958 installation at the World Heritage Centre headquarters of UNESCO.[1]

Mother and Child was carved from green Hornton Stone, a warm toned limestone made fascinating by strange streaks of colour and what appeared to be shells or a fragment of a bone embedded in it. After Roland died it became evident that fifty years of weathering and a massive accumulation of lichen had begun to cause deterioration of the work. I lacked the opportunity to house and conserve her so I sold her to The Henry Moore foundation who in turn presented her to Leeds City Art Gallery[2] where she is to this day and she still continues her travels. Among the loans they generously made was The Hepworth Wakefield for their magnificent 2018 exhibition *Lee Miller and Surrealism in Britain*. My daughter Ami and I were there for the opening. In a way it felt like a family reunion.

Irina, Henry and Mary Moore and Antony Penrose with 'Mother and Child' Sculpture, Farleys garden 1953

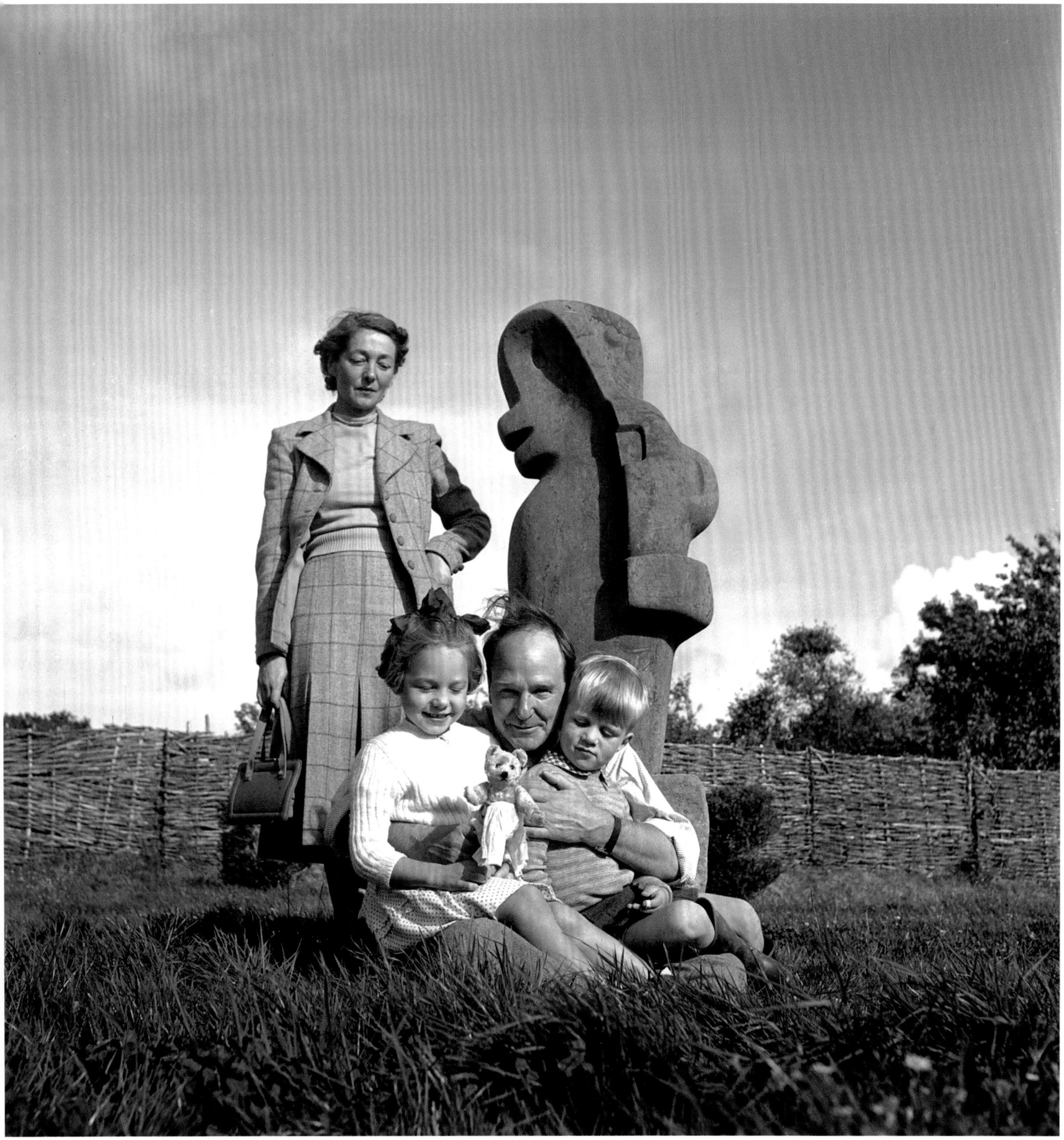

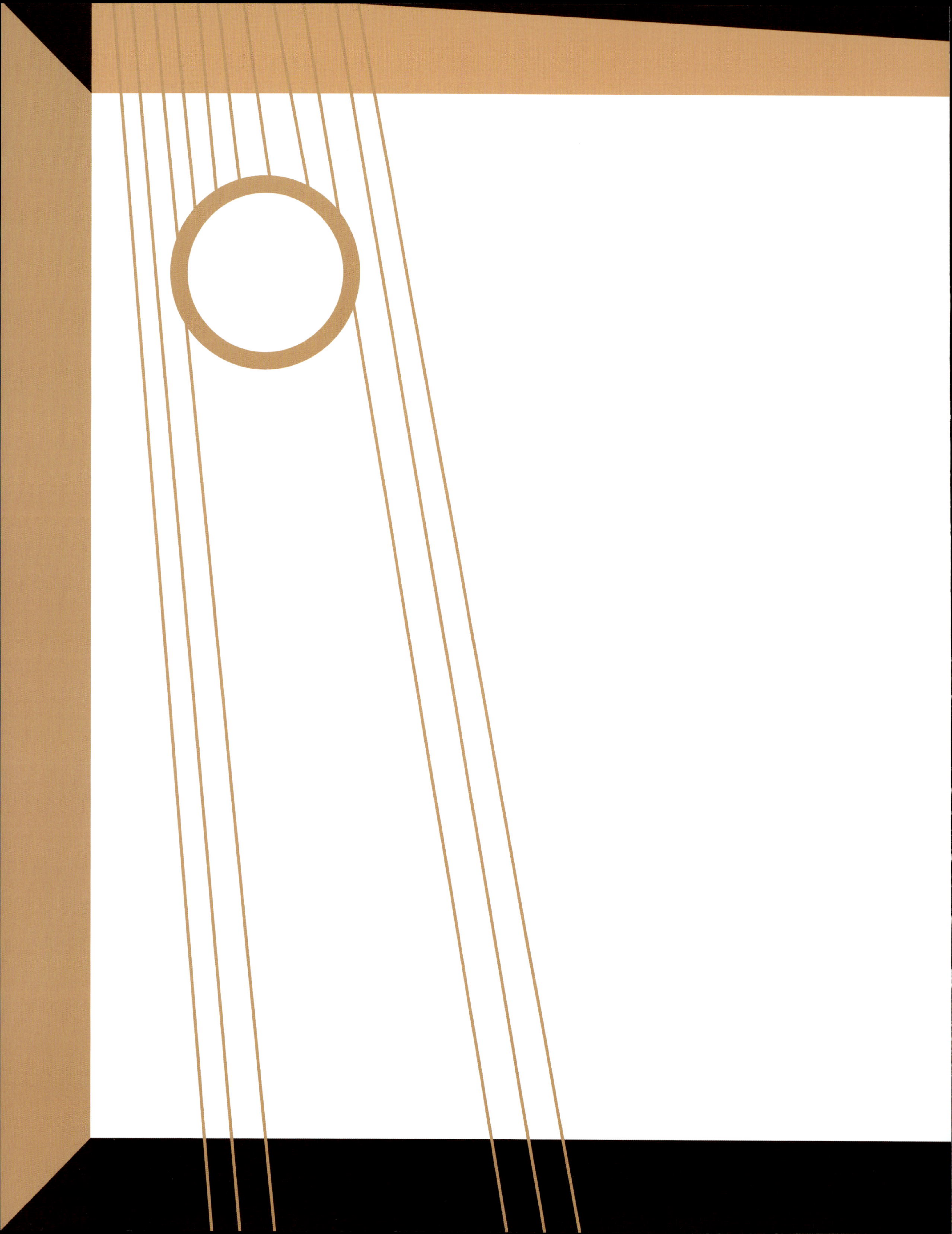

CHAPTER 14

FOR THE SUM OF THREE BIRDS

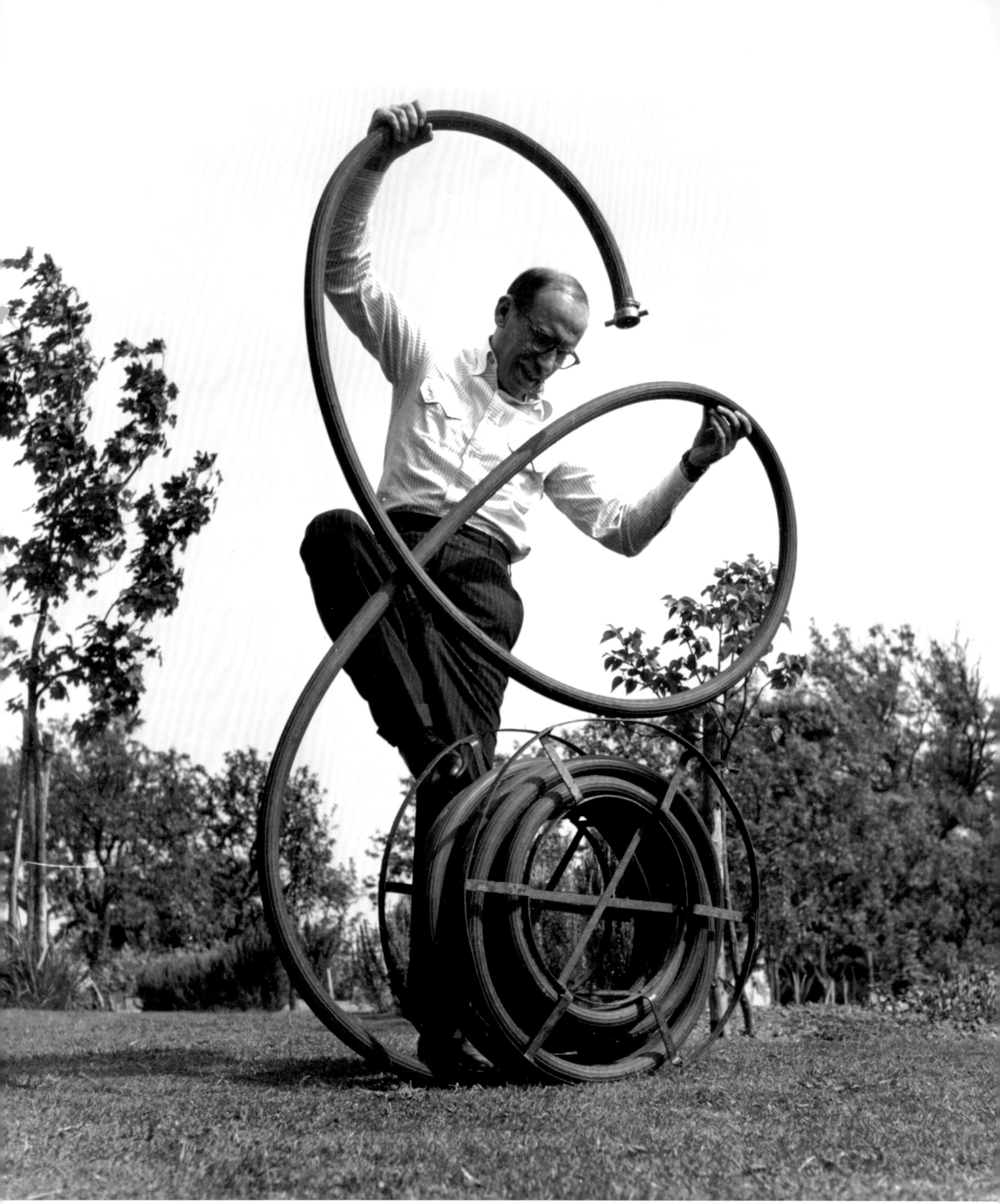

By his own admission Saul Steinberg's drawings defied categorisation. He refused to be confined to one genre and was acclaimed for his drawings, paintings, prints, collages, and sculptures and even jokey false documents, but is most widely known for his covers and drawings in *The New Yorker* magazine.

Steinberg, a Romanian and son of a printer and bookbinder, experienced extreme turmoil in his early years. As a Jew he was denied admission to the school of architecture at the university in Bucharest in 1933, but soon enrolled in the Regio Politecnico in Milan to pursue his architecture studies. His career began as a cartoonist with the humour newspaper *Bertoldo*, moving on to its rival *Settebello*, but by 1938 the Fascist laws against the Jews made it impossible for him to work in any profession. Fortunately, he had become friends with Cesare Civita, an agent for illustrators and artists who was by this time in the USA. Through Civita, Steinberg's work was published in *Harpers*, *LIFE* and other important magazines. In late 1939 Civita mobilised members of Steinberg's family and with them campaigned unceasingly to obtain a visa for him to enter the USA. His departure from Italy reads like a suspense thriller with internment, narrow escapes, thwarted attempts, intense hardship and frustration before he finally got away via Lisbon in 1941 and arrived in the USA after a year in Santo Domingo.[1, 2]

Steinberg's drawings had probably come to the attention of Roland and Lee during their visit to the USA in 1946. They had many friends in common including Alexander Calder, Echaurren Matta, Alfred Barr, Dorothea Tanning, Max Ernst and David E. Scherman of *LIFE*, Lee's wartime buddy and a dear friend of Roland's. Steinberg and his work formed a perfect fit with the surrealist values of my parents. The often-present political undertone, the social commentary and the fantastic leaps of his imagination with his brilliant draughtsmanship made him a firm and enduring friend.

Back in London in 1947, Roland was to be the leading founder of the ICA (Institute of Contemporary Arts), and in 1952 Steinberg was invited to exhibit his work in their newly opened Dover Street gallery. *Steinberg: Drawings*, ran from 1st to 31st May.

Steinberg came over for the opening, then made a trip to France before returning to London. On May 25th he visited Farleys for the day.

Roland had recently bought a garden hose, a clunky great thing that would have looked at home on a fire engine but Steinberg, able to find humour in all kinds of strange situations, immediately saw the possibilities inherent its coils. In Lee's photo he becomes one of his own drawings. Later they drove to nearby Wilmington to see vast hillside drawing of *The Long Man*. Here Steinberg's collaboration with Lee reached a new level. He whipped out his pen and pretended to draw the distant figure. Lee, who since her days in Egypt had accumulated plenty of experience in using her camera to trick perspective, recorded him making his artistic connection to fellow draughtsmen from Neolithic times. Lee's Rolleiflex was not the easiest camera to use for this effect. Being a twin lens reflex, the view finder sees through the top lens and the film is behind the lower one, inevitably giving a slight parallax error. Lee had to guess a compensation movement to close the gap between the pen and the distant fine lines of the figure of *The Long Man*. She just about made it in this shot.

Steinberg wrote to his wife Hedda Sterne;

"Yesterday I went to have lunch at Penroses, nice house, paintings, etc. Went to see a hill in neighbourhood where there's a huge drawing of man – prehistoric (perhaps) drawing made by digging large paths on grass, deep enough to show the white gesso foundation of the hill. Originally the man was in nude with erection. But the grass has been planted to cover those parts now."[3]

Lee was starting to gather material for what was to be her swan song after thirteen years as a contributor to British *Vogue*. It was a witty photo essay titled *Working Guests* for the July 1953 issue, featuring a host of friends, mainly artists and curators fixing up Farleys. One of her shots of Steinberg with the hose found its way into the spread. Many years later when Roland was writing his auto-biography and we had begun cataloguing the sixty thousand negatives of Lee's work found in Farleys attic, we found the other images from this session. We were able to supply him with a newly made print of Lee's shot of Steinberg making friends with the ship's figure head who in those times stood outside our back door[4].

Saul Steinberg,
Farleys garden 1952

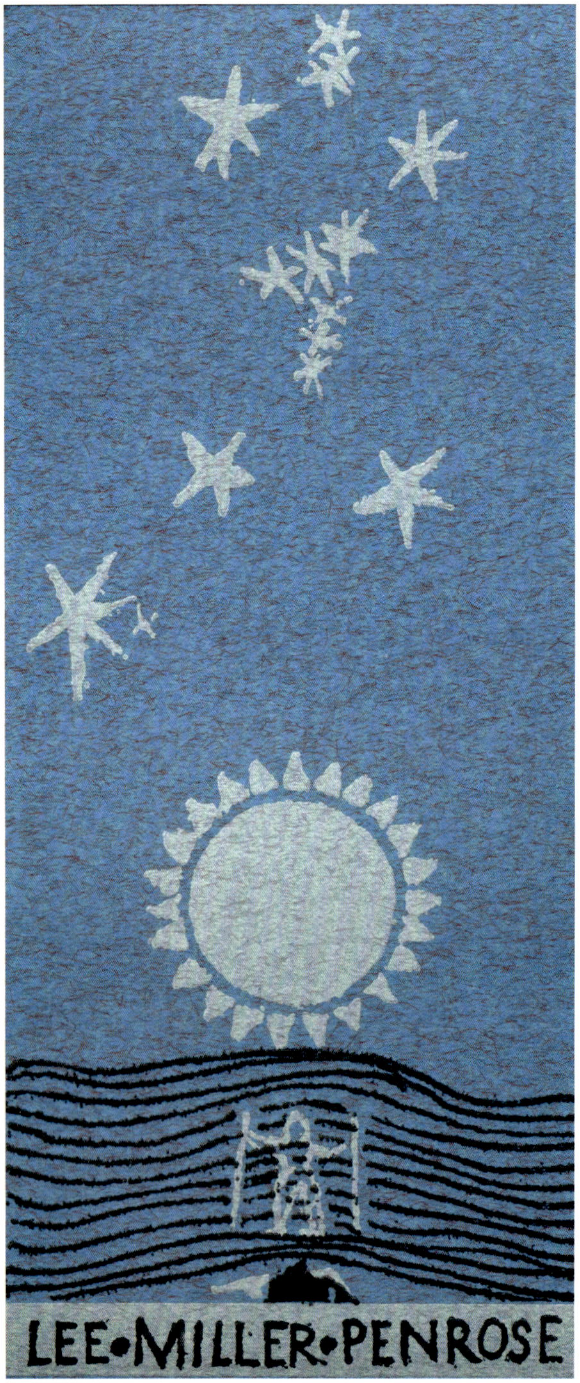

Among Steinberg's works from his travels are series of quick drawings for use in later work. This collection of architectural structures, signs and people were wittily rendered in his notebooks. We see the elegant roof of Brighton railway station with its sweeping curve as the track follows the contour of the hillside and on other pages details of the ironwork. A larger drawing made later in his studio gives us a fantasy pier based on Brighton or Eastbourne or a combination of the two[5]. Roland had trained as an architect and would have known where to go to find the best examples of Victorian grandeur with its elegant cast iron features, so I wonder if he and Lee took Steinberg on a Sussex tour, continuing from *The Long Man* to Eastbourne and thence to Brighton, from where he may have taken the train back to London.

Part of Steinberg's lampooning of authority was his fondness for making outrageously obviously fake documents. Scherman had a large certificate covered in calligraphed copperplate scrolls. It looked magnificently impressive but signified absolutely nothing. In this vein of humour Steinberg asked Roland for the use of his cheque book. Detaching a page, complete with its stub, he proceeded to write Roland a cheque for the sum of three birds. In Steinberg's view, typical of Americans, the British were quaint, bordering on idiotic, with their non-decimal currency. For us, mildly lunatic systems of measurement were the norm. For money we had pounds comprised of twenty shillings which in turn were worth twelve pence and why should their magnitude not be represented by birds? It was a perfect extension of the logic. This cheque appears to be for a substantial value of pounds birds, fewer shillings birds and zero pence birds.

In 1954 Lee returned to her home in Poughkeepsie, New York to help take care of her mother who was near the end of her life. On a side trip to New York, she visited Steinberg and Hedda Sterne. They jointly signed a card to Roland that Steinberg had made. The image of a road passing through a featureless landscape makes a wry counterpoint to the luscious exotic scenes normally depicted on post cards. Perhaps Steinberg's open road is far more significant than the usual hyped post card shot if it is seen as a metaphor for the limitless possibilities inherent in even the dullest scene, given imagination like his.

Lee Miller's bookplate designed by Roland Penrose

Saul Steinberg (Cartoonist), Long Man of Wilmington, East Sussex 1952

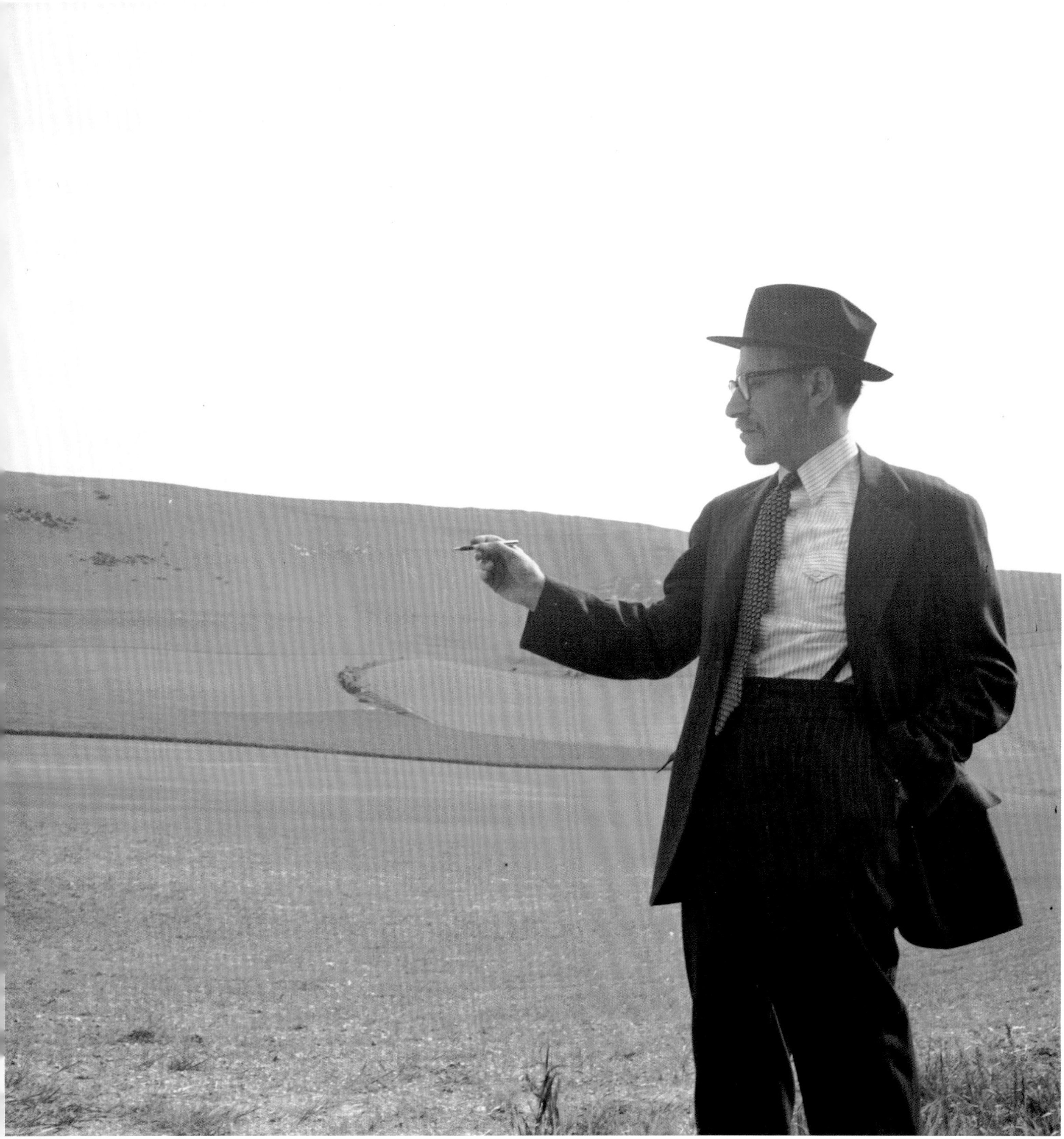

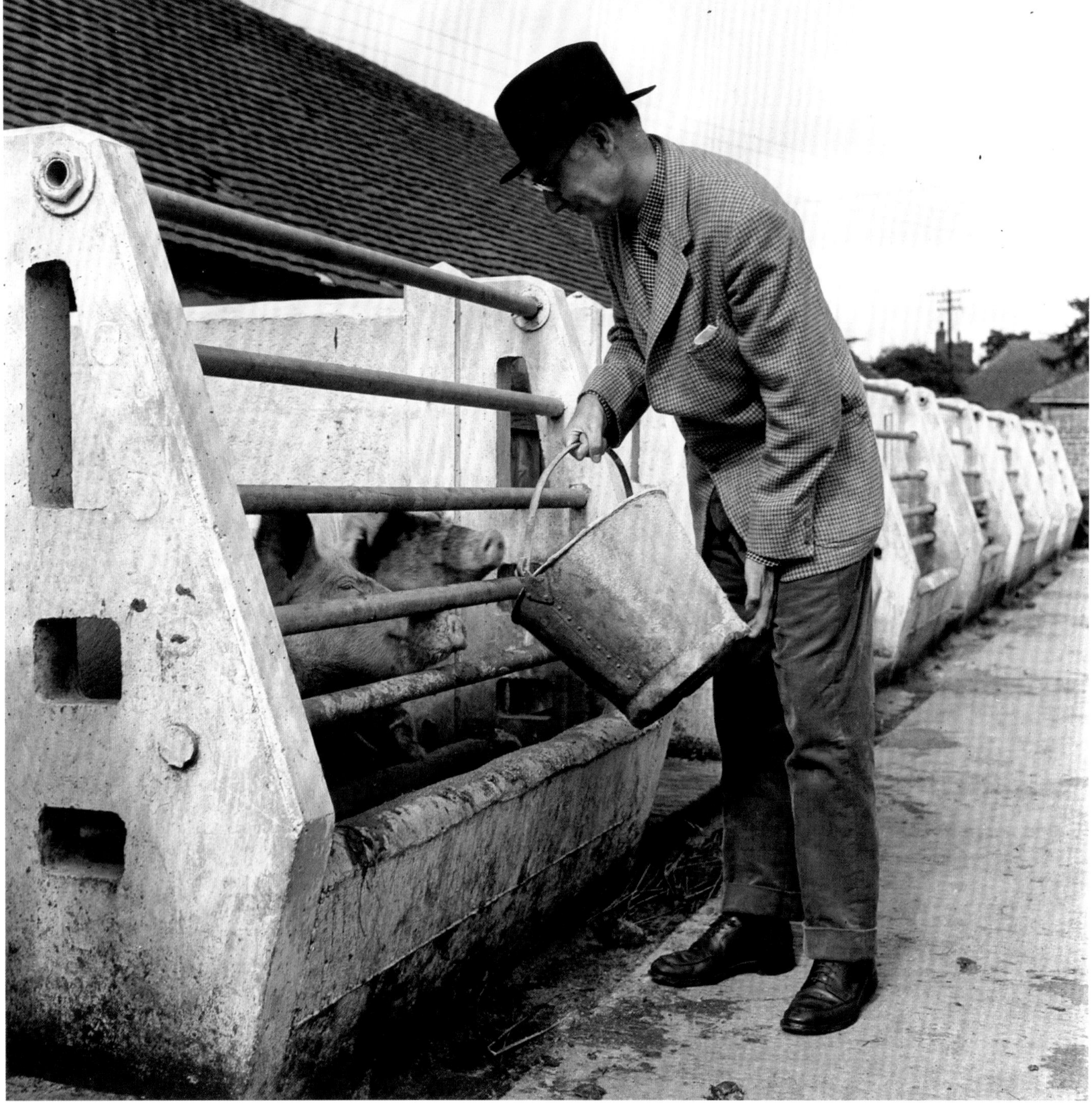

Alfred Barr (Art Historian), Farley Farm 1952

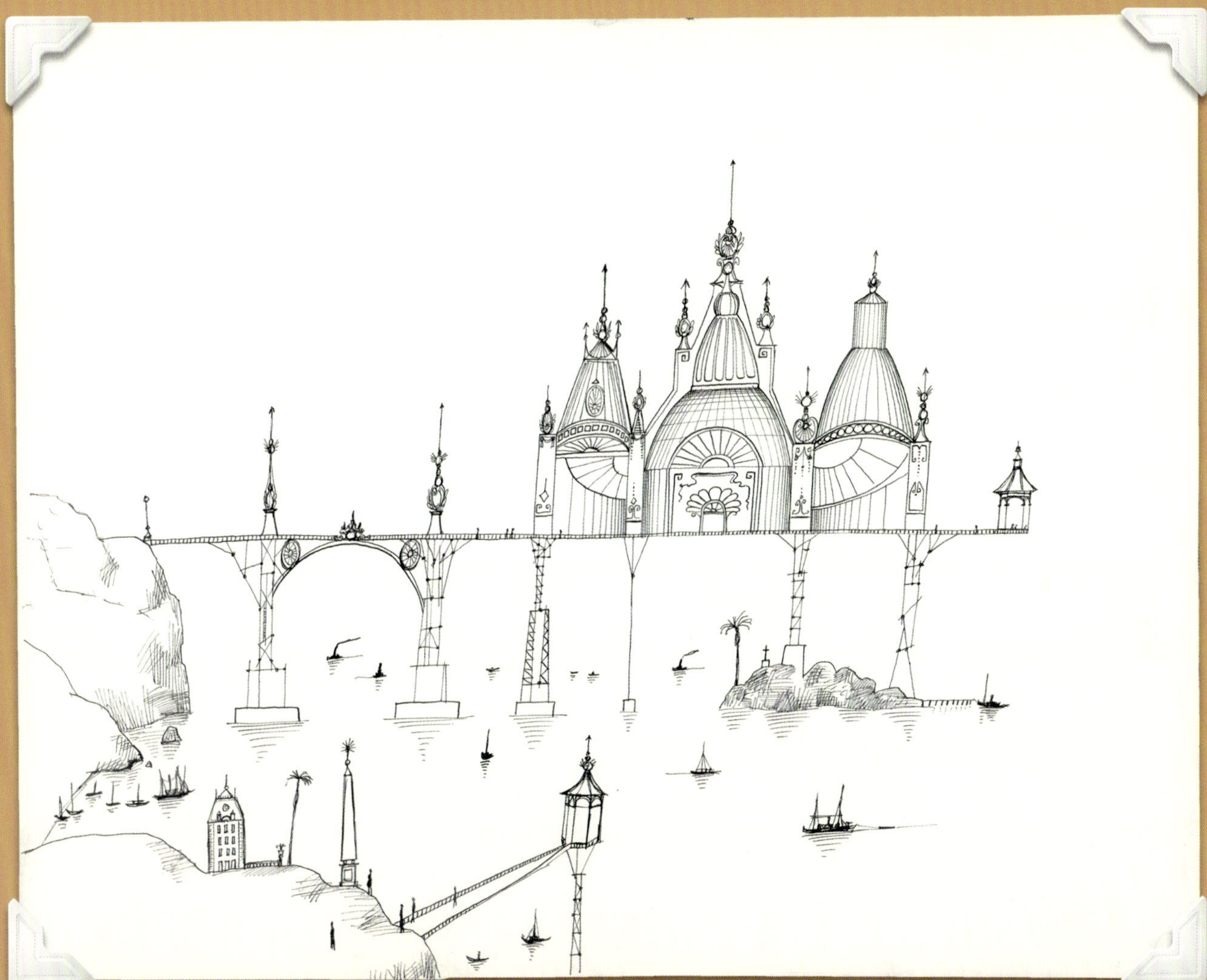

Ironwork Pier, 1952 by Saul Steinberg

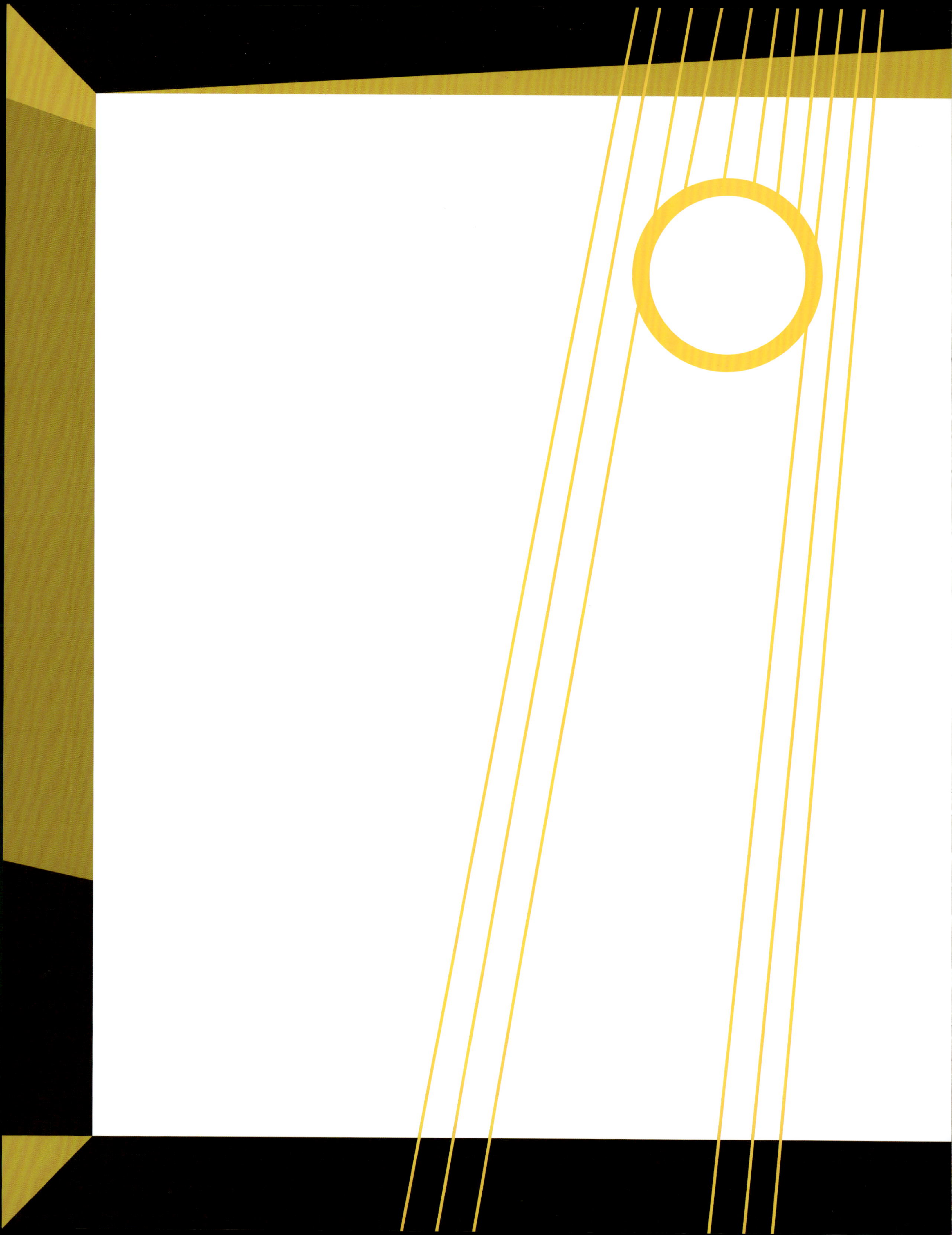

CHAPTER 15

FARLEYS WAS PATSY AND PATSY WAS FARLEYS

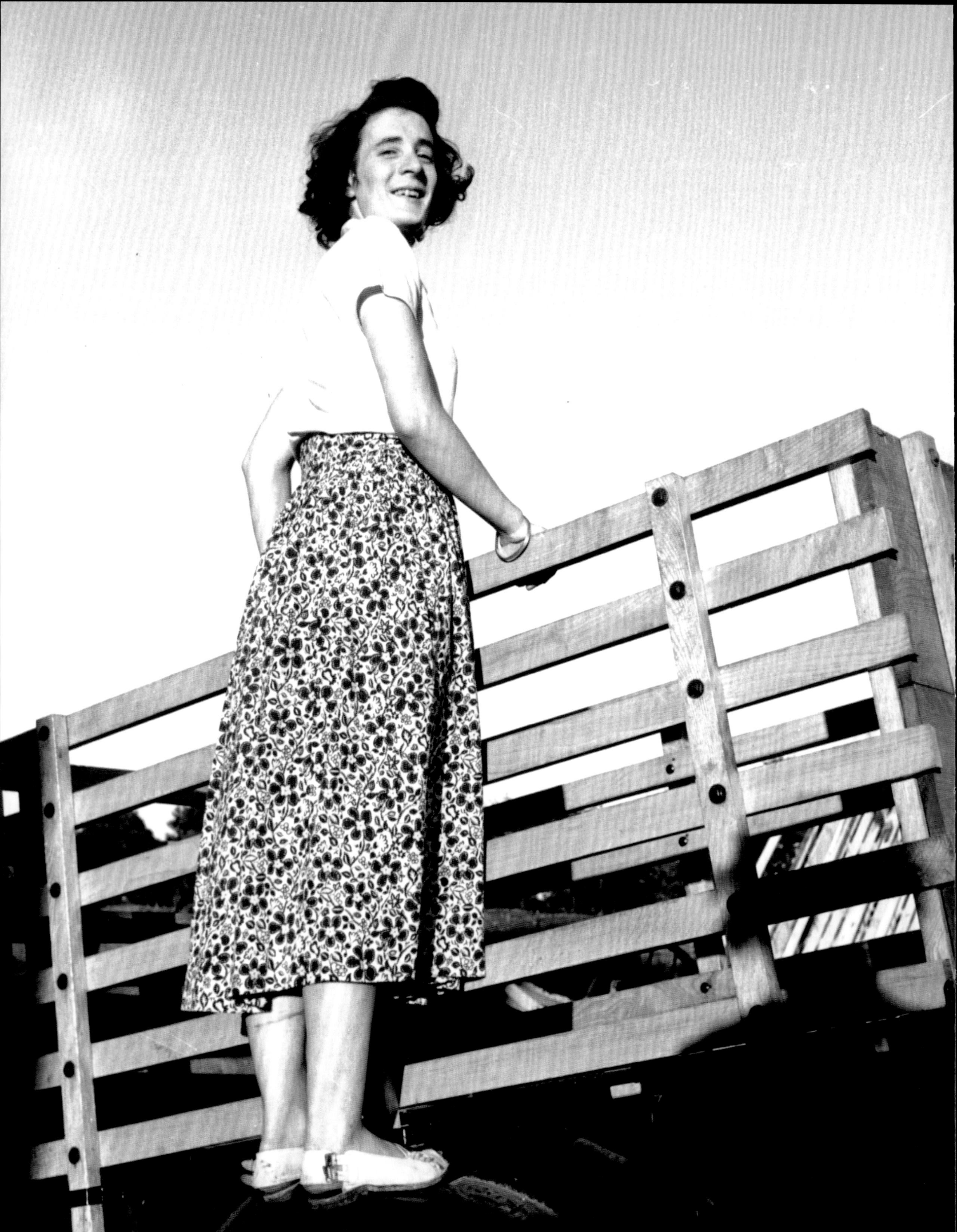

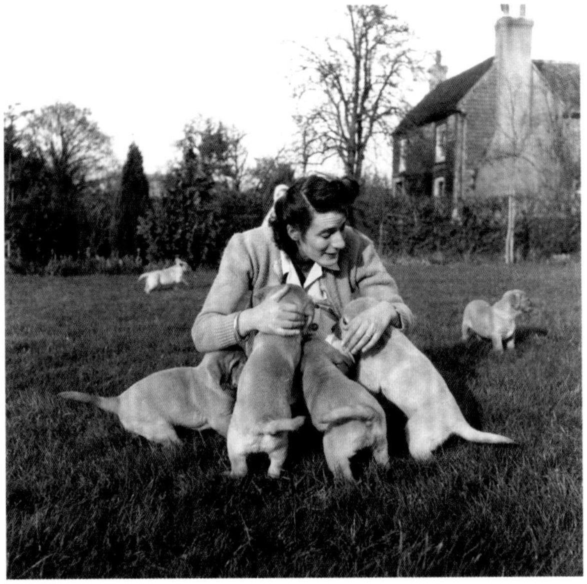

Patsy Murray and Heather's puppies, Farleys garden 1951

Roland was often heard to say in later years, "If it was not for Patsy, I would never have been able to keep Farley Farm". Lee agreed – she wanted no part in the grind of running the home, but loved entertaining her weekend guests from many parts of the world in a sort of informal arts congress. From her early days Patsy asserted a self-styled 'soft power' authority that ensured the place ran smoothly and required only a light touch from Roland and Lee.

Patsy Murray was born in Kent in 1928. Her mother, Paula, was from County Antrim in Ireland. From an early age Patsy was brought up in a kind of commune in Doddington, Kent, run by Dr Josiah Oldfield. He was the physician of Lady Margaret Fruitarian Hospital in Doddington, and a friend of Mahatma Ghandi and Bernard Shaw. Oldfield was an ardent educationalist and insisted Patsy went to school, reached by a two mile walk in all weathers. He chose Patsy's career for her and she became a children's nurse. This strange and often harsh upbringing was a fortuitous preparation for life at Farleys.

At the age of 23 on 14th February 1951, five weeks after the birth of her daughter Georgina, Patsy took the temporary job offered by Roland and Lee as my nanny at Farley Farm. She initially came for two weeks. When she died, she had been part of our lives for a few days more than fifty-seven years.

Of those early days Patsy once told me, "It was such a boost to find liberal minded people who treated me like a human being. They completely accepted me as a person, but it was some time before we became close as friends. After my first week, Georgina became seriously ill. Lee said I should go to her at once, and I did. The doctors advised she should be christened as there was no hope, but as soon I got there she rallied and she survived. Lee then asked me to stay on full time, and I eventually found a foster home for Georgina at Ashurst Wood, not far from Farleys". From that moment on Patsy was the one permanent fixture in my ever-changing world, and Farleys became a real, solid home.

Circumstances changed for Patsy in 1961 and Georgina arrived at Farley Farm. My parents both adored her. As for me, I had to get used to sharing the person I regarded as exclusively MY Patsy, but she soon proved she had enough love for both of us and Georgina became the sister I never had. She stayed at Farleys until she completed her education.

Patsy was wonderfully un-shockable, an important attribute for her life among some highly unconventional people, namely my parents and their friends. Although very tolerant of others she had her own strict moral code. She refused to suffer dishonesty in any form. She stood against cruelty and abuse and for freedom and justice. Mentally she was tough and severe with herself, but for others in her life she had an incredible sympathy and understanding, an embracing warmth and a very earthy wisdom.

In her role at Farleys Patsy became on familiar terms with some of the greatest artists of the 20th Century. She knew the poet Paul Eluard, the painters Joan Miró, Max Ernst, and Antoni Tapiès, Leonora Carrington, Dora Maar, Dorothea Tanning, Maud Westerdhal and Man Ray, who had a particular affection for her. Timmie O'Brien, and Valentine were especially close and a host of others. This made her memories a rich source material for many art historians in later years. She was with us on three of our visits to Picasso's homes in the south of France. Picasso's eldest son Paulo took a big interest in her, but Patsy favoured the company of Picasso's pet goat Esmeralda, preferring conversations with her.

When we moved the archive into Farleys after my father died, Patsy continued to come in everyday to help with whatever was going on, sitting at the kitchen table smoking constantly. Mercifully the laws about smoking in the workplace were not yet enforceable, as how could we have got the cigarettes away from her? To begin with the archive staff, who had the use of the kitchen, found her a little intimidating. She was clearly a matriarch not to be messed with. They soon warmed to her wicked sense of humour and affectionate bonds developed but everyone understood that the kitchen gadgets, saucepans and crockery had to be washed and dried carefully and returned to exactly the right spot.

Patsy Murray, Farleys House 1951

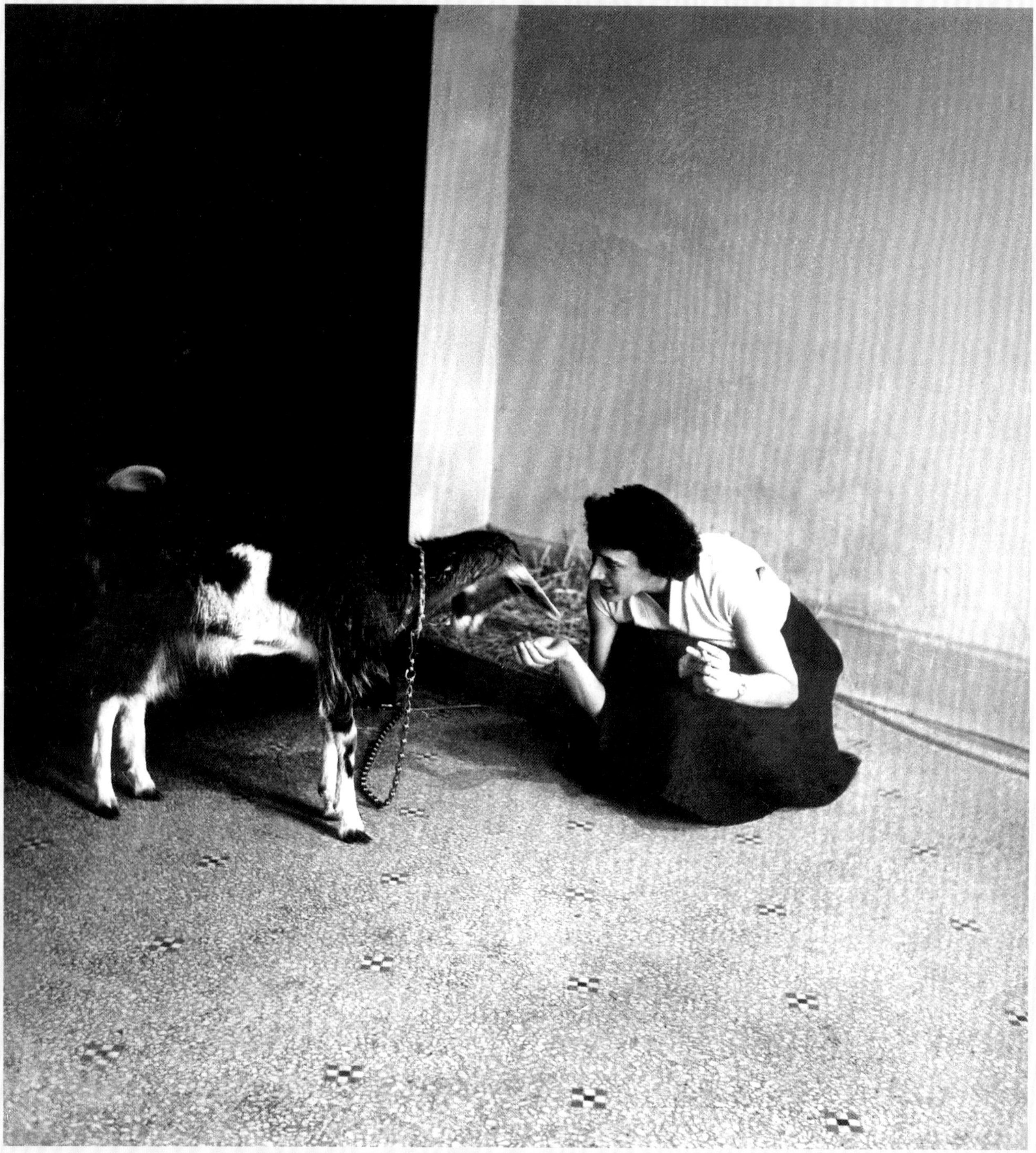

Patsy Murray and Esmeralda the goat, Vila la Californie, Cannes, France 1957

Everyone knew Farleys was Patsy and Patsy was Farleys. The identity of the two was inseparable. I enjoyed introducing Patsy to our tour visitors. I would say – "This is the famous and the original Patsy – they only ever made one. She is still here as my nanny after more than 50 years because she has not finished yet – I am a work in progress". Patsy would go a bit coy, but she loved it, particularly when people would ask her about the old days.

My mother died just after Ami was born to my late wife Suzanna, so it was Patsy who was de facto granny to Ami, her sister Eliza and later to our son Joshua. Likewise, she became the great grandmother to Ami's children, Kahina, Tarik and Amine. My children mattered to Patsy but her happiest moments were when Georgina's two daughters were born.

Patsy's love of animals caused Farleys to be full of pets. The cats were nearly all descended from two strays Lee befriended during the Blitz. Georgina, Patsy and I clamoured to keep our favourites from the new litters of kittens that frequently arrived. Patsy came up with a scheme of keeping the black ones – they all looked alike to my parents and since they were never in the same place at the same time could not be counted. The ruse was discovered late one night when my father encountered all nine gathered to have their supper in front of the Aga. They stayed. In fact, my father always said his ambition was to be reincarnated as one of Patsy's cats. I wonder if he made it.

Patsy spent the penultimate day of her life working at Farleys. Her health had been failing a little but nothing seemed threatening. That evening she called my wife Roz who got her to hospital and soon Georgina arrived. I was in Malaga but arrived back in the early afternoon of the following day. Georgina, Roz and I sat round her bed. She was lucid and making jokes whilst discussing plans for her 80th birthday – only six weeks away. Then overnight she slowly faded, and Georgina and I were holding her hands when she slipped away.

Among her papers Georgina found a letter my father had written to Patsy less than four months before he died. He had suffered some minor strokes, and his eyesight was failing but he painstakingly calligraphed this page in a beautiful cursive script.

Darling Patsy

With whom I have shared so many delights and darknesses. I offer you my love and my lasting gratitude. I appreciate the long and lasting share of heaven and hell you have taken while we have lived together. Your companionship has been a continuous encouragement. Thank you. Your presence is a deep assurance that life is life and worth living.

To you Patsy, my love, Roland

24th December 1983.

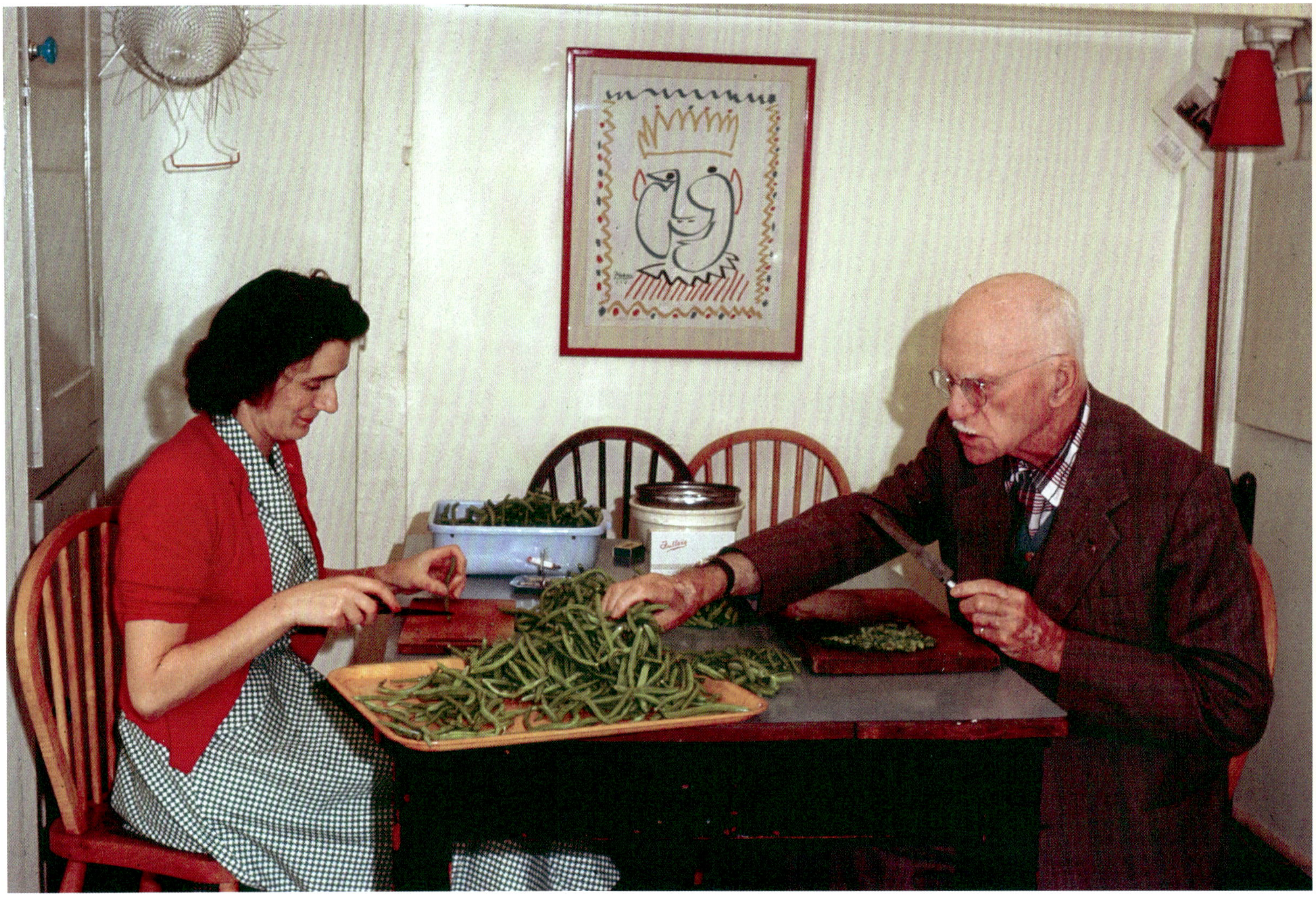

Preparing Beans, Patsy Murray and Theodore Miller, Farleys House 1957

If you visit Farleys and you go in the kitchen you will find that the pots and pans, the herbs and spices and even the bunch of keys hanging from the plate rack are in the exactly same order as they were in my mother's day. For the 31 years after Lee's death that Patsy remained the chatelaine of Farleys, nothing changed. Unwittingly she curated an artist's home of historic importance, holding it until our own staff could take over. In so doing she made a significant contribution to our understanding of the lives all those associated with Farleys.

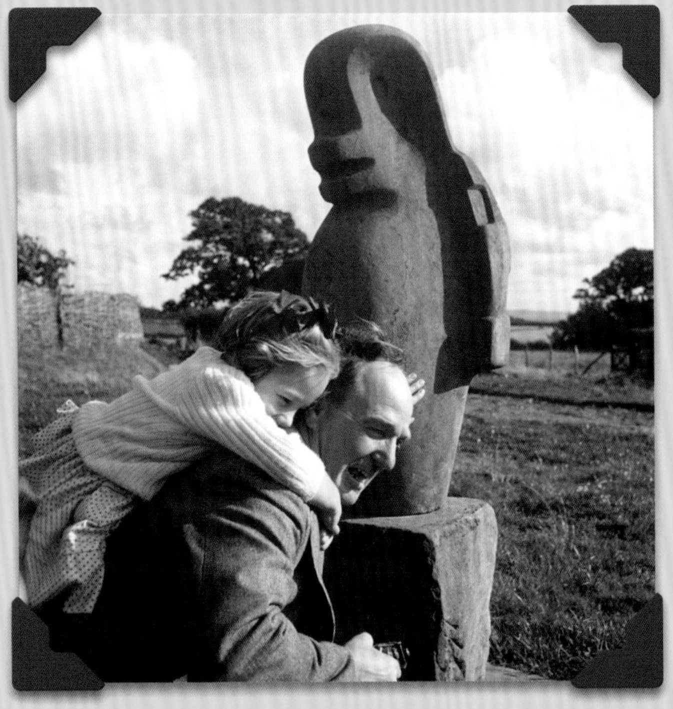

Mary and Henry Moore, Farleys garden 1953

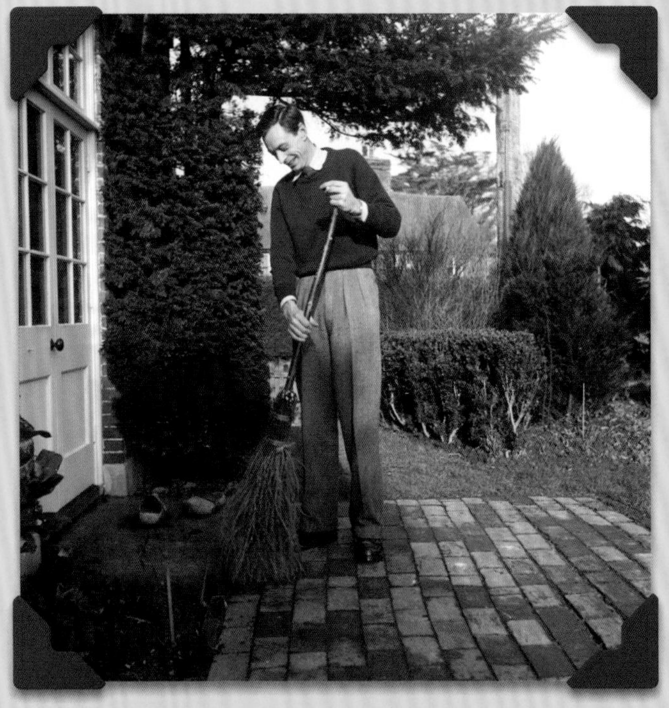

Peter Watson, Farleys garden 1955

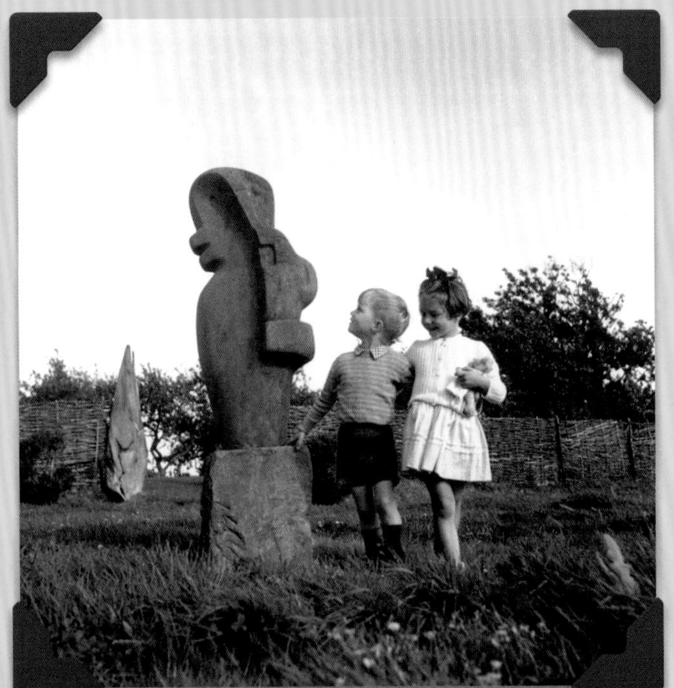

Antony Penrose and Mary Moore, Farleys garden 1953

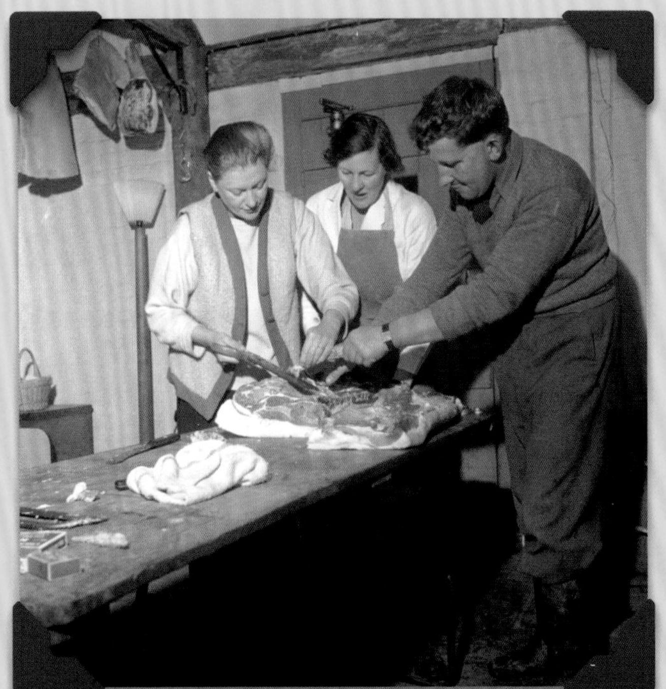

Lee Miller, Unknown and Peter Braden bacon curing, Farleys House 1959 by Roland Penrose

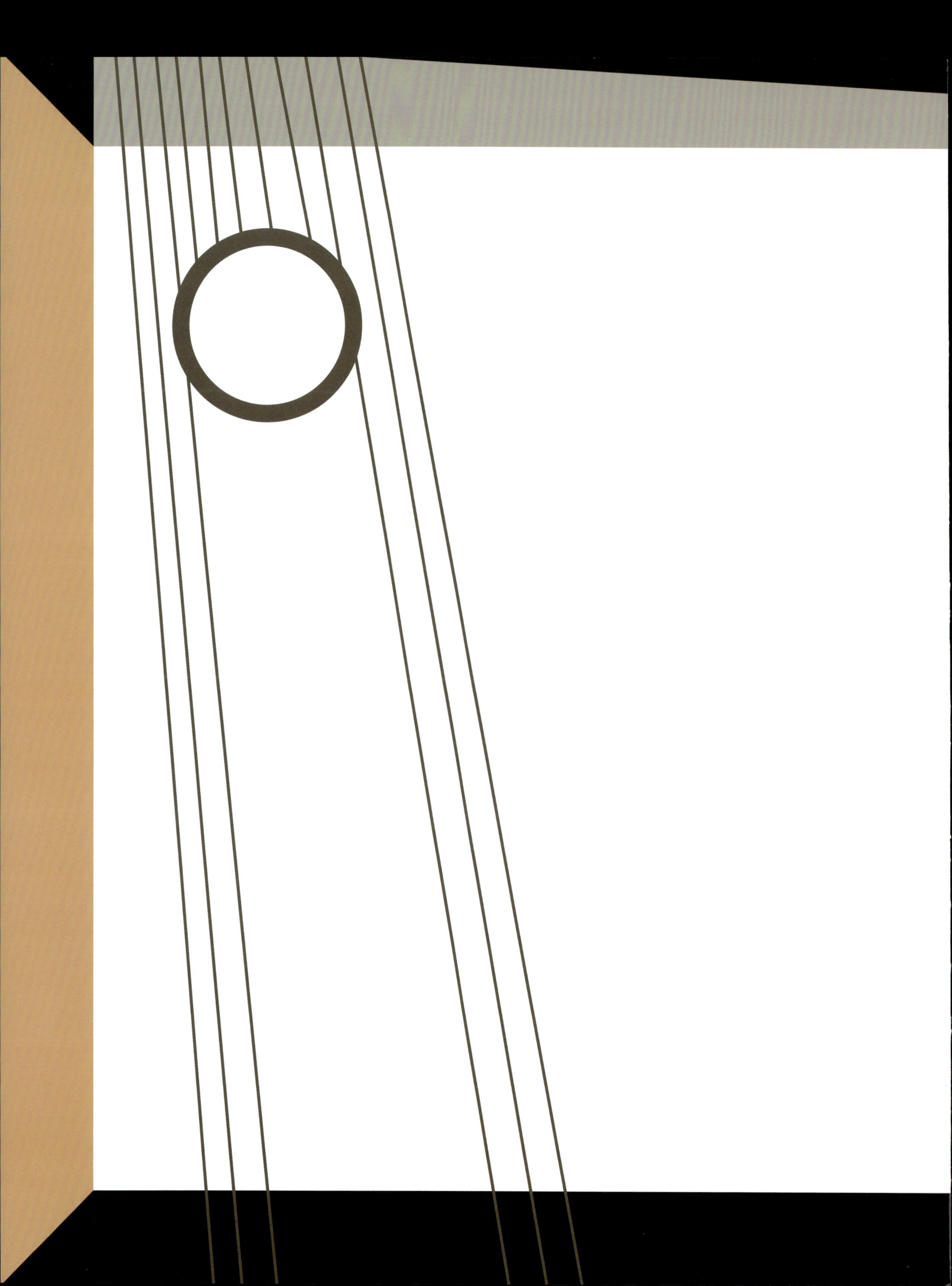

SURREALIST WEEKENDS

FARLEYS IN THE FIFTIES

FOOTNOTES

CHAPTER 01

[1] Lee Miller, original m.s. for her article *Picasso on his seventieth birthday* British *Vogue* November 1951. Coll. Lee Miller Archives, Farleys House and Gallery, Muddles Green, East Sussex.

[2] Ibid.

CHAPTER 02

[1] Letter Lee Miller London to her parents in Poughkeepsie NY, thought to be November 1949. Coll. Lee Miller Archives, England.

[2] The original work is now Coll. National Galleries of Scotland, Modern 1, Edinburgh.

CHAPTER 03

[1] Photograph of Dora Maar at Farley Farm © Lee Miller, Coll. Rene Gimpel, iPhone photo by Louise Baring 27 4 2015.

CHAPTER 04

[1] Lee Miller, *Working Guests*. British *Vogue* July 1953.

CHAPTER 05

[1] Paul Eluard, Farleys House visitor's book, undated. Page 68.

[2] Roland Penrose, *Scrap Book*, Thames and Hudson, London, 1981. Page 291.

CHAPTER 06

[1] Dorothea Tanning inscription on page 5 in *Farleys visitors book* 7/4/1950. Coll. The Penrose Collection, Farleys, East Sussex, UK.

[2] Letter from Dorothea Tanning to Roland Penrose 8/9/1977. Coll. National Galleries of Scotland, Edinburgh. The Roland Penrose Archive.

CHAPTER 10

1 Spurling, Hilary. *The Girl From The Fiction Department,* A Portrait of Sonia Orwell. Page 67. Hamish Hamilton, 2002.
2 Roland Penrose, *Scrap Book*, 1900-1981. Page 192. Thames and Hudson, 1981.

CHAPTER 11

1 Institute of Contemporary Arts, founded by Roland Penrose and Herbert Read in 1947.
2 Sylvan Roumette, 1993, whilst making his documentary on Lee Miller titled *'Crossing the Mirror'*.

CHAPTER 13

1 Henry Moore Foundation Catalogue Number LM 416. *https://en.wikipedia.org/wiki/UNESCO_Reclining_Figure_1957%E2%80%9358*
2 Henry Moore Foundation Catalogue Number LH 171. *https://catalogue.henry-moore.org/objects/22759/mother-and-child*

CHAPTER 14

1 For an excellently informative overview of Saul Steinberg and his work please visit *https://saulsteinbergfoundation.org*
2 *Steinberg: Drawings* ICA. Coll. The Roland Penrose Archive, Scottish National Gallery of Modern Art, Edinburgh, UK.
3 Steinberg's letters to Hedda Sterne, May 26, 1952. Hedda Sterne Papers, Archives of American Art, Smithsonian Institution, Washington DC.
4 Roland Penrose, *Scrap Book*, 1900-1981. Thames and Hudson, London 1981, fig 477.
5 *Ironwork Pier*, Saul Steinberg, 1952 Ink on paper, 23 x 29 in. Coll. The Morgan Library & Museum, New York; Gift of The Saul Steinberg Foundation. © The Saul Steinberg Foundation/Artists Rights Society (ARS), New York.

BIBLIOGRAPHY

Biro, Adam and Passeron, *René Dictionnaire Général Du Surrealisme et ses Environs.* Presses Universitaires de France, Paris 1982
Cowling, Elizabeth. *Visiting Picasso.* Thames and Hudson, London 2006
Man Ray. *Self Portrait.* Little Brown & Co. New York 1963
Massey, Anne and Muir, Gregor et all. *ICA 1946 to 1968.* ICA, London 2014
Penrose, Roland. *Scrap Book.* Thames and Hudson, London 1985

Other publications written by Antony Penrose:

The Lives of Lee Miller. Thames and Hudson 1984
Foreward by David E. Scherman, *Lee Miller's War.* Thames and Hudson 2007
The Home of The Surrealists. Lee Miller Archives Publishing 2019
The Boy Who Bit Picasso. Thames and Hudson 2010
Miró's Magic Animals. Thames and Hudson 2016
Surrealist Lee Miller. Lee Miller Archives Publishing 2019
Roland Penrose. The Friendly Surrealist. Lee Miller Archives Publishing 2020

Further reading published by Lee Miller Archives Publishing:

Bouhassane, Ami. *Grim Glory. Lee Miller's Britain at War.* 2019
Bouhassane, Ami, Muir, Robin and Butchart, Amber. *Lee Miller, Fashion in Wartime Britain.* 2020
Penrose, Roland. *The Road is Wider than Long 1938.* 2020
Bouhassane, Ami. *Lee Miller, A life of Food Friends and Recipes.* 2021

ACKNOWLEDGEMENTS

Text by Antony Penrose
Rights Management by Kerry Negahban
Digital Imaging by Lance Downie
Design and Print by Katie Smith and Richard Shaw. FOURLY
Exhibition organised by Antony Penrose, Ami Bouhassane and Tracy Leeming

Special thanks to the Lee miller Archives and the Farleys Team:

Jenny Batty
Kahina Bouhassane
Kate Henderson
Lori Ingles-Hall
Jeni Longley
Jane Parsons
Elaine Wardekker-Obrien

FARLEYS HOUSE TOURS

For more information regarding visiting Farleys House,
the home of Lee Miller & Roland Penrose and Farleys Gallery
please go to **www.farleyshouseandgallery.co.uk**

lee miller Roland Penrose
FARLEYS HOUSE & GALLERY
HOME OF THE SURREALISTS

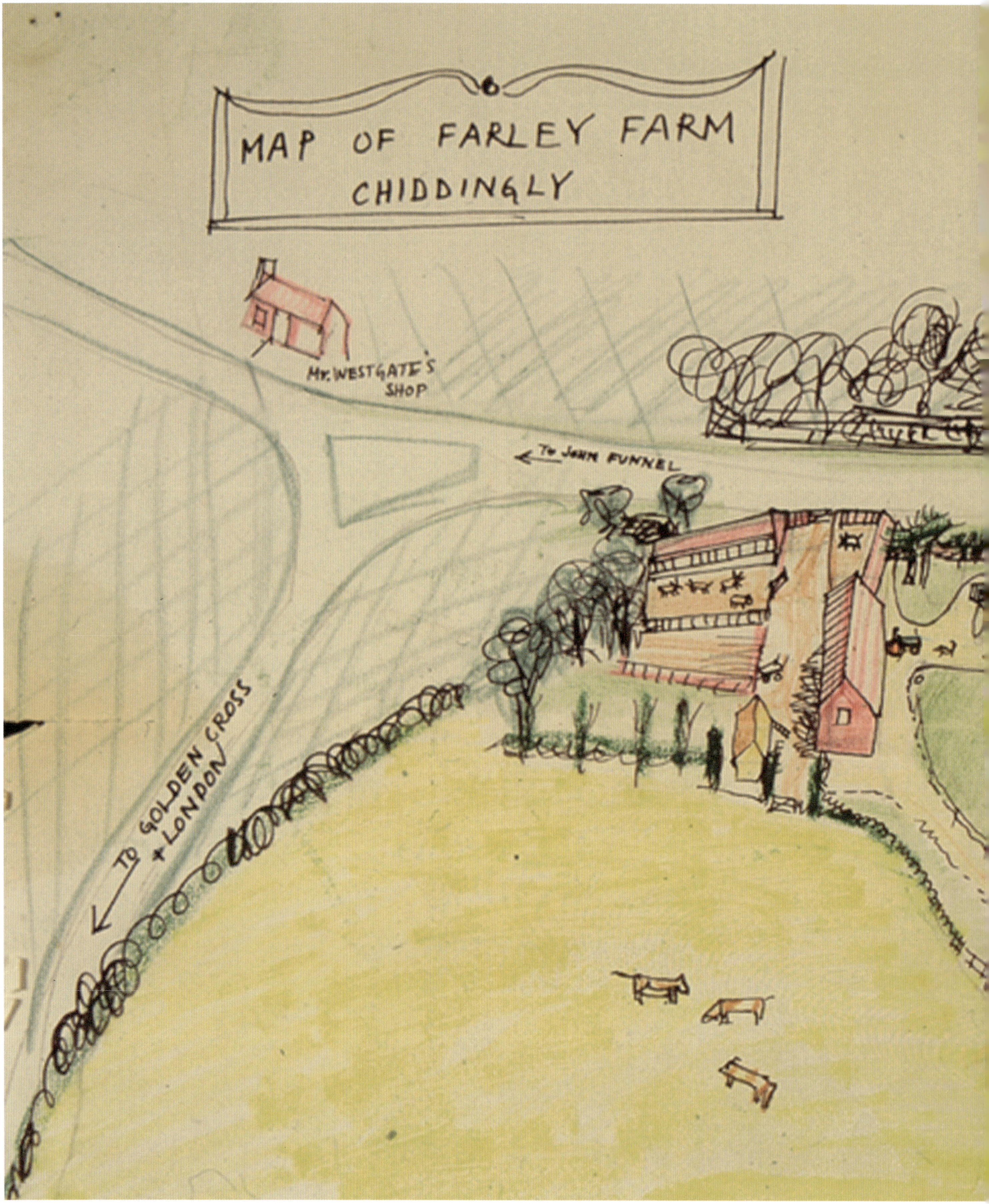
MAP OF FARLEY FARM
CHIDDINGLY
Mr. WESTGATE'S SHOP
TO JOHN FUNNEL
TO GOLDEN CROSS + LONDON